A REVIEW

OF

The Causes and Consequences

OF

THE MEXICAN WAR.

BY WILLIAM JAY.

EIGHTEENTH THOUSAND.

BOSTON:
AMERICAN PEACE SOCIETY.

1853.

PRESS OF ABNER FORBES,
37 Cornhill, Boston.

INTRODUCTION.

The writer is a believer in the Divine authority of the Scriptures—he acknowledges no standard of right and wrong but the Will of God, and denies the expediency of any act which is forbidden by laws dictated by Infinite Wisdom and Goodness. This avowal will prepare the reader to find in the following pages many opinions not having the stamp of public approbation. Patriotism, honor, glory, and national prosperity, are terms to which the Christian and the mere politician attach different ideas, and estimate by different standards. He who admits the authority of the Bible will not readily acknowledge that whatever is "highly esteemed among men" must be right, nor that what is unpopular is, of course, wrong.

In the following Review, the *public* conduct and opinions of *public* men are freely and fearlessly canvassed, but in no instance, it is hoped and believed, at the expense of truth. In justice to the writer, the reader is earnestly entreated to bear in mind the distinction between the statement of a *fact*, and the expression of *an opinion.* Conscious of his own anxious and often laborious efforts to secure accuracy of detail, and of quotation, the author flatters himself that his facts will be found incontrovertible—for his opinions he claims no infallibility, and anticipates no general assent.

The Review has far loftier objects than those of an historical record. It aims to recommend and enforce the duty of preserving Peace, by exhibiting the wickedness, the baseness, and the calamitous consequences of a victorious War, effecting all the ends for which it was waged. It seeks to warn the country against that admiration of military prowess, which, by degrading in the public estimation the virtues which conduce to the happiness and security of society, and by fostering the arts and passions which minister to human destruction, is corrupting the morals and jeoparding the liberties of the Republic. It strives to excite the abhorrence of the good for that statesmanship which seeks the aggrandizement of the country in defiance of the laws of God; while by presenting a true portrait of the patriot, it would fain afford some aid in detecting spurious resemblances.

Such are the purposes for which the design of the Review was conceived and executed. The author hopes for a hearing, not from the selfish throng ignobly struggling in the political arena for office, and power, and money, and lavishly squandering in the strife their own truth and honor, and the public good; but from that small, yet increasing number, who are inquiring how far their relations to the State are to be governed by the precepts of Christianity.

The maxim that "all's fair in politics," and the monstrous frauds, falsehoods, and forgeries, attending almost every important election, illustrate the lamentable *fact*, that in general "Religion has nothing to do with politics." But religious people in vast numbers have much to do with politics, and too often seem to think that in their character of office-holders, or office-seekers, they have received a dispensation from the obligations of the Moral Law. Such persons, should they deign to read the ensuing pages, may possibly be reminded with profit, that moral responsibility is not attached solely to such of our actions as may be termed private and domestic, but that "God will bring *every* work into judgment"—works done in political meetings, at elections, and even on the floor of Congress: and, that as there is an express prohibition against following "a multitude to do evil," no majority, however great, can be pleaded in justification. of crime, or in mitigation of punishment.

CONTENTS.

REVIEW OF THE MEXICAN WAR.

CHAPTER I.

EARLY EFFORTS TO WREST TEXAS FROM MEXICO.

LOUISIANA was ceded by France to Spain in 1762, and restored to the former power in 1800. Three years after, it was ceded by France to the United States. In none of these cessions, was there any specification of boundaries. The territory was a vast undefined region west of the Mississippi; and with rare exceptions, untenanted by civilized inhabitants. It, of course, adjoined the Spanish dominions in Mexico, but the separating line could not easily be ascertained. As the American settlements in Louisiana extended, the question of boundary necessarily became a matter of discussion, between the governments of Spain and the United States. This question was finally settled in 1819, by a treaty with Spain, in which the contracting powers severally ceded to each other all claims to territory beyond their respective sides of a defined line.

In 1820, the State of Missouri, formed out of the Louisiana territory, was admitted into the Union as a slave State. To facilitate its admission, and to overcome the formidable opposition of the Northern States, to the incorporation into the confederacy of another slaveholding State, the slaveholders proposed and effected the celebrated Missouri compromise, a law declaring that in future slavery should be prohibited north of 36° 30″ north latitude.

It was not long however, before it was discovered that this Missouri compromise, together with the southern boundary of the United States, as defined in the Spanish treaty of 1819, had reduced within comparatively narrow limits, the area from which slave States might hereafter be formed; with the exception of Florida, the territory south of the Missouri compromise line, was not probably sufficient for more than two States.

The State of Louisiana was separated from the Spanish province of Texas by the Sabine river, and the soil, climate, and position of that province, rendered it a desirable acquisition to the slaveholding interest. Various expedients were from time to time devised, to obtain possession of this coveted territory—forcible seizure—colonization—purchase—independence, and annexation. The first was attempted soon after the Spanish treaty had extinguished all claims of the United States to Texas, as included within the territory of Louisiana.

A man named James Long, with about seventy-five lawless adventurers, left Natchez on the 17th June, 1819, and proceeded to Nacogdoches, about forty miles within the limits of Texas. On the 23d of the same month, he there issued a proclamation which may be regarded as the first step in that career of fraud, falsehood, and violence, which ultimately led to the annexation of Texas, and the war against Mexico. In this document, which was probably prepared in the State of Mississippi, Long, styling himself President of the Supreme Council of Texas, declared "that the citizens of Texas have long indulged the hope that in the adjustment of the boundaries of the Spanish possessions in America, and of the territories of the United States, they should be included within the limits of the latter." As this hope had been dissipated by the recent treaty, the proclamation proceeds to announce the independence of the REPUBLIC OF TEXAS. This paper, was of course, intended as an invitation to American citizens to repair tc Long's standard, and participate with him in the intended plunder; and it was consequently published in the *Louisiana Herald*, printed in New Orleans.

In a little while, the whole party were dispersed, some being killed, and the others taken prisoners by the Spaniards.*

The plan of colonization was next adopted. Moses Austin of Missouri, in 1821, obtained leave from the Spanish authorities, to introduce three hundred families into Texas, on certain conditions. The permission was granted, as is said, on the representation of Austin, that Catholics were oppressed in the United States, and it was agreed that all the settlers to be introduced by him should be of the oppressed religion. Austin dying, the grant was in 1823, renewed to his son, who commenced a colony on the Brazos, with emigrants from Tennessee, Mississippi, and Louisiana. By the renewed grant, the settlers, it is asserted, were to be exclusively Catholics; but whatever was their creed in other respects, they were believers in the right of man to hold property in man, and accordingly carried their slaves with them.

In 1826, a body of emigrants from the United States, settled about Nacogdoches, again raised the standard of insurrection under a man of the name of Edwards, and published a declaration of independence. They were, however, soon crushed by the Mexican forces.

At the date of the boundary treaty, Mexico was a

* Speech of Mr. Severance in H. of R., Feb. 4, 1847.

slaveholding country, and its near propinquity to our own settlements, was on that account viewed with less jealousy by southern statesmen.

The planters, as we have seen, might cross the line with their slaves, and pursue the cultivation of sugar and cotton; nor was any difficulty apprehended with regard to the recovery of fugitives slaves from the States.

These border relations were, however, changed by a decree of the Mexican Congress of 13th July, 1824, prohibiting the introduction of slaves from foreign countries. The Mexican Constitution, adopted the same year, declared that no person should hereafter be *born* a slave; thus providing for the gradual but total abolition of slavery throughout the Republic.

The United Provinces of Coahuila and Texas, formed one State, and its Constitution adopted in 1827, contained an article giving freedom to all who should be hereafter born, and prohibiting the introduction of slaves. The work of emancipation was completed by a decree of the Mexican Congress of 15th September, 1829, manumitting every slave in Mexico.

These successive measures not only frustrated the views of the colonists, and discouraged further emigration from the slave States, but greatly irritated and alarmed the whole slaveholding interest. The future area of slavery had been greatly contracted by the boundary treaty, and the Missouri compromise; and now that area was to be bounded on the south and east, as well as on the north, by an unlimited AREA OF FREEDOM. Under such circumstances, American slavery was doomed. The influence of the free States would soon predominate in the general government, and the growing spirit of abolition would not only extend into the south itself, but would in various ways, endanger the security and permanency of slave property. The colonists in Texas were at present too feeble to break the yoke of freedom imposed on them by the Mexican Government. Against that Government, the United States had no pretext for war; and the treaty of boundary was too recent and too explicit to permit any claim being made to the territory of Texas. But one resource was left, and that was *purchase.*

The government as early as the 15th March, 1827, instructed Mr. Poinsett, our Minister in Mexico, that we wished to *change* the existing boundary, making it begin at the mouth of the Rio del Norte (Rio Grande), thence up the river to the Rio Puereo, and then with the last river to its source; thence North to the Arkansas, and with this to the 42° North Lat.; and that for this change of boundary we would give one million of dollars. This modest proposal included almost the whole of Texas as at present claimed.

The idea of purchase now took strong hold of the southern mind; and great efforts were made to enlighten public opinion on the importance of Texas, and the necessity of its acquisition. In 1829 a series of newspaper essays on the subject appeared from the pen of Mr. Benton, a distinguished Senator from Missouri. Of the character of these essays some opinion may be formed from the following notices of them in the journals of the day.

The *Edgefield Carolinian*, speaking of Texas, remarked, "Some imposing Essays, originally published in the St. Louis *Beacon*, with the signature of 'Americanus,' and attributed to Col. Benton of the Senate, explaining the circumstances of the treaty of 1819, and displaying the advantages of the *retrocession*, have operated on the public mind in the West with electrical force and rapidity. The writer produces strong circumstantial proof that the surrender of Texas resulted from the subserviency of our

2

negotiator to Spain in her contest with Mexico, together with the powerful subsidiary motive of hostility to the southern and western sections of our country. Americanus exposes the evils to the United States of this surrender under twelve distinct heads. Two of them of particular interest to this section of the country, that *it brings a non-slaveholding empire in juxta-position with the slaveholding South-west,* and diminishes the outlet for the Indians inhabiting the States of Georgia, Alabama, Mississippi, and Tennessee."

A Baltimore paper, speaking of the essays of "Americanus," says, "One of the reasons that he assigns for the purchase of Texas is, *that five or six more slaveholding States* may thus be added to the Union. Indeed, he goes farther than this in one of his calculations, and estimates, that 'NINE MORE STATES *as large as Kentucky,*' may be formed within the limits of that province."

A Charleston paper treating of the same subject, observed, "It is not imposssible that he (President Jackson) is now examining the propriety and practicability of a retrocession of the vast territory of Texas; an enterprize which could not fail to exercise an important and favorable influence upon the future destinies of the South, *by increasing the votes of the slaveholding States in the United States Senate.*"

Judge Upsher, of Virginia, afterwards Secretary of State under President Tyler, remarked, the same year, in the Virginia Convention, "If Texas should be obtained, which he strongly desired, it would *raise the price of slaves,* and be a great advantage to the slaveholders of that State." Mr. Doddridge, in the same debate, asserted, "The acquisition of Texas will greatly enhance the value of the property in question." *Debates, p.* 89. Mr. Gholston, of the Virginia Legislature in 1832, said, "He believed the acquisition of Texas would raise the price of slaves fifty per cent. at least." Virginia being a breeding State, these gentlemen were anxious to obtain Texas as a new and extensive market for their staple commodity. To stimulate the action of the Government, rumors were set afloat of the intentions of Great Britain to possess herself of Texas; an artifice practised without intermission from 1829 to the day of annexation. The following from the New Orleans *Creole*, of 1829, is a specimen: "A rumor reached us by the last packet from Mexico, that a company of British merchants had offered to advance $5,000,000 to the Mexican Government on the condition that the Province of Texas *should be placed under the protection of Great Britain.*"

President Jackson entered fully into the views of the slaveholders, and on the 25th August, 1829, Mr. Poinsett was instructed to offer five millions for Texas. Although this bid so greatly exceeded the former, it was promptly rejected. The offer was, according to a Mexican journal, followed by another: "When he (Poinsett) found his offer objectionable, he further insulted the nation by proposing a loan of TEN millions (as a pawnbroker would) upon the *pawning* of Texas until repaid, which insidious proposal was meant to fill the country of Texas with Anglo-Americans and *slaves*, and to hold it after in any event."

The failure of Mr. Poinsett to obtain from Mexico a stipulation to surrender fugitive slaves, gave a new stimulus to the efforts of the slaveholders to possess themselves of Texas

CHAPTER II.

INDEPENDENCE OF TEXAS.

THE insurrectionary efforts under Long and Edwards having failed, the Colony under Austin having yielded as yet no aid to the slaveholding interest in the United States, all hopes of acquiring Texas by purchase being now abandoned, and no pretext for war with Mexico existing, the slaveholders, as a last resort, determined to effect the separation of the Province from the Mexican Republic, as a necessary preliminary to annexation. Coming events were thus shadowed forth in an article published in 1830, in the Arkansas *Gazette:* "No hopes need be entertained of our acquiring Texas (by purchase) until some party more friendly to the United States than the present, shall predominate in Mexico; and perhaps not until the *People of Texas* shall throw off allegiance to that government, which they will no doubt do, so soon as they have a reasonable *pretext* for doing so. At present they are probably subject to as few exactions and impositions as any people under the sun." It will be observed that the writer takes for granted that *we* shall acquire Texas, as soon as the American settlers shall have a pretext for revolting from Mexico. At a Congressional election held about this time in the State of Mississippi, the following interrogatories were addressed to certain of the candidates—"Your opinion of the acquisition of Texas, and how—whether by force or treaty; and whether the law*

* Passed by Mexico in 1830, and repealed in 1833

preventing the emigration of Americans is not evidence of apprehension that that province wishes to secede from the Mexican Government, and whether, if requested, we ought to give the seceders *military assistance;* and what would be the effect of the acquisition of Texas upon the *planting interest?*"

"The South," said the Mobile *Advertiser* at this time, "wish to have Texas admitted into the Union for two reasons; first, to equalize the South with the North; and secondly, as a convenient and safe place calculated from its peculiarly good soil and salubrious climate, for a *slave population.*" The same year, Mr. Samuel Houston of Tennessee, disclosed to a friend (Robert Mayo, M.D.), who communicated the intelligence to the President, that he was organizing an expedition with recruits from the United States, for the purpose of wresting Texas from Mexico; and soon after it was announced in a Louisiana paper, that Houston had gone to Texas, the editor adding, "we may expect shortly to hear of his raising his flag."

One mode of effecting a revolution was to enlist the pecuniary interests of as many American citizens as possible in the independence of Texas. Vast grants of land had been made by the State Legislature to a few individuals. These grants were of course worthless till sold out in parcels. Many of the patentees resided in the United States, and joint-stock companies were formed for the sale of these lands. Three of the most notorious of these companies, viz.: "The Galveston Bay and Texas Company," "The Arkansas and Texas Company," and "The Rio Grande Company," were established in New York. Care was taken to enlist prominent politicians in these companies; and great efforts were made to distribute the *scrip,* or certificates of partial purchases, as widely as possible. This scrip was of little value while Texas continued under the government of Mexico, but in case of independence followed by annexation might prove a fortune to the holder. In this manner, a powerful pecuniary interest was excited in the free States in behalf of Texas.*

The plans of the conspirators in Texas were aided in 1832, by the withdrawal of the Mexican troops, in consequence of one of those political revolutions with which the Republic had been frequently afflicted since its independence. In this state of things, fresh emigrants found no difficulty in entering the territory with their slaves. The colonists, however, experienced an obstacle to their views in their union with Coahuila, in as much as their representatives were in a minority in the joint Legislature. The first step, therefore, to independence, was the dissolution of the connection between the two provinces. For this purpose, the colonists in 1833 organized themselves into a distinct and separate State. This organization was in direct and palpable violation of existing laws. The Mexican Congress refused to recognize the separate State of Texas. A small body of troops was sent into the insurgent territority, and driven out. The standard of rebellion was raised. Texan agents traversed the United States, addressing public meetings, enlisting troops, and despatching military supplies to the revolted province. On the 2d March, 1836, the insurgents issued their declaration of independence,† and fifteen days after adopted a Constitution establishing PERPETUAL SLAVERY.

* After the Texan revolution, an alderman of the New York Corporation introduced a resolution, overflowing with patriotism, and calling upon Congress to acknowledge the independence of Texas. The surprise occasioned by this extraordinary attempt in a civic body to influence the foreign relations of the national government, was dissipated by the discovery, that the mover of the resolution was secretary to one of the Texan land companies

† Of the fifty-seven signers to this declaration, fifty were emigrants from the *slave States*, and only three Mexicans by birth, and these, it is said, largely interested in Texan land speculations.

CHAPTER III.

PROFESSIONS AND CONDUCT OF THE FEDERAL GOVERNMENT IN REFERENCE TO THE WAR BETWEEN MEXICO AND TEXAS.

THE Government of the United States has at all times been liberal in its professions of neutrality in regard to belligerents, and has on various occasions endeavored to prevent its citizens from engaging in hostilities against friendly powers. In 1793, President Washington issued his proclamation warning American citizens against "committing, aiding or abetting hostilities against any of the Powers at war," and threatening with prosecution all who should "violate the laws of nations," with respect to the belligerents. Washington's subsequent acts abundantly evinced the sincerity of his proclamation.

In 1806, President Jefferson issued a proclamation declaring, that "sundry persons, citizens of the United States, are conspiring and confederating together to begin and set on foot a military expedition against the dominions of Spain; fitting out and arming vessels in the western waters of the United States; collecting arms, military stores and other means;" and he commands all such persons to cease all further proceedings as they will "incur prosecutions with all the rigor of the law." He moreover enjoined it upon all military officers of the army and navy of the United States, "to be vigilant in bringing to condign punishment persons engaged in those unlawful enterprizes."

In 1815 a similar proclamation was issued by President Madison against persons chiefly in Louisiana, who were preparing to invade the Spanish provinces.

In 1838, President Van Buren by proclamation informed the citizens of the northern frontier who were aiding the Canadian rebels, that, by compromitting the neutrality of the Government, they would render themselves liable to arrest and punishment, "under the laws of the United States, which will be rigidly enforced."

It thus appears that from 1793 to 1838, our Government had acknowledged the duty, and professed the ability, to punish its citizens for violating the neutral obligations of the nation.

In 1835 and 1836, Texas was at open war with Mexico, part of the time as an insurgent province, and part of the time as a separate Republic. The first official act of the government manifesting its sympathy for the insurgents, was the appointment in 1835 of *four* consuls to reside among them. The appointment was of itself insulting to the Mexican government, and was undoubtedly made for the purpose of stationing in Texas confidential agents who might facilitate the progress of revolt, independence, and annexation.

The embarrassment and perplexity into which Mexico was thrown by the revolt of Texas, and the aid openly furnished the insurgents from the United States, encouraged the Cabinet at Washington once more to press their proposal for purchase, and Mr. Butler, the minister in Mexico, was instructed (16th August, 1835), to negociate for a cession of the territory bounded by the Rio Grande from its source to the 37th degree north latitude, and thence to the Pacific including the whole of Texas, Santa Fé, and a large portion of California !*

* Ex. Doc. 1st Sess., 25th Congress

It may readily be supposed that the Federal administration was not very zealous in prohibiting succor to the Texans, who were laboring to secure to the United States a very large portion of this coveted territory.

On the 29th October, 1835, the Mexican Minister informed the Secretary of State that no less than twelve vessels were about to sail from New York and New Orleans with military stores, and that on the 10th of the month an armed schooner had sailed from New Orleans for Texas, without papers from the Mexican Consul, and he demanded the interposition of the Government to prevent such breaches of neutrality. In consequence of this application, the Secretary (Mr. Forsyth) addressed a circular to various United States' Attorneys, directing them to "prosecute all violations of those laws of the United States which have been enacted for the purpose of preserving peace and of fulfilling the obligations of treaties with foreign nations." The cold generality of this circular indicated the temper and wishes of its author, which were no doubt perfectly understood by the prosecuting officers to whom the order was addressed. Notwithstanding the publicity and notoriety of the "violations," not an individual was ever punished for participating in them, nor was an officer of the Government ever dismissed or censured for treating the circular as a mere matter of form. A few months after the date of the circular, Mr. N. C. Read, United States' District Attorney in Ohio, addressed a public meeting in that State, called in aid of the Texans, and proposed the following resolution, which was adopted :—"Resolved, that no law, human or divine, except such as are framed by tyrants, and for their benefit, forbids our assisting the Texans ; and such law, if any exists, we do not as Americans choose to obey." At the same meeting, a Committee was openly appointed "to assist Captain Lawrence in raising recruits and funds for the cause of Texas." We have no evidence that the extraordinary conduct of the Ohio prosecuting officer impaired the confidence the Government had placed in him. Nevertheless, Mr. Forsyth assured the Mexican Minister that "all measures enjoined and warranted by law *have been and will continue to be taken* to enforce respect by the citizens of the United States within their jurisdiction to the neutrality of this Government."

The declaration of Mr. Van Buren, the personal friend of General Jackson, and his successor in office, is a singular commentary on this official and solemn pledge. "Nothing is either more true or more extensively known, than that Texas was wrested from Mexico, and her independence established through the instrumentality of citizens of the United States." *

To a second remonstrance from the Mexican Minister against the aid so openly and scandalously afforded by American citizens to the Texans, Mr. Forsyth returned, 29th January, 1836, the following most extraordinary reply: "No sooner was it apparent that the *dispute* between Texas and the *dominant party* in the other Mexican States would be carried to extremities, and indications observed of a design in some of the citizens of the United States to take a part in the struggle, *all the measures in his power* were adopted by the President to prevent any interference that could by possibility involve the United States in the dispute, or give just occasion for suspicions of an unfriendly design on the part of the Government tc intermeddle in the domestic quarrel of a neighboring State."

Six days *before* these solemn and official assurances were given, a course of measures had been commenced

* Printed Letter to Mr. Hammet, 20th April, 1844.

by the President which exhibits the very peculiar view he was pleased to take of neutral obligations.

On the 23rd January, General Gaines was directed to take a position near the western frontier of the State of Louisiana, to prevent the contending parties from entering into the United States' territory! He was reminded that, by treaty with Mexico, each power is required to prevent by force, "all hostilities and incursions on the part of Indian nations within their respective boundaries." Supposing this order to have been given in good faith, its sole object could have been to protect the Texans from assaults by *American* Indians. There was no reason whatever to apprehend that the Texans, Americans themselves, and daily receiving supplies from their countrymen, would make hostile incursions into the American territory. The Mexicans had neither the disposition nor the ability to invade the United States. There was, moreover, no proof that the American Indians intended any aggressions upon the Texans. The army was stationed on the frontier of Texas for objects very different from those which were avowed. Commanded by a General devoted to the cause of annexation, it gave countenance and support to the Texans in their struggle; and, should more efficient aid be needed, no small portion of its men, arms, and ammunition, would readily find their way into the Texan camp. It is to be observed, moreover, that Gaines was not directed to prevent *American* citizens from compromitting the neutrality of the Government. Regiments raised in the Southern States might freely pass his tent on their way to wage war against a friendly power. In deference to our treaty stipulations, Indians were to be restrained from entering Mexico; but foes far more dangerous to the Mexicans than savages were to have free admittance. General Gaines was a willing instrument; and, in acknowledging the receipt of the orders sent to him, showed that he thoroughly understood the purposes for which they were issued. "Should I (said he in his letter to the Secretary of War of 29th March, 1836,*) find any disposition on the part of the *Mexicans* or *their red brethren* to menace our frontier, I cannot but deem it my duty, not only to hold the troops of my command in readiness for action in defence of our slender frontier, but to *anticipate* their lawless movements by crossing our *supposed or imaginary* national boundary, and meeting the savage marauders *wherever* they may be found in their approach towards our frontier." In other words, he would march to the rescue of Texas, should the Mexican forces advance into the revolted province. A few days after the date of this letter, the General, in his hot zeal, made a requisition on the Governors of Louisiana, Mississippi, Alabama, and Tennessee, each for a battalion of volunteers to *protect the frontiers!* The General and the Cabinet acted in perfect unison. The former had hinted his readiness to cross the *imaginary* boundary, for the purpose of *anticipating* the approach of the Mexicans. The latter, on the 25th April, informed him there was reason to believe the Indians would be induced to join the Mexicans, and in that case, should the contending parties *approach* the frontier, he may advance as far as NACOGDOCHES. On the 4th May, he is informed "that the Secretary of War had written to the Governors of Louisiana, Mississippi, Tennessee, Kentucky, and Alabama, requiring them to furnish him with such militia force as he may require to protect the Western frontier of the United States from hostile incursions." The General had, on his own responsibility, called for four battalions from four States. The President, still more provident,

* Ex. Doc., 1st Sess. 24th Cong. Vol. 6.

gives him power to call for an unlimited number of Militia from no less than *five* States. And why were these vast powers confided to Gaines?—and what and where was the enemy against whom this unnumbered Militia was to be poured forth by all these States? Not an Indian, not a Texan, not a Mexican, had invaded our territory. The country was at peace; nor were there even rumors of approaching war. To understand the management of Gaines and his employers, it must be recollected that adventurers were now flocking to Texas, and that Texan agents were organizing in the Southern States military expeditions to rescue the province from the dominion of Mexico. A letter from one of these men, Felix Houston, dated Natchez, Mississippi, 4th March, 1836, and published in the journals of the day, will suffice to show the character of these expeditions. "I contemplate starting for Texas about 1st May next, and expect to take with me about five hundred emigrants. I am making preparations for arms, ammunition, uniforms, &c., &c , *at an expense of* $40,000. I shall have a rendezvous, and begin to send on supplies by the 1st May." Of course, such expeditions were a drain upon the pockets of slaveholders, as well as upon the treasury of Texas. The device of the Cabinet, in permitting General Gaines to collect volunteers on the frontier of Texas, from no less than five States, at the *public expense*, obviated the only serious difficulty experienced in raising within the United States a military force for wresting Texas from Mexico. Recruits for Texas might now, under the requisitions of the President, and the plenipotentiary discretion of the General, be equipped and transported from the neighboring States to Nacogdoches, in Texas, at the cost of the United States. When once in Texas, they might fight the Mexicans if they pleased, but they were sent there to "*protect the frontier*;" and, in sending them for such a purpose, the President of course violated none of the obligations of neutrality, and afforded the Mexicans no cause for complaint! General Gaines had been authorized to advance as far as Nacogdoches; but circumstances might occur to render it expedient for him to go still farther, and the administration boldly reserved to themselves the privilege of sending him and his army wherever they pleased. The Mexican Minister very naturally remonstrated against the invasion of Mexican territory by the American army. Mr. Forsyth very coolly replied (May 10th), "that to *protect Mexico* from American Indians, and to protect our frontiers from Mexican Indians, our troops might, if necessary, be sent *into the heart of Mexico.*"

It would seem that neither General McComb, the Commander-in-Chief of the army, nor the Governor of Louisiana, had been admitted into the secrets of the Cabinet. On the 26th of April, the former addressed a letter to the Secretary of War, from New Orleans, informing him that the Governor insists that it is unnecessary "to send to the frontiers of the State *any troops*, as the country was not invaded, nor likely in his opinion to be invaded; and further, he was impressed with the belief, that it was a scheme of those interested in the Texan speculations, who had been instrumental in making General Gaines believe that the Mexican authorities were tampering with the Indians within our boundaries; and at the same time exciting, by false representations here, the sympathies of the people in favor of the Texans, with a view of inducing the authorities of the United States to lend their aid in raising in this city a force composed of interested persons, who should move to the Texan frontier under the call of General Gaines, *and afterwards, under false pretensions, actually march into Texas, and take part in the war now waging between the Texans and the Government of Mexico; and all this at the expense of the United States, and consequently with the implied sanction of the Government.*"

This letter affords an amusing instance of the simplicity of the commanding General, who supposed he was giving *information* to the Government when detailing the natural and intended consequences of its own measures. The General did not know what is proved by official documents, that the device of placing an army on the frontiers of Texas originated with the Cabinet, and not with Gaines.

The troops, in obedience to orders from Washington, marched *into Texas*, and took a position at Nacogdoches. Immediately, Houston, the Texan President, issued his proclamation, pretending that the Indians were about to attack Nacogdoches, and calling on the militia "to sustain the United States troops at this place," and *to report themselves to the United States Commander.* The object of the proclamation was two-fold, first, to impress both Texans and Mexicans with the military aid to be granted the former by the United States,—and secondly, to array, as soon as possible, the Texan militia under the American General.

An American officer at Nacogdoches, indignant at the perfidious conduct of the Government, thus gave vent to his indignation in a letter published at the time in the *Army and Navy Chronicle.* Speaking of the object of taking their present position, he remarked, "It is to create the impression in Texas and Mexico, that the Government of the United States takes a part in the controversy. It is in fact lending to the cause of Texas all the aid which it can derive from the countenance and apparent support of the United States, besides placing our troops in a situation to take an active part in aid of the Texans, in case a reverse of their affairs should render aid necessary."

One of the practical results of sending troops into Texas is given in the following extract from the *Pensacola Gazette*:—"About the middle of last month, General Gaines sent an officer of the United States army into Texas, to reclaim some deserters. He found them already enlisted in the Texan service, to the number of TWO HUNDRED. They still wore the uniform of our army, but refused, of course, to return. *This is a new view of our Texan relations.*"

When our troops were no longer needed in Texas, they were withdrawn, and sent to fight the Seminoles in Florida. General Gaines now issued a proclamation, offering *a full pardon* to those who had "absented themselves from their regiments," provided they returned by a certain day. As these absentees, commonly called deserters, had been serving the cause of slavery in Texas, the mercy of the General was cordially extended to them.

When the Government thus evinced its sympathy for Texas, and sent its army among the insurgents to countenance, and, if necessary, protect them, it could not be expected that the partisans of Texas in the United States, would be very regardful of the laws of neutrality. A few extracts from the journals of that day will show the publicity with which the people of the United States made war upon a friendly power:—

"WHO WILL GO TO TEXAS? Major J. W. Harvey of Lincolnton, has been authorized by me, with the consent of Major-General Hunt, an agent in the western counties of North Carolina, to receive and enrol volunteer emigrants to Texas, and will conduct such as may wish to emigrate to that Republic, about the 1st October next, *at the expense of the Republic of Texas.*

"J. P. HENDERSON,

"Brig.-Gen. of the Texan Army."

"THREE HUNDRED MEN FOR TEXAS. General Dunlap of Tennessee is about to proceed to Texas with the above number of men. *Every man is completely armed*, the corps having been originally raised for the Florida War."

"This morning more than 200 men, commanded by Colonel Wilson, and on their way to Texas, passed this place in the Tuskina, with drums beating and fifes playing. They will be followed by 300 men more, all from old Kentucky."

In vain did the Mexican Minister, from time to time, call the attention of the Government to these violations of neutrality. Notwithstanding the solemn and repeated assurances given by the Secretary of State, not a serious effort was made to arrest the tide of war which was rolling from the United States upon the Mexican territory. No proclamation was issued, warning our citizens of their duties and responsibilities; no instructions were given, as in former instances, to military officers, to arrest the violators of our neutrality. Jefferson had succeeded in bringing a man, lately one of the highest functionaries in the country, to trial, for secretly planning an invasion of the Spanish dominions. Jackson, one of the most energetic Presidents that ever occupied the executive chair, never enforced the penalties of the law on one individual of the many thousands who openly perpetrated the crime which Burr had only designed.

When commanding in the southern department, *General* Jackson thought proper to put to death two foreigners, named Arbuthnot and Ambrister, accused of aiding the Indians in their hostilities, and thus expressed himself in his order for their execution:—" It is an established principle of the law of nations, that any individual, of any nation, making war against the citizens of another nation, they being at peace, forfeits his allegiance, and becomes an outlaw and a pirate."

The "established principle of the law of nations," announced by the General, was not recognized by the President when his own personal and political friends were the outlaws and pirates, and were struggling to effect an object most dear to his own heart. On the 10th May, 1836, General Gaines transmitted to the President the news of the victory of the Texans at San Jacinto, over Santa Anna, and indulged the anticipation that in consequence of the victory, "THIS MAGNIFICENT ACQUISITION TO OUR UNION" would grace his administration.

CHAPTER IV.

EFFORTS OF THE ADMINISTRATION TO EXCITE A WAR WITH MEXICO.

THE distracted and exhausted state of Mexico, the energy and rapidily increasing numbers of the Texans, the vast supplies they were daily receiving from the United States, together with the presence of a friendly army, ready, when necessary, to interpose between them and the enemy, all combined to render the issue of the struggle certain. Texas, it was seen, would become independent of Mexico. But her *independence* would not necessarily add to the political power of the slave-holding interest in the United States. For this purpose *annexation* was indispensable. But annexation could not be effected at present, without drawing after it a war with Mexico, and this obvious consequence strengthened the objections entertained to the measure at the North. It was well ascertained that no treaty of annexation, especially at the price of a Mexican war, would at present receive the sanction of Congress. But, if Mexico could be induced to *commence* hostilities against the United States, or should her conduct justify a declaration of war against her, then one powerful obstacle to annexation would be removed, and Texas would become ours, by right of conquest, and with the unanimous consent of her inhabitants. Every attempt to purchase Texas had failed, and all hope of acquiring it by this means, was abandoned on the termination of Mr. Butler's fruitless mission. From this time, the policy of the administration was to *force Mexico into a war.* The commencement of this new policy was the advance of American troops into Texas, on the pretence of protecting the frontier against Indians.

On the 5th of August, 1836, the President, in a letter to the Governor of Tennessee, countermanded a requisition by Gaines for troops, assigning this remarkable reason: "*There is no information to justify the apprehension of hostilities to any serious extent from the Western Indians.*"

The victory of San Jacinto had now been won, and the President probably thought that General Gaines's zeal in behalf of Texas was putting the country to unnecessary expense. Why the order countermanding the General's requisition was not given through the Secretary of War does not appear. Possibly it was deemed most prudent not to put the important admission we have quoted, on record in the War Office, and it is to some accident or carelessness that we are indebted for this letter, among the official documents published by Congress. Let its date be kept in mind. *5th August,* 1836.

On the 10th of the succeeding September, the Mexican Minister at Washington wrote to the Secretary of State, and, referring to some newspaper statements that the United States troops had invaded the Mexican territory, averred that, if this invasion was sanctioned by the Government, his mission must terminate. And what reply was returned? Did the Government apologize for the invasion as having been induced by false reports? Did it acknowledge, that there was now "no information to justify the apprehension of hostilities to any serious extent from our Western Indians," and that therefore the troops should be immediately recalled? Far different was the response returned. The Secretary of State admitted that American troops were then stationed at Nagadoches, and further, that on the 4*th* of that month the President had instructed General Gaines to enter the Mexican territory, if he shall be satisfied, "that any body of Indians who disturb the peace of the frontier of the United States, receive assistance or shelter within the Mexican territory."

The Minister denied that Mexico had any wish to excite the Indians against the United States, and he formally demanded the withdrawal of the troops from the Mexican territory (Texas). This demand was, on the 13th October, met by a flat refusal—a refusal coupled with insult. The Minister was informed by our Secretary of State, that by treaty each party was bound to restrain its own Indians from making hostile incursions upon the territories of the other; and, as Mexico had not the ability to fulfil her engagement, the United States had the right in self-defence to occupy her territory. Not a particle of evidence was adduced to show that the frontiers of the United States were menaced by Mexican Indians—not an argument advanced to prove the necessity of our army advancing into Texas in *self-defence*, and the whole pretext is stamped with the brand of impudent falsehood, by the confession made to the Governor of Tennessee by the President in the letter we have quoted.

Two days after this insult to Mexico, her Minister demanded his passports.* This was a great point gained by the administration. Diplomatic intercourse with Mexico was so far interrupted; and the rupture, if properly managed, might result in war, and consequently in annexation. While in the very act of inflicting the grossest outrages upon Mexico, and amid professions of neutrality as ardent as they were false, the administration thought it

* See Ex. Doc., 2d Sess., 24th Cong. Vol I.

expedient to raise a note of wailing for the injuries committed by Mexico upon American citizens, accompanied with the most obstreperous clamors for compensation.

The public have heard much, but understood little, about "Our claims upon Mexico." It is not probable that one in a thousand of those who declaim about Mexican outrages, as justifying the war against that Republic, know whereof they affirm. Before entering upon an examination of our claims upon Mexico, it may be well to state two of the general principles which, by the laws and usages of nations, limit the interference of a government in behalf of the demands of its citizens upon foreign powers for the redress of alleged grievances.

Complaints growing out of *contracts* entered into by citizens of one country with the Government of another, are not properly subjects for international discussion. Our Government would not tolerate for a moment, a remonstrance from the British Cabinet in behalf of an Englishman employed in our arsenals or ship-yards, who complained that he had not been paid his stipulated wages.

Where by *treaty* a foreigner is entitled to seek redress in the courts of the country in which his alleged injury has been received, his Government is not permitted to convert his wrong, whether real or imaginary, into a national grievance. Should an English subject be assaulted in our streets, defrauded by his debtor, or falsely imprisoned by a police officer, his Government could not demand of ours redress for his sufferings. Were these two principles to be disregarded, and were Governments to insist on sitting in judgment on the contracts their subjects might form with foreign powers, or on the quarrels in which they might be involved abroad, it is very evident that the peace of the world would be perpetually disturbed. Yet these principles, as we shall see hereafter, have been set at naught in many of the claims preferred by the American Government on that of Mexico.

But the subject of these claims is so important in itself, and so indicative of the determination of the Cabinet at Washington to provoke a war with Mexico, as to demand a separate chapter.

CHAPTER V.

CLAIMS ON MEXICO, AND WAR RECOMMENDED BY THE PRESIDENT TO ENFORCE THEM.

On the 20th July, 1836, shortly after the victory of San Jacinto, and the captivity of the President of Mexico, the Secretary of State sent to Mr. Ellis, our Minister, a list of fifteen complaints against the Republic, accompanied with the strange acknowledgment that "the Department is not in possession of *proof* of all the circumstances of the wrong done in the above cases, as represented by the aggrieved parties." The Cabinet deemed it expedient to prefer the complaints without loss of time, and to seek afterwards for proof to establish them.

But the most extraordinary part of this procedure, and which reveals the anxiety of the Government to bring on a rupture with Mexico, is the course prescribed to Ellis. He is ordered to demand such reparation "as these accumulated wrongs may be found to require." If no satisfactory answer shall be given in *three weeks*, he was to announce, that, unless redress shall be afforded without unnecessary delay, his further residence would be useless. If this threat proved unavailing, he was to notify the Government that, unless a satisfactory answer was returned in *two weeks*, he should ask for his passport, and at the expiration of the fortnight, he is to return home, if no satisfactory answer is received. The Mexican Minister had already, for the reasons we have stated, left Washington; and here we see a contrivance for withdrawing our

Minister from Mexico in a manner highly irritating and insulting. All diplomatic relations between the two countries being thus interrupted, and for the alleged reason that Mexico had *refused* to pay our just demands, the way would be open for *reprisals*, and consequently *war* would follow.

It will be observed, too, that the responsibility of taking the momentous step which was almost necessarily to lead to hostilities, was adroitly thrown upon the *discretion* of a Mississippi slaveholder, eager to enlarge the slave territory by the annexation of Texas. Mr. Ellis was to judge whether the reparation offered was such as our "accumulated wrongs" required; *he* was to decide what was unnecessary delay, and *he* alone to determine whether the answers he received were or were not satisfactory.

We will now notice the fifteen grievances, the redress of which in a manner which Mr. Powhatten Ellis might deem sufficiently *satisfactory* and *prompt*, was to be the *sine qua non* of peace or war. We entreat the reader's patience while we enumerate these grievances, and the replies to them, because as he will see hereafter, it was for *these* that our diplomatic intercourse with Mexico was broken off, and that the President recommended to Congress, a measure equivalent to a declaration of war. The claims *afterwards* urged, can of course afford no justification or apology for the conduct of the administration, founded exclusively on the *fifteen* transmitted to Mr. Ellis. They were in substance as follows:

1. An American, of the name of Baldwin, had in 1832, unjust judgments given against him in the Mexican courts, and on one occasion, on account of an altercation between him and a magistrate, he was sentenced to the stocks. He resisted, and attempted to escape, and fell and injured

his leg. He was thereupon seized, put into the stocks, and afterwards imprisoned.

2. The American vessel Topaz, was chartered by the Mexican Government in 1832, to convey troops. The master and mate were murdered by the soldiers, the crew imprisoned, and the vessel seized and used in the Mexican service.

3. The American vessel Brazoria, was seized in 1832, and employed in a military expedition, without compensation.

4. Two American steamboats were taken possession of by Mexican officers, and used without compensation, in 1832.

5. Capt. McKeigé was imprisoned at Tabasco, in 1834, and an enormous fine imposed upon him, " without cause."

6. The American vessel Paragon, was causelessly fired into by a Mexican schooner, in 1834.

7. The American brig Ophir, was seized and condemned in 1835, at Campeachy, because by some mistake, the proper papers were not shown at the Custom-house.

8. The American vessel Martha, was seized at Galveston, in 1835, for alleged violation of the revenue laws, and the passengers, accused of an intention to use fire arms against a guard placed on board, were put in irons.

9. The American vessel Hannah Elizabeth, stranded in 1835, on the coast, was boarded by soldiers, and the crew imprisoned, and pillaged of their clothes. The crew were afterwards released.

10. Two American citizens were arrested in Metamoras, in 1836, by a party of soldiers, who struck one of them in the face with a sword. They were temporarily confined on suspicion of an intention to proceed to Texas. Sentinels were placed at the Consul's door, under false pretences. Soldiers broke into his gate, searched his house, and took from his yard a mare and two mules.

11. Mr. Slocum, bearer of despatches, was in 1836, detained and fined, for carrying official letters.

12. The American schooner Eclipse, was in 1836, detained at Tabasco, and her master and crew, mal-treated by the authorities.

13. The American schooner Compeer, and other vessels, were in 1836, forcibly detained at Metamoras.

14. The United States revenue-cutter Jefferson, in 1836, arrived off the harbor of Tampico, and was forbidden to enter. An officer and boat's crew, on landing, were temporarily arrested.

15. The American vessel Northampton, was wrecked in 1836, near Tabasco, and taken possession of by Custom-house officers and soldiers. The crew remonstrated, and the captain was wounded. More than half of the goods saved from the wreck were pillaged, and lost, by the revenue officers and soldiers. The Consul complained, but obtained no redress.

Such are the fifteen "accumulated wrongs," complained of by the American Government, and ordered to be formally presented by Mr. Ellis. It will be observed, that not one of them is alleged to have been committed by the Mexican *Government*. No law, no act of the *Government*, is complained of. Custom-house officers may act illegally, and soldiers may commit outrages, police officers and magistrates may be guilty of oppression, and yet the Government be wholly ignorant of the offences committed. Millions and millions of American property have been seized, by virtue of orders issued directly by the Governments of England and France; yet in no instance, did the American Cabinet venture to hazard the peace of the country, by demanding reparation within a specified number of *days*. On the contrary, the settlement of our claims upon other nations, was preceded by protracted negotiations. Our claims for the value of slaves carried away by the British forces, in 1815, were not settled and paid, till 1826. Indemnity for French spoliations on our commerce, from 1806 to 1813, was not received till 1834. In these cases, our claims were not a pretext for war, and consequently their payment was not hazarded by an insulting demand for a satisfactory reply in *two weeks.*

Several of the fifteen complaints we have enumerated, if well founded, did not justify national interference, being injuries for which the sufferers were entitled to seek redress in the Mexican courts; others were proper subjects for inquiry and remonstrance; not one afforded a legitimate cause for war, for not one had been ordered, or as yet justified by the Mexican Government.

The extreme haste with which Mexico was required to redress these complaints, is the more extraordinary when we recollect, that the alleged grievances were mostly of recent date. The complaint of Baldwin, was the oldest, viz.: five years standing; three others occurred four years before, two in 1834, three in 1835, and the other *nine* within less than twelve months of the instructions to Mr. Ellis.

It so happened, that before Mr. Forsyth's despatch reached the minister, *two* of the fifteen wrongs, the eleventh and fourteenth, had been settled to the satisfaction of the latter. Through the ignorance of a Post-master, Mr. Slocum had been fined $6, for a supposed violation of the law in carrying letters. The government, on learning the affair, censured the Post-master, and remitted the fine. The revenue cutter Jefferson was refused admittance into the harbor of Tampico, only because the port was closed against all foreign vessels, without exception; and the commander of Tampico, had been removed for his harshness in temporarily confining the American officer and crew who had landed.

On the 26th September, Ellis laid before the Mexican Minister in writing, the *thirteen* remaining grievances, and was promptly assured that they would be investigated. As most of these complaints related to acts recently committed by Custom-house officers and other officials, it was probable that the letter of the 26th September, was the first notice of them, that the Government had ever received; yet on the 20th October following, less than *four weeks* from the date of the first letter, Ellis announced to the Government, that unless the wrongs complained of, are redressed without unnecessary delay, "his farther residence in Mexico would be useless."

To this insulting missive, a calm, dignified reply was returned the *next* day. Ellis is reminded that a delay in answering a note is not a sufficient cause for breaking off a negotiation; and that, to decide on the grievances presented, documents were to be collected from various offices in different parts of the Republic. He was informed, that measures had already been taken to procure the requisite documents, and promised that, when these were received, the decision of the government would be communicated to him. Well did John Quincy Adams remark in a note to his printed speech in Congress in 1838, "From the day of the battle of San Jacinto, every movement of the administration of this Union appears to have been made for the express purpose of breaking off negotiations, and precipitating a war, or *of frightening Mexico into the cession of not only Texas, but the whole course of the Rio del Norte, and five degrees of latitude across their continent to the South Sea.* The instructions of the 20th July, 1836, from the Secretary of State to Mr. Ellis almost immediately after the battle, were evidently premeditated to produce rupture, and were but too faithfully carried into execution. His (Ellis's) letter of the 20th October, 1836, to Mr. Monasterio was the premonitory symptom, and no true-hearted citizen of this union can read it, and the answer to it on the next day by Mr. Monasterio, without blushing for his country." But neither Ellis nor his employers were in the habit of blushing; and on the 4th November the Minister, in pursuance of his instructions, gave formal notice that, unless his complaints were satisfactorily answered in *two weeks*, he should demand his passports!

It was only to a feeble nation, and one whose hostility was courted for ulterior designs, that the administration would have hazarded such insolence. Mexico, sensible of her feebleness, did not resent the insult, and Mr. Ellis received an answer within the number of days he had assigned. The Mexican Secretary remarked that, by the existing treaty, citizens of either country were entitled to bring their grievances before the tribunals of the other, and hence it was unnecessary for their respective governments to interfere to procure that justice for them which the courts of law were ready to afford;* and that complaints against

* The 14th Art. of the treaty between the United States and Mexico guaranteed protection to the persons and property of the citizens of each, "leaving open and free to them the tribunals of justice for their judicial recourse, on the same terms which are usual and customary with the natives or citizens of the country in which they may be." Mr. Forsyth availed himself of this article of the treaty in his reply (January 29th, 1836), to a demand from the Mexican Government for the punishment of the Captain of an American armed ship, for an alleged outrage committed by him on a Mexican vessel. The Secretary remarked, "*That the courts of the United States are freely open to all persons in their jurisdiction, who may consider themselves to have been aggrieved in contravention of our laws and treaties.*" This application of the treaty to Mexican complaints was exceedingly convenient; but its application to *American* complaints was indignantly refused by Mr. Ellis in his reply of the 15th November of the *same* year. He declared that "the opinion ex-

officers of the customs should not be made subjects of negociation, for the reason that Americans have the same means of redress in the tribunals of the country as the Mexicans themselves. Nevertheless, the government will not decline to examine the complaints preferred by Mr. Ellis. These, it will be recollected, had been reduced to thirteen, and they were thus answered :

1. As to Mr. Baldwin, whatever may have been his wrongs, he ought to have sought redress in Mexican courts. It was probable his behavior had been improper, as six criminal prosecutions were pending against him. The government had no power to interfere between litigant parties in courts of justice ; but it had signified to the authorities the wish that justice might be awarded to Baldwin with promptitude and impartiality.

2. The government understands that the Topaz which was chartered to convey troops, was wrecked ; that, after she was stranded, and while the soldiers were in the hold, the American crew shut the hatches upon them, and murdered three Mexican officers who were upon deck. That the object of the crew was to carry off the money on board ; that the soldiers forced the hatches, attacked the crew, killed one, and secured the others for trial.

3. The Brazoria was pressed into the service of the Texan colonists by Austin, and had been abandoned by her owner with protest for loss and damages. The Minister of War had ordered her to be sold, and the proceeds paid into the treasury. On proof of ownership, the Government was ready to pay an equitable indemnity.

4. As to the steam-boats detained, the government had

pressed by the Hon. Mr. Monasterio which limits the citizens of the United States having certain claims against the Government, to resort to the judicial tribunals of Mexico for indemnity, is wholly indefensible."

Ex Documents, 24th Congress, 2 Sess., Vol. 3., Doc. 139.

a contract with the owner, who is now in debt to the Government. Nothing is due to him; but if he thinks otherwise, let him establish his claims before the tribunals.

5. The case of Captain Keigé has been investigated, and the Government has ordered the offending officer to be prosecuted, and will indemnify Captain Keigé.

6. Orders have been given for the trial of the officer who fired into the Paragon; but the result of the trial is not yet known.

7. In the case of the Ophir no wrong was done. The vessel was properly condemned for want of the necessary papers. An appeal was taken to a higher court, before which the missing papers were produced, and the vessel discharged.

8. The Government is wholly ignorant of the case of the Martha, and has called for, but not yet received, information upon the subject.

9. In regard to the case of the Hannah Elizabeth, the government had called for, but not yet received, a statement of the transaction.

10. The Government is ignorant of the proceedings at Metamoras, and has called for information.

This information was soon after received, and Mr. Ellis was informed that, on the arrival at Metamoras of the commander of that city, he understood that two strangers had just departed, who were supposed to be Texan spies. He sent four dragoons after them, who saw them enter a house in the outskirts of the city. Finding a mare and two mules in the yard, the soldiers removed the animals to prevent the escape of the strangers. The soldiers then entered the house, and arrested the two men, who on examination were found to have passports, and were allowed to proceed on their journey, and the animals were returned. It was not till after the affair that the commandant learned that the house was occupied by the American Consul.

11. The Government was uninformed of the affair of the Eclipse, but would make the proper inquiries.

12. The Compeer and other vessels were detained a few days at Metamoras, in consequence of a general embargo on all vessels without distinction, imposed by the Commander of that department, without the knowledge of the Government, which disapproved of and revoked it.

13. The Government knows nothing of the case of the Northampton, but has called for information.

Such were "the accumulated wrongs" for which the Cabinet determined to break off all intercourse with Mexico. It is rare, indeed, that diplomatic history exhibits a series of national complaints so trivial in themselves, urged with so much spleen and arrogance on the one side, or met with so much fairness and good temper on the other. To the thirteen grievances forwarded from Washington, Mr. Ellis had thought proper to add *five* more without instructions, and we therefore continue the catalogue of grievances, viz.:

14. The American Consul at Tampico had, May 26th, 1836, been summoned by the authorities to authenticate certain papers, and on his refusal had been threatened with imprisonment.—To this it was replied, that the Government was ignorant of the circumstances, but would investigate the matter.

15. The American vessel, Peter D. Vroom, being wrecked on the coast, June, 1836, the American Consul had the cargo brought to Vera Cruz, where the consignee abandoned it to the underwriters. Whereupon the Mexican Court appointed an agent for the underwriters, who sold the cargo, and the demand of the American Consul

to receive the proceeds was refused.—To this the Mexican Secretary replied, that as the underwriters had appointed no agent, the Court did right to appoint one for them, and that the Consul had no official authority in the premises.

16. Ellis complained that copies of certain judicial proceedings in the case of the brig Aurora had been refused to the American Consul.—He was informed that the copies were offered to him, but that he refused to pay the legal fees charged for making the copies.

17. The American vessel Bethlehem was seized by a Mexican armed vessel on the 2nd September, 1836, and the crew detained twenty days, and then landed, the vessel confiscated, and the captain refused a copy of the proceedings.—The Government knew nothing of the affair, but would make inquiries.

18. The American vessel Fourth of July had been taken possession of by Mexican soldiers.—It turned out that the vessel had been built for the Mexican Government. The agent had contracted before a notary for the sale; but a party of soldiers had been sent on board previous to the delivery of the bill of sale. The owner had been paid for his vessel, and made no complaint.*

We have now the sum-total of all the complaints against Mexico, which the joint efforts of Messrs. Forsyth and Ellis could collect. We can readily imagine the storm of indignation and resentment which such a budget presented by the British Government to that at Washington, with a demand for a satisfactory answer in fourteen days, would raise throughout the length and breadth of the Federal

* Mr. Forsyth having heard of this case, wrote to Ellis, December 9th, 1836, as "the owners of the brig Fourth of July are content," he is not to insist on the restoration of the vessel, but only to demand satisfaction for the insult offered to the American Flag!!

Republic. The tone assumed by Mr. Ellis was not less offensive than the pretended grievances themselves. Of that tone, we may form some opinion from the dignified conclusion of the Mexican answer:

"Your Excellency, after specifying all the subjects which have been thus replied to, goes on to say, that the Mexican armed vessels have fired upon and insulted the flag of the United States, that her consuls have been maltreated and insulted by the authorities, private citizens assassinated, arrested, and scourged, like malefactors, their property condemned and confiscated, &c., &c. But as these charges are made in terms so general, the Supreme Government of the Republic desires that they may be specified, before taking them into consideration."

Let us now see the character of the eighteen *specified* grievances, as explained by the Mexican Government. The cases of the Topaz (No. 2), Brazoria (No. 3), Captain Kiegé (No. 5), the Paragon (No. 6), the Ophir (No. 7), the affair at Metamoras (No. 10), the case of the Compeer (No. 12), the Peter D. Vroom (No. 15), the Aurora (No. 16), and the Fourth of July (No. 18), are utterly divested of all wrong and injustice on the part of the Mexican Government.

There remain only eight of the whole budget which afford the least room for complaint; and of these the Government professed entire ignorance in the case of the Martha (No. 8), the Hannah Elizabeth (No. 9), the Eclipse (No. 11), the Northampton (No. 13), the treatment of the Consul at Tampico (No. 14), and the Bethlehem (No. 17). It was not pretended that the injuries complained of in these six cases had been inflicted by *orders* from the Government; and it might readily be believed that the Government was not acquainted with every abuse of power by its officials. But in each of these cases, an inquiry was promised; and it is difficult to conceive what more could have been reasonably demanded. We have now left only *two* cases within the knowledge of the Government, at all open to the suspicion of injustice and oppression—the case of Baldwin (No. 1), and of the detained steamboats (No. 4). *Apparently* neither was a fit subject of negotiation; for the complaints in the first case were made against judicial decisions, which can never be properly brought into question by a foreign government, except when founded on some *great principle* contradicted by treaty or national law, and not on mere issues of fact. The complaint in the second instance appears to have grown out of a *contract* over which our own Government had no legitimate cognizance.

The Cabinet had relieved themselves from breaking off the negotiations by throwing the responsibility of it upon Mr. Ellis. Their confidence in this gentleman was not misplaced. *After* receiving from the Mexican Secretary of State the explanations and assurances already mentioned, he demanded (7th December) his PASSPORTS! The Mexican Government begged to know *for what cause* he took a step so calculated to affect the relations of the two countries. It would not do to give the *true* reason: it was difficult to frame a plausible one; and Mr. Ellis remained silent.

The Mexican Minister had left Washington on account of the march of American troops into Texas, and the claim advanced by the Government of the right to send an American army into the heart of Mexico, if necessary, to guard against *Indian hostilities.* Mr. Ellis had terminated his mission in Mexico in the exercise of the discretion allowed him, adjudging the answers made to the eighteen complaints *unsatisfactory.* Negotiations being at an end, satisfaction for the eighteen grievances, and as many more as we could find, could of course be obtained only by force, which would necessarily lead to war, and that as necessarily to the immediate annexation of Texas. Accordingly, on the 6th February, 1837, the President having received Mr. Ellis's report, sent a Message to Congress on the subject of our claims upon Mexico. In this document, complaining of the conduct of the sister Republic, he observed: "The length of time since some of the injuries have been committed, the repeated and unavailing applications for redress, the wanton character of some of the outrages upon the property and persons of our citizens, upon the officers and flag of the United States, *independent* of recent insults to this Government and people by the late extraordinary Mexican Minister, would justify in the eyes of all nations IMMEDIATE WAR. That remedy, however, should not be used by just and generous nations, confiding in their strength, for injuries committed, if it can be honorably avoided; and it has occurred to me that, considering the present embarrassed condition of that country, we should act both with wisdom and moderation, by giving to Mexico one more opportunity to atone for the past, before we take redress into our hands."

"To avoid all misconception on the part of Mexico, as well as to protect our national character from reproach, this opportunity should be given with the avowed design and full preparation *to take immediate satisfaction,* if it should not be obtained on a repetition of the demand for it. To this end, I recommend that an act be passed, authorizing *reprisals and the use of the naval force of the United States,* by the Executive, against Mexico, to enforce them, in the event of a refusal by the Mexican government, to come to an amicable adjustment of the matters in controversy between us, upon another demand thereof, made on *board one of our vessels of war, on the coast of Mexico.*"

The cruelty of this attempt to involve the two countries in war, was aggravated by the very character of the recommendation. No specification is made of the injuries we have received, no notice is taken of the answers returned to the eighteen complaints, no mention made of the *amount* of money claimed. The President is to be armed with power to take immediate satisfaction, and for this purpose the navy is to be placed at his disposal. But to what amount the navy is to plunder the commerce and sea-ports of Mexico, is not stated. However, before a system of robbery is commenced, a demand for satisfaction (but how much no one knows,) is to be sent to the Government of Mexico, from a ship of war off Vera Cruz, and "a satisfactory answer" to be retnrned, of course, in a certain number of days. No one can fail to see that the President intended WAR, and that a compliance with his recommendation by Congress would have been equivalent to its declaration. The country was not yet prepared to commence a system of human butchery, for the purpose of facilitating the acquisition of Texas; and General Jackson's belligerent proposition found but little favor with either house of Congress.

But the reader is as yet only partially acquainted with the extreme wickedness of this proposal. He is yet to learn that only *six months* before the date of this message, the President had himself acknowledged that Mexico was guiltless of the conduct he now imputed to her. We must again advert to the letter of the 5th August, 1836, already quoted in the preceding chapter. This was a sort of semi-official, semi-confidential epistle, written, not at Washington, but at the President's residence in Tennessee, and addressed to the Governor of that State. Governor

Cannon was, doubtless, no less anxious than his friend, for the annexation of Texas, even at the cost, if necessary, of a war with Mexico. General Jackson seems to have written the letter, to excuse himself for countermanding Gaines's order for troops, and for not facilitating annexation, by making war on Mexico. On the first point he tells the Governor "there is no information to justify the apprehension of hostilities to any serious extent, from the western Indians." But was not the frontier endangered by the Mexicans? Was not Mexico virtually waging war upon us? Listen to the solemn assertions made by the President's ambassador Ellis, in his letter to the Mexican Secretary of State, on the 26th September, only a few weeks after the communication made to Governor Cannon:—"The flag of the United States has been repeatedly insulted, and fired upon by the public armed vessels of this Government; her consuls, in almost every port of the Republic, have been maltreated and insulted by the public authorities; her citizens, while in the pursuit of a lawful trade, have been murdered on the high seas, by a licentious and unrestrained soldiery. Others have been arrested and scourged in the streets by the military, like malefactors—they have been seized and imprisoned under the most frivolous pretexts—their property has been condemned and confiscated in violation of existing treaties, and the acknowledged laws of nations, and large sums of money have been exacted of them, contrary to all law." Now, in such a state of things, how did General Jackson excuse himself to his friend, for not vindicating the rights of his country? Very easily. All the grievances we could muster were but *eighteen*, and Ellis's vituperation was intended for the purpose of insult and exasperation. The President well knew, as the result proved, that Congress could not be prevailed on to declare war against Mexico at present, and hence he tells Governor Cannon: "*Should* Mexico insult our national flag, invade our territory, or interrupt our citizens in the lawful pursuits which are guaranteed to them by treaty, *then* the Government will promptly repel the insult, and take speedy reparation for the injury. BUT IT DOES NOT SEEM THAT OFFENCES OF THIS CHARACTER HAVE BEEN COMMITTED BY MEXICO."* Let it not be forgotten, that this confession was made about two weeks *after* the date of the instructions to Ellis already mentioned, and which were obviously intended to produce a rupture of the diplomatic intercourse between the two countries, as preparatory to war.

* See this remarkable letter in *Ex. Doc.* 2 *Sess.* 24 *Cong. Vol.* 1, *No.* 2. It was probably intended as a *private* letter, but almost immediately found its way into the newspapers, most likely through the indiscretion of Governor Cannon. Being thus made public, Mr. Forsyth made use of it, *the* 31*st of the same month*, in his correspondence with the Mexican Minister, sending him a *newspaper copy of the letter*, as evidence of the President's friendly disposition towards Mexico!

CHAPTER VI.

ACKNOWLEDGMENT OF THE INDEPENDENCE OF TEXAS.

THE colonists of Texas being American citizens, at no time wished to remain a separate and independant nation. Their highest aspiration was to see their lone star admitted into the American constellation. The slave-holders also were adverse to the rise of a small independent State on their southern borders—a State that in time might form a barrier to the progress of slavery. It was the policy of the Texans to stimulate the desire of the slave-holders for annexation, and hence within fifteen days after the declaration of independence, they adopted a constitution giving the rights of citizenship to all white emigrants, after a residence of six months, authorizing emigrants to bring their slaves with them, and rendering human bondage perpetual, by depriving the legislature of the power to abolish it. A boon was held out to the breeding States, by granting them the monopoly of the Texan market, the importation of slaves being prohibited, *except from the United States.* Free negroes and mulattoes, it is well known, are regarded by the slave-holders as a dangerous population. In Texas, no colonization society was needed to remove such nuisances from the country. By the Constitution, every negro and every mulatto, now or in future, remaining on the soil of Texas, was doomed to bondage. There was still one more lure held out to the South. Mr. Benton had calculated that nine slave States might be carved out of Texas; but his vision of the future was confined to the Mexican province of that name. The American insurgents, however, resolved to offer to the slave-holding interest, not a single province only, but parts of Coahuila, Tamaulipas, and New Mexico; and accordingly voted themselves, on the 19th December, 1836, the vast territory included between the United States and the Rio Grande, from its source to its mouth. To proclaim, moreover, their eagerness to transfer themselves and their immense domain, now consecrated to slavery, to the Federal Union, a poll was held in 1836, at which the electors were required to express their wish for annexation, or for a separate government. The result was, 3279 votes for annexation, and 91 against it. This vote is also important, as showing the diminutive population of the insurgent State. These various manifestations were not made to unwilling or unobservant spectators.

The President, while full of complaints against the aggressions of Mexico, sent an official agent (Henry M. Morfit,) into Texas, whose report of the good land, it was hoped, would excite the American people to go up and take possession. On the 22d December, 1836, the President laid before Congress a communication from his agent, on the "Political, military, and civil condition of Texas." This document reveals the following important facts:—"The boundaries claimed by Texas will extend from the mouth of the Rio Grande, on the east side, up to its head waters, thence on a line due north, until it intersects that of the United States, and with that line to the Red River, on the northern boundary of the United States, then to the Sabine, and along that river to its mouth, and from that point westwardly with the Gulf of Mexico to the Rio Grande. *It was the intention of the Government, immediately after the battle of San Jacinto, to have claimed from the Rio Grande along the river to* 30 *degrees of latitude, and then west to the Pacific.* It was, however, found that this would not strike a convenient point on the California, that it would be difficult to control a wandering population so distant, and that the territory now determined upon would be *sufficient* for a young Republic. *The political limits of Texas proper, previous to the last revolution, were the Nueces river on the west, along the Red River on the north, the Sabine on the east, and the Gulf of Mexico on the south.*"*

The report of his agent in Texas was accompanied by the President with certain remarks highly characteristic of the policy pursued from the first by the Federal Government towards that province. "It is known," said the President, "that the people of Texas have instituted the same form of government with our own; and have, since the close of your last session, openly resolved, on the acknowledgment by you of their independence, to seek admission into the Union as one of the Federal States. *The title of Texas to the territory she claims is identified with her independence.* She asks us to acknowledge that title to the territory with an avowed design immediately to transfer it to the United States." Thus we have a direct appeal to the avarice of the American people in behalf of annexation. The extravagant claims of Texas to Mexican territory are spread before Congress, and that body is reminded that the title to these vast domains *is identified* with the independence of Texas. Let us acknowledge that independence, and we thereby acknowledge the goodness of her claims; and, as soon as the acknowledgment is made, all Texas, and part of Coahuila, Tamaulipas, and most of New Mexico, will be ours. The influence of the tempter was in no degree lessened by a little commonplace cant about the duty of avoiding all suspicion of acting from *interested* motives. It was now obvious that, as

* Ex. Documents Vol. 2. 24 Cong. 2 Sess.

Texas could not be purchased, and as Mexico would probably not be provoked into war, the acknowledgment of Texan independence was a necessary preliminary to annexation. But there was a powerful and vigilant hostility at the North against every measure leading to the acquisition of more slave territory. Pains were, therefore, taken first to weaken this opposition by considerations of personal and party interest, and, secondly, to lull its apprehensions by false and deceptive suggestions and assurrances. Thus President Jackson, in the Message already quoted, after showing how exceedingly profitable to the United States the acknowledgment of Texan independence would certainly prove, proceeded to allay the alarm of the North which his own representation awakened, by pretending that such acknowledgment must be indefinitely postponed. "Prudence," said he, "seems to dictate that we should still stand aloof, and maintain our present attitude, if not till Mexico or one of the great foreign powers shall recognize the independence of the new Government, at least until *the lapse of time, or the course of events, shall have proved, beyond all cavil or dispute*, the ability of that country to maintain their separate sovereignty, and to uphold the Government constituted by them."

This declaration, so frank and explicit, and made at the beginning of the Session of Congress, tended to prevent all demonstration of popular opinion against the acknowledgment, and all pledges on the subject from the Representatives to their constituents.

On the 1st of March, two days before the close of the Session, and in the absence of six members, a resolution passed the Senate acknowledging the INDEPENDENCE OF TEXAS. Allusion was made in debate to the objections made by the President on the 22d of the preceding December to such a measure. To the astonishment of the public, the mover of the resolution, Mr. Walker, from Mississippi, declared in his place that he "had it from the President's own lips that, if he were a Senator, he would vote for this resolution." Thus *the lapse of time and course of events*, contemplated by the President in his Message, were ascertained to be eight weeks, and a majority in Congress. The resolution was adopted by the lower House, and the American Colonists in Texas were thus received into the family of nations as forming an Independent Republic.

CHAPTER VII.

NEW CLAIMS ADVANCED AGAINST MEXICO.

It will be recollected that President Jackson, in his Message of the 6th February, 1837, proposed that he should be authorized to make reprisals against Mexico, and for that purpose to employ the naval force of the nation, provided Mexico did not come "to an amicable adjustment of the matters in controversy between us, upon another demand thereof made on board one of our vessels of War."

Now, "the matters in controversy between us" were, in fact, no other than the eighteen grievances already specified. It was stipulated by the existing treaty with Mexico, that neither party shall "order or authorize *any act of reprisal*, nor declare war against the other on complaints of grievances or damages, until the said party considering itself offended shall first have presented to the other a statement of such injuries or damages, verified by *competent proof*, and demand justice and satisfaction, and the same shall have been either refused or *unreasonably* delayed." Whatever claims and grievances we might have against Mexico, they were not "*matters in controversy*" until after they had been presented, and by the express terms of the treaty could not warrant either reprisals or war, until they had been *verified*, and the Mexican Government had either refused or unreasonably delayed justice.

Notwithstanding this treaty stipulation, the President

laid before Congress a schedule of grievances amounting in number to FORTY-SIX.* Of the original eighteen claims, only one dated as far back as 1831, in the new schedule *thirty-two* are founded on acts alleged to have been committed *prior* to 1832. Having given the reader a specification of each of the original claims, we will not now trespass on his patience by noticing in detail the additional ones which the administration now found it convenient to disinter from the oblivion of past years, and which had been in fact buried by the treaty ratified 5th April, 1832, which proclaimed the friendship existing between the two Republics. It may be well, however, to give a few samples of these claims to show the determined efforts of the American Government to quarrel with Mexico.

"Mexican Company, Baltimore, 1816; amount of claim not stated. This was an association of individuals that furnished General Mina with the means of undertaking his invasion of Mexico, which amount they aver has never been repaid to them."

"Mrs. Young, 1817; amount of claim not stated. The claimant is the widow of Col. Guilford Young, who was a partner of Mina, and was killed while fighting in 1817. The claim is understood to be for arrears of pay."

These claims it will be observed, are for insurrectionary services *against the Spanish Government,* seven or eight years before that Government was succeeded by the Mexican Republic.

"John B. Marie, 1824; amount of claim not stated. Goods seized upon pretext of having been introduced contrary to a Mexican law. The claimant says he was ignorant of the law."

"T. E. Dudley, and J. C. Wilson, 1824; amount

* Ex. Doc., 24th Cong., 2d Sess., vol. 3.

claimed not stated. The claimants robbed of a part of their property by the Camanche Indians, on their return from a trading expedition to Mexico."

The proposition to employ the naval force of the Union in making reprisals to enforce *such* claims was deemed too hazardous to be wise. It would necessarily bring on a war; and a war waged on pretexts so scandalous, might destroy the popularity of the party, and augment the anti-slavery feeling of the North. It was evident the nation was not yet prepared to incur the calamities of war for the sole purpose of hastening the annexation of Texas; and moreover, such a war, to receive the concurrence of the North, must at least be *commenced by Mexico.* A course was therefore adopted, more sagacious than that urged by the fiery impatience of the President. Committees of the two Houses of Congress, made reports well calculated, by exaggerating the misconduct of Mexico, to exasperate the ill-feeling already existing, but recommending that one more demand should be made for reparation.

On the last day of the Session, an appropriation was made for the salary of a Minister to Mexico, "whenever in the opinion of the President circumstances will permit a renewal of diplomatic intercourse honorably with that Power." It was only in the preceding December that the Diplomatic intercourse had been broken off by instructions from the President, on the ground that it could not honorably be continued; and yet, on the 30th of March, without any circumstance having occurred in the interval to invite a renewal of that intercourse, except the refusal of Congress to go to war, the President nominated a Minister to Mexico! "And who," to use the language of J. Q. Adams, "was this Minister of peace, to be sent with the last drooping twig of olive to be replanted and revivified in the genial soil of Mexico? It was no other than Powhattan Ellis, of Mississippi, famishing for Texas, and just returned in anger and resentment from an abortive and abruptly terminated mission to the same Government. His very name must have tasted like wormwood to the Mexican palate; and his name seems alone to have been used for the purpose of giving a relish to these last resources of pacific and conciliatory councils. But though appointed, he was not permitted to proceed upon his embassy. He was kept at home, and in his stead was despatched a courier of the Department of State, with a budget of grievances good and bad, new and old, stuffed with wrongs as full as Falstaff's buck basket with foul linen, to be turned over under the nose of the Mexican Secretary of State, with an allowance of ONE WEEK* to examine, search out, and answer concerning them all."

In politics as in commerce, the supply is regulated by the demand. The Cabinet were in urgent want of claims upon Mexico, and, as it was, possible money might be extorted on these claims, there was, of course, no lack of claimants.

On the 20th July, 1836, the "accumulated wrongs" for which Mr. Forsyth instructed Ellis to demand satisfaction, and, if not received in a limited time, to ask for his passports, amounted, as we have seen, to fifteen in number, but as two had been already settled, in fact only to *thirteen.* These, by the zeal and industry of Ellis, were increased to eighteen. On the 6th February, 1837, the accumulation was swelled to *forty-six,* and on the 20th July, 1837, the anniversary of Mr. Forsyth's celebrated despatch to Ellis, the "courier of the department of

* "The messenger bearing the budget was instructed to remain in the city of Mexico *one week.*" Rep. of Cong., 1st Sess., 29th Cong., Vol. 4.

State," appeared in the city of Mexico, bending beneath a load of FIFTY-SEVEN wrongs, for which, in the name of the American Government, he demanded "justice and satisfaction."

Of these complaints, it may readily be imagined, many were in the highest degree most insolent and ridiculous. Let one suffice:—In 1829, Mexico was invaded by a Spanish force, and a printing press in Tampico, said to have been American property, was destroyed by the invaders. Eight years after the occurrence, Mexico is for the first time informed that she is held responsible by the Federal Government, for an act committed by her enemies in time of war. We can judge of the effect of such a claim upon the Mexicans, by supposing a demand of the French king upon the American Government, for payment of injuries received by one of his subjects, from the British troops while in possession of the city of Washington.

The temporary detention of two citizens at Metamoras, and the pretended abduction of two mules and a mare, although so abundantly and satisfactorily explained, again figure among the national grievances for which the "courier" demanded satisfaction.

That our Government had no desire whatever, to bring their dispute with Mexico to an amicable termination, is perfectly obvious from the extraordinary course it pursued on this occasion. Congress decided not to go to war, but to renew negotiations, and furnished money for the salary of a minister. A minister is appointed personally odious to the Mexicans, but detained at home, while a messenger is sent with a list of fifty-seven grievances, of which not more than eighteen at most had ever before been brought to the notice of the Mexican Government. This messenger was forbidden to remain for more than *one week*. No opportunity was afforded to Mexico to make explanations, or even to ascertain what reparation would be satisfactory. She had no minister in the United States. The American Minister, appointed in obedience to the wishes of Congress, was not dispatched; and hence, admitting our claims to have been just, and admitting Mexico to be willing to allow them, the very measures adopted by the Cabinet precluded all adjustment of the points in controversy Our demands were in truth intended only to irritate, and to furnish stronger pretexts than had yet been found for *reprisals and war*.

Before this "buck basket," with its fifty-seven grievances reached Mexico, that Government—which knew of no other than the eighteen causes of complaint against it specified by Mr. Ellis, and on account of which he had terminated his mission—had passed an Act offering to submit to the award of a friendly power, the claims of the United States.*

* Ex. Doc., 25th Cong., 2 Sess. Vol. 8.

CHAPTER VIII.

TREATY OF ANNEXATION PROPOSED AND REJECTED.

Just twelve months after the declaration of Texan independence, that independence was acknowledged by the United States. A minister representing the Federal Government, was immediately despatched to the insurgents, and one in return was received from them. Mr. Hunt, recently an American citizen, and now "Envoy Extraordinary and Minister Plenipotentiary of the Republic of Texas," appeared among his old friends at Washington, and in August, 1837, proposed, in behalf of the yearling Republic, a treaty of annexation. Mr. Van Buren had, the preceding 4th of March, assumed the reins of Government. This gentleman had, on various occasions, shown so much anxiety to conciliate the South, as to be stigmatized by his opponents as "the Northern man with Southern principles." Mr. Hunt was therefore warranted in believing, that he would have no personal objection to extending the slave region by the addition of Texas. But very sufficient obstacles existed to the proposed treaty. Such a treaty would necessarily involve a war with Mexico, and in such a war the country was not yet prepared to engage. The treaty moreover, could not be ratified, because it was well ascertained, that more than one-third of the Senators would withhold their assent. A fruitless attempt to negotiate such a treaty would be a political blunder which Mr. Van Buren was too sagacious to commit—a blunder which would inevitably destroy the popularity of the administration, and have a most disastrous influence on the ensuing election. The Texan proposition was therefore politely declined on the ground that annexation at the present time must result in a war with Mexico. This was a reason which could give no offence to the South, especially as there were good grounds for hoping that the dextrous management of our claims would ere long remove the only alleged obstacle to annexation. The pear was not yet quite ripe, and Mr. Van Buren was at the time ignorant of the Mexican offer, which was destined to postpone its maturity.

CHAPTER IX.

TREATY OF ARBITRATION—ACTION OF THE SLAVEHOLDERS.

MEXICO, anxious to preserve peace with the United States, not only proposed to refer the claims of the latter to arbitration, but once more sent a Minister to Washington. This gentleman arrived in October, and, as is said, from a misapprehension that the Mexican proposition had already been communicated to the American Government, did not officially announce it till the 22d December, 1837. The proposition itself was a sore disappointment to the partisans of annexation. It tended to avert, or at least to postpone war. It was a proposition so fair and honorable, so pacific, and so directly appealing to the moral sense of the community, that it could not be rejected, without bringing great odium upon the administration; and the party of which it was the representative, had but little popularity to spare. Still it was received in sullen silence, and no other notice taken of it at the time, than a formal acknowledgment of its receipt.* No less than three times after this acknowledgment, did Mr. Forsyth (Secretary of State), press upon the Mexican Minister new claims, and new demands without deigning even a passing allusion to the very important proposal he had received. *Four months* elapsed, and this Government had yet given no intimation of its willingness to adopt an equitable and pacific mode of obtaining redress for "the accumulated wrongs" under which it professed to be suf-

* See Ex. Doc. 25th Cong., 2 Sess., Vol. 12.

fering. In the meantime, the Mexican offer had become public, and petitions had been presented to Congress praying its acceptance;* and at least forty thousand citizens had laid before that body their remonstrances against annexation. At length on the 21st April, 1838, Mr. Forsyth informed the Mexican Minister, that the President "is too anxious to avoid proceeding to extremities," not to accept the offer! Negotiations were now commenced at Washington, which resulted, on the 10th of September, 1838, in a convention between the two Governments, by which it was agreed, that all the claims against Mexico should be referred to a board of four Commissioners, two to be appointed by each party. The board to meet in Washington three months after the exchange of ratifications, and to sit not more than eighteen months. The award of the Commissioners to be final, but the cases on which they could not agree were to be decided by an umpire to be named by the King of Prussia. Should the Mexican Government not find it convenient to pay the amount awarded in cash, the payment was to be made in so much government stock as would, at the market price in London, be equal to the award. The Mexican ratification of this Convention not having been exchanged within the time limited, it was renewed with slight modifications in 1840; the most important of which was, that the sum awarded was to be paid, one half in cash, and the other in Treasury notes bearing eight per cent. interest, and receiveable for Mexican duties.

The determination of the Executive to refer the Mexican claims to arbitration, and the delay necessarily caused by such a reference, seemed to excite the slaveholders to increased energy in forwarding their favorite object. Mississippi had already, by its Legislature, demanded the an-

* See Ex. Doc. 25th Cong., 2 Sess., Vol. 12.

nexation of Texas, avowedly for the benefit of the slaveholding interest. The State of Alabama now did the same. The Legislature of Tennessee joined in the demand, but refrained from the indecency of resting it on the extension of human bondage. Three days after the acceptance of the Mexican offer, Mr. Preston, a senator from South Carolina, introduced a resolution, declaring the expediency of annexing Texas to the Union. On the 14th June, 1838, Mr. Thompson of the same State proposed a joint resolution in the Lower House, directing the President to take proper steps for the annexation of Texas, "as soon as it can be done consistently with the treaty stipulations of this Government."

At the South there was little or no difference between the two political parties on the question of annexation. As a specimen of the recklessness and profligacy with which the measure was then urged, we may quote the following language held by a prominent whig journal, "We have heretofore asserted, and we repeat it again, that Texas should be made a component part of our country *at all hazards*, peaceably if she was willing, and forcibly, if she was reluctant."*

The North, however, was not silent. The whig party were nearly united in their opposition to Texas, and they were in many instances joined by portions of their political opponents. The States of Vermont, Maine, Massachusetts, Connecticut. Rhode Island, New York, and Pennsylvania, all protested, through their Legislatures, against annexation. It is not, therefore, surprising that Mr. Van Buren departed from the policy of General Jackson in referring the claims of Mexico to arbitration instead of the sword.

* Frankfort (Ky.) *Commonwealth*, May 2d, 1838.

CHAPTER X.

RESULTS OF THE TREATY OF ARBITRATION.

It is not to be inferred, from what has been heretofore said of the claims upon Mexico, that none of them were founded in justice. Unquestionably some of the most legitimate were nevertheless of a character which, according to the laws and usages of nations, were not fit subjects of *national* controversy, such for instance as were founded on contracts or on torts within the cognizance of the ordinary tribunals of the country. Nor is it surprising that, during the many military revolutions by which Mexico had for years been convulsed, subordinate officers should occasionally have exceeded their powers, and for military purposes have trespassed on the neutral rights of American residents. The admiralty courts of Mexico, had condemned American vessels, taken with arms and munitions of war intended for Texas. These articles of contraband were by treaty liable to forfeiture; but the vessels themselves, together with such parts of the cargo as were not contraband, were by treaty exempted from condemnation. Had the intentions of the American Government been equitable, and their measures temperate, there is no reason to believe that any serious difficulty would have been experienced in recovering compensation where it was justly due.

The Board of Commissioners appointed under the Treaty commenced their session in Washington, 17th August, 1840; and by 26th May, the next year, a period of about nine months, they had passed upon *every claim* that had been presented to them, accompanied with the necessary vouchers, *a fact deriving great importance from subsequent events.* In February, 1842, the Commission was dissolved by the limitation prescribed in the Treaty, having sat eighteen months. The King of Prussia had named his Minister at Washington, Baron Roenne, as umpire.

Total amount of Claims presented, - - -	$11,850,578
Of these submitted too late to be examined,	3,336,837
	8,513,741
Referred to Umpire, and undecided by him for want of time, - - - - - - - -	928,627
Amount of Claims adjudicated, - - - -	7,595,114
Rejected by Commissioners and Umpire, -	5,568,975
Allowed do. do. - -	$2,026,236

This statement invites various remarks. The Federal Government had been for years espousing the cause of the Mexican claimants. Session after session had the Executive Messages brought before Congress, not the particulars but *the subject* of Mexican outrages. Committees had reiterated the lamentations of the President over our accumulated wrongs. A minister had been withdrawn from Mexico, because redress had been withheld; and war had virtually been recommended by General Jackson to obtain, by force of arms, that justice for our citizens which Mexico denied them. Finally, a solemn Treaty proposed to afford the long-desired but denied reparation. A Court, composed of two American and two Mexican citizens, were to sit in judgment on these claims; and, where the Court could not agree, an impartial umpire was to award the amount justly due. The Court commenced its session about *two years* after its first appointment. Surely the claimants had abundant notice to prepare and present their claims; and they had also timely notice that the term of the Court was limited to eighteen months. For the convenience of the claimants, the Court assembled in Washington, contrary to the wishes and remonstrances of the Mexican Government. Under such circumstances, it is not surprising that, after the Court had been in session nine months, only one-half of the time to which it was limited, it had disposed of *every case* that had been presented with proper vouchers. But at the termination of the next nine months, we find claims to the amount of $3,336,837, that were presented too late to be even examined! The magnitude of these claims, and the astonishing delay in presenting them, after the unwearied solicitude of the Government to swell the demand against Mexico, clearly indicate their fraudulent and speculative character. We find, moreover, that of those claims which were passed upon, about THREE-FOURTHS OF THE AMOUNT CLAIMED WAS REJECTED as not due. Unquestionably the strongest claims were first brought forward; and if these were three-fourths spurious, we may judge of the character of those introduced at the close of the session. We have seen the eagerness with which the Government welcomed and pressed every claim, however stale and absurd. It is obvious that the Court of Claims, if we may so name it, was a lottery in which magnificent prizes might be drawn, and in which the tickets cost nothing. Every man who had been in Mexico for the last twenty years, and could manufacture a wrong, was virtually invited to come forward and try his luck. There is also strong reason to believe, that, when at the end of the first nine months, all the cases ready had been heard, it was found that the result would be so insignificant as to cast contempt and ridicule upon the Cabinet; and that, therefore, great efforts were made to induce reckless speculators and adventurers to come forward with claims which would at least swell the unliquidated demand, and furnish ground for continued and irritating complaint. But supposing the unsettled claims to have been not less worthless than those which were adjudicated, then one million more would have been added to the award, making a debt due by Mexico of three instead of the eleven millions claimed.

Congress lately passed a bill for paying to American claimants five millions, due from the French Government, but which ours did not choose to go to war to collect. It was only of feeble Mexico, with her unprotected territory, that the Federal Cabinet was ready to collect debts at the mouth of the cannon.

It may not be amiss to give some specimens of the shameless profligacy of many of these claims, which politicians, for selfish purposes, have found it convenient to magnify into grievous wrongs.

A. O. de Santangelo was a schoolmaster and printer in Mexico. In one of the revolutionary struggles, he was obliged to flee, abandoning his school and press. He came to New Orleans, and thence to New York, where he became *a naturalized citizen of the United States*, and in that capacity brought in a bill of $398,690 against the Mexican Government for damages! The Mexican Commissioners denied that anything was due; the American Commissioners allowed him $83,440—which the Umpire cut down to $50,000, one-eighth of the demand. On what principle this eighth was allowed, it is difficult to imagine.

Rhoda McCrae claimed $6,694.04 for a pension for her son killed in the Mexican service. The American Commissioners to their shame allowed the claim, and the Umpire to his credit rejected it.

Sophia M. Robinson claimed, for services rendered by her husband in Mexico—then a province of Spain—in 1817, (!) $16,000, and as much more for interest. The American Commissioners allowed her $32,000 ! The Umpire most righteously refused her a cent.

John Baldwin claimed for a *trunk of wearing apparel*, seized by a Mexican custom-house officer, $1170. Interest $311.50: $1481.50. *All* allowed by American Com missioners. Undecided by Umpire.*

Mr. Pendleton, of Virginia, in a very able speech in Congress, 22nd February, 1847, on these claims, thus comments on one of them: "There is one particular item —a beauty of its kind—which I will mention. The item is for fifty-six dozen bottles of porter. I believe the best London porter can be purchased in any part of the world for something like three dollars a-dozen; and I estimate this porter, therefore, very liberally, when I put it down at two hundred dollars. What do you suppose is charged for it in this account? Why, sixteen hundred and ninety dollars! But that is reasonable, compared with the interest charged upon the price. That is for less than six years set down at $6,570; making for fifty-six dozen bottles of porter the nice little sum of $8,260! I do not say that all these accounts are of that sort; but this I will say, that many of them are *more* unreasonable."† One of the claims left undecided was preferred by a Texan land company for the comfortable sum of $2,154, 604; and one individual claims $690,000 for erroneous decisions against him in Mexican courts! It is creditable to the justice and moderation of Mexico, that, when such unscrupulous audacity was countenanced by our Government, the demands manufactured against her reached to no more than eleven millions of dollars.

* Ex. Doc., 27th Cong., 2nd Sess. No. 21.
† App. Cong. Globe.

CHAPTER XI.

NEW TREATIES WITH MEXICO ABOUT CLAIMS.

THE Treaty of Arbitration had deprived the Administration for some time of all pretexts of complaint against Mexico, and probably postponed the annexation of Texas. Fortunately for the designs of the Cabinet, the accumulation of claims towards the close of the Commission had, as we have seen, left a large nominal amount undecided. Of this surplus, the Administration eagerly availed itself to renew a harassing negotiation. No Minister had been sent to Mexico since Mr. Ellis thought it expedient to demand his passports, and to decline specifying the reasons of so ungracious a measure. The Commission under the Treaty terminated, as we have seen, in February, 1842; and the next March, Mr. Tyler, who as Vice-President had succeeded to the Executive Chair on the death of President Harrison, appointed Mr. Waddy Thompson, of South Carolina, Minister to Mexico. In selecting this gentleman, he was no doubt influenced by the same motives which had led to the appointment of Messrs. Poinsett, Butler, and Ellis. He was a slaveholder, devoted to the cause of Texas. He had, moreover, on the floor of Congress, introduced a resolution directing the President to take measures for the annexation of Texas, as soon as it could be done, consistently with the Treaty stipulations of the Government—an act which necessarily rendered him personally offensive to the Mexican Government.

It will be recollected that by the treaty of arbitration the award was to be paid half in cash, and half in treasury notes *at par,* bearing eight per cent. interest, and receivable for duties. Mr. Thompson found the Mexican credit very low, and treasury notes at a discount of about seventy per cent. His diplomatic correspondence has been published only in part, and we are therefore ignorant by what means he succeeded in negotiating, 30th January, 1843, a *new* convention or treaty by which Mexico agreed to pay on the 30th April of the same year, all the interest then due, and the award itself in five years, in equal quarterly instalments. This arrangement has been represented as a *boon* granted to Mexico,* and therefore aggravating her ingratitude. The assertion, like most others made in vindication or apology of the Mexican war, is untrue. Says Mr. Calhoun, Secretary of State, writing to Mr. Shannon, minister in Mexico, June 20th, 1844—"The convention (of 1839), provided that the claims which should be allowed, might be discharged by payment of Mexican treasury notes, but as these were much depreciated in value, it became a *matter of importance* to effect some other arrangement by which *specie* should be substituted in their stead. To this end your predecessor (Thompson), was empowered and *instructed* to enter into a negotiation with the Government of Mexico, and a convention was concluded, 30th January, 1843." Mr. Thompson, in his " Recollections of Mexico," speaking of this convention, says, p. 223, " the market value of the treasury notes was about thirty cents on a dollar, and, if this additional two millions had been thrown upon the market, they would have been depreciated still more. The owners of these claims knew this, and were *anxious* to make some other arrangement." Hence the " boon"

* Report of C J. Ingersol, Chairman of Com. of Foreign Affairs, June 24th, 1846.

was extorted from Mexico, and probably through the menaces of the negotiator.

But the new convention did more than regulate the payment of the award. It stipulated for the negotiation of *another arbitration treaty*, and one more comprehensive than the last, for it was to provide for the settlement of all claims made by the Government of Mexico *against the United States*, as well as the claims of the Government and citizens of the United States against the Republic of Mexico. Here was at least the *appearance* of fairness. The United States consented by this treaty, which was duly ratified, that the wrongs the Government and it citizens had done to Mexico should be submitted to a court of referees. What claims the *citizens* of Mexico had against the United States do not appear; but the claims of the *Government* were numerous and important.

Vessels captured by Mexican ships of war for being engaged in contraband trade, had been forcibly seized and carried off by American armed vessels, and a Mexican national vessel had been audaciously captured and brought to the United States by one of the vessels of our navy; and frequent had been the insults which American functionaries had offered to the Mexican authorities. It must, therefore, have been a grateful reflection to the Mexicans, that the wrongs they had themselves suffered, were to be examined and redressed by a tribunal more impartial than the Cabinet at Washington. Whether it was through inadvertence, or with a view of *inducing Mexico to provide for the settlement of the vast amount of claims left undecided* that the American Government accorded this unusual justice to the sister Republic, is uncertain. The treaty stipulated for by the convention of 30th January, 1843, was concluded in Mexico on the 20th November of the same year. The respective claims of the citizens and Governments of the two countries were to be referred to a joint commission to sit in Mexico; and where the commissioners should not agree, the award of an umpire, to be named by the king of Belgium, was to be final. This treaty was sent to Washington, accompanied by a letter from Thompson to the Secretary of State, in which he tells him "the place of meeting of the board, you will see, is in Mexico, and not in Washington. The Mexican plenipotentiaries said that the last commission met in Washington, and that it was their right to insist that this one should meet in Mexico. The only reply that I could make was, that the claims presented to that commission were all against Mexico, and that nearly all the claimants resided in the United States; to which they replied that this commission will also be charged with the claims of the Government and citizens of Mexico against the United States, and that they could not concede this point. I thought there was much reason in their demand; and, as it was matter of punctilio, and as with a Spaniard punctilio is everything, I was well satisfied it would be a *sine qua non*, and therefore yielded it, in *consideration of their allowing me to name the arbiter*—a much more important consideration."

The mere details of this treaty were of course matters of discretion to which the Government at Washington had the strict right of objecting. But the United States had, by a solemn convention duly ratified, agreed that the complaints of the Government and citizens of Mexico should be referred by treaty to a tribunal for settlement; to refuse therefore to consent to such a reference, was a breach of faith plighted by treaty. Yet of such a breach was the Senate of the United States guilty. The treaty was conditionally ratified by the Senate, first striking out of it the right of each Government to prefer before the commission claims against the other; and secondly, altering the place of meeting to Washington.* There was nc dispute about the treaty of 30th January, 1843. Mr. Upshur, Secretary of State, in his correspondence with Thompson, acknowledged and regretted the obligation it imposed, of referring to a tribunal wholly judicial in its character a subject "strictly diplomatic." Yet, in defiance of a plain treaty stipulation, the Senate refused to refer the claims of the Mexican Government to the decision of the commissioners and umpire. The place of meeting was changed by the Senate to *Washington*, although the Government had been warned by its own agent, that the sitting of the commission in Mexico was a *sine qua non*, and a point of national pride. The treaty thus mutilated, and conditionally ratified, was sent back to Mexico, where no farther notice of it was taken. Hence arose the cry from the partisans of Texas, that Mexico *refused* to settle the claims advanced by the citizens of the United States. President Polk in his labored vindication of the war against Mexico, contained in his message of December, 1846, had the temerity to charge Mexico with "violating the faith of treaties, by failing or refusing to carry into effect the sixth article of the convention of January, 1843"!!

* Report of Com. on Foreign Affairs, June 24th, 1846.

CHAPTER XII.

THE SEIZURE AND SURRENDER OF MONTEREY, IN CALIFORNIA, BY COMMODORE JONES.

On Mr. Thompson's appointment, an attempt was made in the House of Representatives, to defeat his mission by a motion to strike out from the supply bill the appropriation for a salary to the Minister to Mexico. In opposing this motion, Mr. Wise, of Virginia, the administration leader in the House delivered, 14th April, 1842, a characteristic speech, of which the following is an extract:

"Texas had but a sparse population, and neither men nor money of her own to raise and equip an army for her own defence; but let her once raise the flag of foreign conquest—let her once proclaim a crusade against the rich states to the South of her, and in a moment volunteers would flock to her standard in crowds from all the States in the great valley of the Mississippi—men of enterprise and hardy valor before whom no Mexican troops could stand an hour. They would leave their own towns, arm themselves and travel at their own cost, and would come up in thousands to plant the lone star of the Texan banner on the Mexican capital. They would drive Santa Anna to the South, and the boundless wealth of captured towns, and rifled churches, and a lazy, vicious, and luxurious priesthood, would soon enable Texas to pay her soldiers, and redeem her State debt, and push her victorious arms to the very shores of the Pacific.

"And would not all this extend slavery? Yes, the

result would be, that, before another quarter of a century, the extension of slavery would not stop short of the Western Ocean.

"To talk of restraining the people of the great valley from emigrating to join her armies, was all in vain. They had gone once already. *It was they that conquered Santa Anna at San Jacinto;* and three-fourths of them after winning that glorious field, had peaceably returned to their homes. But once set before them the conquest of the rich Mexican provinces, and you might as well attempt to stop the wind. Let the work once begin, and he (Mr. Wise) did not know that this House would hold *him* very long.

"Give me five millions of dollars, and I would undertake to do it myself. Although I don't know how to set a single squadron in the field, I could find men to do it; and, with five millions of dollars to begin with, I would undertake to pay every American claimant the full amount of his demand with interest, yea, fourfold. *I would place California* where all the powers of Great Britain, would never be able to reach it. SLAVERY SHOULD POUR ITSELF ABROAD WITHOUT RESTRAINT, AND FIND NO LIMIT BUT THE SOUTHERN OCEAN. The Camanches should no longer hold the richest mines of Mexico; but every golden image which had received the profanation of a false worship should soon be melted down, not into Spanish milled dollars indeed, but into good American eagles. Yes, there should more hard money flow into the United States than any exchequer or sub-treasury could ever circulate. I would cause as much gold to cross the Rio del Norte as the mules of Mexico could carry; aye, and make a better use of it than any lazy, bigoted priesthood under Heaven. I am not quarrelling with the particular religion of these priests; but I say, that any priesthood that has accumulated and sequestered such immense stores of wealth, ought to disgorge, and, it is a benefit to mankind, to scatter their wealth abroad where it can do good. Texas had proclaimed a blockade against all the coast of Mexico; and though she had no fleet to enforce it, she would be able to make it good by hewing her way to the Mexican capital. Nor could all the vaunted power of England stop the chivalry of the West, till they had planted the Texan star on the walls of the city of Montezuma. Nothing could keep these booted loafers from rushing on till they kicked the Spanish priests out of the temples they profaned. War was a curse; but it had its blessings too. He would vote for this mission as the means of preserving peace; but, if it must lead to war, he would vote it the *more* willingly."

The author of such a speech was, of course, admirably fitted for the Mexican mission; but, as that was already filled, the President (Tyler) expressed his obligation to the Orator, by appointing him Minister to France. A Whig Senate recoiled at the idea of sending Mr. Wise to represent American morality and refinement in Europe, but consented that he should discharge that function in Brazil. Amid the vulgarity and profligacy of this speech, there is much that merits attention as indicative of the views and anticipations of the slaveholders. We see what visions of plunder the idea of a war with Mexico raised before their excited imaginations; we see what boundless regions were in their hopes to be consecrated to human bondage, and with how little cost and danger, the chivalry expected to gather a golden harvest from both mines and churches. Mr. Wise was chairman of the naval committee, and high in the confidence of the administration; and hence his reference to *California* was peculiarly significant, and shadowed forth coming events. The annexation of Texas was the immediate object of the slaveholders; but California was looming in the distance, and many wistful eyes were gazing upon it, as the means of carrying slavery to the "Western Ocean."

Mr. Upshur, the Virginian who in 1829 wanted Texas to raise the price of slaves, and now Secretary of the Navy, in his report of December 4th, 1841, announced to Congress, that "In Upper California there were already considerable settlements of Americans, and others are daily resorting to that *fertile and delightful* country. Such, however, is the unsettled condition of that whole country, that they cannot be safe either in their persons or property, *except under the protection of our naval power.*" He also declared that, "It is highly desirable that the Gulf of California should be fully explored, and that this duty alone will give employment a long time to one or two vessels of the smaller class." Here was a beautiful device for forcing Mexico into a war and wresting California from her. Our ships of war were to be continually hovering on the coast, and their officers surveying the harbors and interfering in every controversy between the Mexican authorities and American squatters and adventurers.

A few days after this report, Commodore Jones, also a Virginian, was dispatched with a squadron to the Pacific. He was specially instructed to keep one or more vessels occasionally or constantly cruising upon the coast, and within the Gulf of California, and the officers were "to pay particular attention to the examination of the bays and harbors they may visit, and to lay down their positions correctly." The subsequent conquest of California bears testimony to the foresight of Messrs. Tyler and Upshur. It is not to be supposed that Commodore Jones was permitted to depart without being acquainted with the wishes and hopes of his employers. He undoubtedly well understood, although not formally instructed, that he was to avail himself of any good opportunity of getting a foothold in California.

In May, 1842, the Mexican Secretary of State sent a circular to the diplomatic corps, declaring that the Mexican Government protested against the aid afforded to the Texans by citizens of the United States with the toleration of their own Government. At the same time the Secretary addressed a letter to Mr. Webster, American Secretary of State, formally protesting against the allowance by the Federal Government of the violation, on the part of its citizens, of the obligations of neutrality in the open aid afforded to the insurgents of Texas. These two letters were published in a Mexican journal, and fell into the hands of Commodore Jones at Callao, together with a *Boston* newspaper, giving from a *New Orleans* paper one of those common lies about English interference, which had for years been plentifully manufactured by the partisans of annexation.

The lie which now caught the eye of the Commodore was, that Mexico had ceded California to Great Britain for $7,000,000! It so happened that three British armed vessels were at this time in the Pacific, and the watchful Commodore did not know their business, nor where they were going. The Mexican documents induced him to guess, that war had been declared between the United States and Mexico, and the rumor given from the New Orleans paper, led him to guess, that Great Britain had purchased California; and as he had not been informed where the three British vessels were going, he guessed they had gone to take possession of the newly purchased territory. He accordingly left Callao on the 7th September, 1842, "crowding all sail on the direct coast of Mexico" (California). The *next* day he summoned a council of his officers, submitted to them his documents, at the same time expressing his belief that the British squadron was there on its way to Panama, "where it will be reinforced by troops, &c., from the West Indies (!!) destined for the occupation of California." Under these circumstances, he asked for the advice of his three captains, as to the "employment of the small naval force (three vessels), at my disposal so as to best promote the interests and honor of our country, *thus suddenly jeopardded!*" The three marine statesmen assembled in the cabin of the United States frigate, thus intrusted by the Commodore with the weighty question of peace and war, advised that the squadron, already "crowding all sail" for California, should continue its course; and moreover announced, as the result of their deliberation, that, "in case of war between the United States and Mexico, it would be their (the officers) bounden duty to take possession of California," and that they "should consider the military occupation of the Californias by any European power, but more particularly by our great commercial rival England, and especially at this particular juncture, as a measure so decidedly hostile to the true interests of the United States as not only to warrant, but to make it our duty, to forestall the designs of Admiral Thomas, if possible, by supplanting the Mexican flag with that of the United States at Monterey, San Francisco, and any other tenable points within the territory said to have been recently ceded by secret treaty to Great Britain."

These naval expounders of the laws of nations would have regarded the expression by any European power of a doubt of the right of the United States to purchase territory in either of the four quarters of the globe, as an insult to the national sovereignty; but they calmly determine, without consulting their own government, to rob

England of a territory they supposed she had acquired by treaty, although they well knew that by such a robbery they would, of course, involve their country in a war with their great and powerful "commercial rival."

The three officers composing the Council, as well as the Commodore, and the Secretary of the Navy under whom they were acting, were all from the *slave* States.

On the 19th October, the Commodore entered the harbor of Monterey. The Mexican and not the British flag met his sight, and of course he achieved an easy conquest. He landed, and, without opposition, took possession of the fort, and unfurled the stars and stripes. The provident Commodore had brought with, him for the edification of the Californians, whom he intended instantly to transform into American citizens, *printed* proclamations in the Spanish language, which were without loss of time distributed among the inhabitants. "These stripes and stars," said the proclamation, "infallible emblems of civil liberty, of liberty of conscience, with constitutional right and lawful security to worship the great Deity in the way most congenial to each one's sense of duty to his Creator, now float triumphantly before you, and *hence and for ever* will give protection and security to you and your children, and to countless unborn thousands." Amid all this fustian we distinctly discover, that the *immediate and permanent* annexation of California was the object of the expedition.

It does not appear where this magnificent proclamation was prepared and printed. Printing presses are not, it is believed, included in the ordinary equipments of ships of war, and it is therefore a natural inference that the proclamation was printed either in Washington, or at Callao, the port from which the Commodore had departed for Monterey. In either case, it seems that the conquest of California was deliberately resolved on *before* the Commodore convened his officers to sanction by their *advice* the enterprise he had already commenced. On the 13th September, six days after he had left Callao, and while on his course to Monterey, he wrote to Mr. Upshur, "In all that I may do (in reference to California), I shall confine myself strictly to what I may suppose would be *your views and orders*, had you the means of communicating them to me." Mr. Upshur's well-known sentiments, and the character of the ultra pro-slavery party to which he belonged, leave no doubt that the Commodore perfectly comprehended his wishes.

The day after Jones had distributed his proclamation with all its fine promises, he discovered that, instead of robbing Great Britain of a territory she had purchased, he had seized upon a possession of a neighboring Republic still at peace with his own country. The "infallible emblems of civil liberty," &c., &c., were therefore lowered, and a due apology was made to the Mexican commander; and the succeeding day, the Commodore, abandoning the task of converting the Californians into American citizens, returned to the more inglorious but more innocent occupation of exploring the coast and bays of California, preparatory to another and less transient conquest.

The Government at home was, of course, compelled to disavow Jones's act; but in vain was his punishment demanded by Mexico. She was informed that he "intended no indignity to the government of Mexico, nor anything unlawful to her citizens."

CHAPTER XIII.

NEGOTIATION AND REJECTION OF TREATY OF ANNEXATION WITH TEXAS.

The treaty concluded with Great Britain in 1842, by removing all apprehension of collision with that power respecting the north-eastern boundary, gave a fresh impetus to the partisans of annexation. It had been foreseen that a war with England, by diverting the forces of the United States, and by giving Mexico a powerful ally, might enable the latter to repossess herself of Texas. This danger being passed, Messrs. Tyler and Upshur determined that annexation should no longer be delayed. Texas, moreover, had been acknowledged by France and England. With the latter she had entered into a treaty for the suppression of the slave-trade, thus nominally yielding what the United States had sternly refused. This very treaty was alarming to the slaveholders, who became apprehensive that, if Texas was left to herself, owing to emigration from abroad, the time might come when slavery would be abolished within her borders, and this apprehension seems to have been shared by some of the Texan leaders themselves. General Lamar, recently President of the Republic, about this time addressed a letter to his friends in Georgia warning them that, unless annexation shall be effected, "the anti-slavery party in Texas will acquire the ascendancy, and may not only abolish slavery by a constitutional vote, but may change the whole character of the constitution itself.

"At present the anti-slavery party is in the minority;

but it would be dangerous, even now, to agitate the question with much violence, for the majority of the people of Texas *are not owners of slaves.* Texas, if left to stand alone, there is every probability that slavery will be abandoned in that country. The negroes are yet but few in number, and would be emancipated in the country without the slightest inconvenience, and indeed would continue to be useful in the capacity of hirelings." He then goes on to remark that, as to the southern States, annexation "would give stability and safety to their domestic institutions, and thereby save them FOR EVER from the unparalelled calamities of abolition."

The very idea of freedom in Texas aroused the slaveholders to new and more resolute efforts for immediate annexation. So unequivocal had become the indications of a determination on the part of the south, to brook no longer delay, that at the close of the session of Congress in March, 1843, J. Q. Adams, and twelve other representatives published an address to the people of the United States, warning them of the machinations of the administration to secure the extension of slavery, by adding Texas to the Union—pointing out the gross violation of our neutral obligations towards Mexico, and calling upon the free States for renewed and increased activity to avert the calamity with which the country was threatened. Subsequent events speedily confirmed the foresight of this address, with a single exception. The address declared that the annexation of Texas would be a measure in such violation of the Constitution, and for a purpose so odious and profligate, as "not only *inevitably to result in a dissolution of the Union,* but fully to justify it." How far this prediction was uttered in the spirit of prophecy, it is yet too soon to determine.

Mr. Upshur, whose sympathies for Texas were, as we have seen, connected with the price of Virginia negroes, was called by Mr. Tyler to the office of Secretary of State, and, availing himself of the facilities afforded by his new office, prosecuted with vigor the work of opening another and most extensive slave market.

On the 13th September, 1843, he informed Mr. Thompson of the intention of the Government to remonstrate, in a formal manner, with Mexico, unless she shall make peace with Texas, or shall show a disposition and ability to prosecute the war with respectable forces. This was only another device to provoke a quarrel. The idea of our being offended with Mexico, because she was dilatory in killing our friends and brethren in Texas, was too ridiculous to be seriously pressed, even by Mr. Tyler's administration. A letter written by Upshur, a few days before, to Murphy, our agent in Texas, reveals the true reason why the Cabinet had indulged the thought of bullying Mexico into a *peace* with Texas. On the 8th September, he tells Murphy, there is a rumor of a plan in England, to raise money for the Texan government, wherewith to abolish slavery, by indemnifying the masters, and that the English capitalists were to take Texan land in payment. "Such an attempt," said the Secretary, ever anxious for the anticipated market for Virginia slaves, "upon any neighboring nation, would necessarily be viewed by this Government with very deep concern; but when it is made upon a nation whose territory joins the slave-holding States of our Union, it awakens still more solemn interest. It cannot be permitted to succeed withous most strenuous efforts on our part to avert a *calamity* so serious to every part of our country. Few calamities could befal this country more to be deplored than the establishment of a predominant British influence, and the ABOLITION OF DOMESTIC SLAVERY IN TEXAS."*

* Ex. Doc., 1st Sess., 28th Cong. No. 271

The correspondence between Upshur and Murphy is one of the most humiliating to a true-minded American, of any that has ever disgraced the annals of his country. "So far as this *Government* is concerned," writes Upshur, September 22d, 1843, "we have every desire to come to the aid of Texas in the most prompt and effectual manner. How far we shall be supported by the people, I regret, is somewhat doubtful. There is no reason to fear there will be any difference of opinion among the people of the SLAVE-HOLDING STATES." Murphy, in his reply, September 24th, 1843, takes the liberty of giving the Secretary of State some shrewd advice,—"Say nothing about abolition;" and again, in another letter, "Do not offend our fanatical brethren of the north. *Talk about civil and political and religious liberty.* This will be found the safest issue to go before the world with." In other words, go before the world with a lie in your mouth about the rights and liberty of Texas, which is already as free as we are, and conceal from the people of the north, that our only object is to extend and perpetuate negro slavery. The advice was partially followed, and the cry of "extend the area of freedom" was raised by the slave-holders and their northern allies. But "out of the fulness of the heart the mouth speaketh," and before long, all disguise was set aside, and the true object boldly and unblushingly avowed "before the world," both by the Government and by southern legislatures and popular meetings. The story of the contemplated pecuniary contribution in England to advance the cause of human liberty in Texas, was unfortunately without foundation; like a multitude of similar falsehoods in relation to the anti-slavery interference of England, it was intended to facilitate annexation. On the 17th October, Upshur proposed to the Texan agent a treaty of annexation. The

Mexican Minister at Washington, aware of the intrigues of the Cabinet, gave notice, that if Texas were received into the Union, he must ask for his passports. Mr. Upshur replied in an insulting tone, declining all explanation, and treating with scorn the intimation of Mexican hostility. In the mean time, the Texans having shown less eagerness to enter into the proposed treaty than Upshur had anticipated, he became alarmed, and thought proper to menace even the free and independent Republic of Texas. He wrote to Murphy (January 16th, 1844,) of course for the information of the Texan leaders, that in case annexation should be declined by the latter, "Instead of being, as we ought to be, the closest friends, it is inevitable we shall become the bitterest foes;" and he warns them, that without annexation, Texas "cannot maintain that institution (slavery) *ten* years—probably not half that time." To remove all apprehension, that, if Texas should consent to a treaty of annexation, she might be subjected to the mortification of having the treaty rejected for want of the constitutional majority of two-thirds of the Senate in its favor, he hazarded, in his desperation, the following most extraordinary assertion:—"Measures have been taken to ascertain the opinions and views of Senators upon the subject, and *it is ascertained that a clear majority of two-thirds* are in favor of the measure!!" The *fact* that this very Senate, whose votes Mr. Upshur professed to have canvassed, *rejected* the treaty, by a majority of more than two-thirds, throws a painful suspicion upon the personal veracity of the American Secretary; and the more so, as no explanation was ever given to the public of the wonderful discrepancy between his canvass and the actual vote.

Great Britain thought proper to disavow the machinations which it had been deemed expedient by the partisans of Texas to ascribe to her. Our Government was, on the 8th April, officially informed, that it was indeed well known to the whole world that Great Britain desired the abolition of Slavery wherever it existed, but that she would not unduly interfere to accomplish it—that she aimed at no dominant influence in Texas, and that, in striving for human liberty, the Government would not "openly nor secretly resort to any measures which can tend to disturb the tranquillity, or thereby affect the prosperity of the American Union." This avowal, so frank and honorable, so becoming a free and a christian people, perhaps hurried the conclusion of the treaty, as it removed one of the pretended reasons alleged for its necessity. Four days after the British document was received, Mr. Calhoun, as Secretary of State, to which office he had been appointed on the death of Mr. Upshur, had the gratification of signing a treaty with Texas, by which that State was annexed to the American Union.

In the proud elation of feeling caused by so signal a triumph in the cause of human bondage, Mr. Calhoun replied on the 8th April, 1844, to the communication from the English Minister. He declared that the President viewed with deep concern, the desire avowed by Great Britain for the abolition of slavery; that in his opinion, Texas by herself, could not withstand a compliance with this desire, and therefore "It is the imperative duty of the Federal Government, the common representative and protector of the States of the Union, to adopt, in self-defence, the *most effectual means to resist it;*" and that, in obedience to this obligation, a treaty of annexation had been concluded. "And this step" (he asserted) "had been taken as the most effectual, if not the only means of guarding against the threatened danger." The next day he addressed a letter to the American Agent in Mexico, announcing the conclusion of the treaty, a step, he says, "*which was forced on the Government of the United States in self-defence, in consequence of the policy adopted by Great Britain in reference to the abolition of slavery in Texas.*"

The audacious mendacity of this declaration is the more remarkable, as Mr. Calhoun's own language bears witness to its falsity. The readers of these sheets have already had abundant proof, that the annexation of Texas was prompted by other motives than "self-defence" against the anti-slavery policy of Great Britain, as manifested in that Republic. So early as the 27th May, 1836, immediately after the rumor of the battle of San Jacinto, and even *before* the official account of the victory had reached Washington, and while Great Britain was wholly ignorant of the existence of such a Republic as Texas, Mr. Calhoun, in his place in the Senate, proposed the recognition of the Independence of Texas, and her immediate admission into the Union!! In his speech on the occasion, he remarked, "There were powerful reasons why Texas should be a part of this Union. The southern States, owning a slave population, were *deeply interested in preventing that country from having the power to annoy them.*"* A revolted province was in actual war with the parent country, and, while the slain in the last battle were still unburied, this champion of slavery proposes the instant incorporation of this province into the Union for the benefit of the slaveholders—utterly reckless of the wickedness of the act, trampling under foot the obligations of neutrality, and regardless of the calamities of war which such a measure would inevitably inflict upon his country.

But it is not enough that Mr. Calhoun's statement

* Cong. Globe—29th Cong., 2d Sess., p. 495

should be falsified by himself. We summon a witness far more competent, and quite as credible as himself. General Houston may well be called the father of the Texan Republic, having commanded its army on the field of San Jacinto, and afterwards presided over its councils as President. The treaty with England was negotiated under his direction, and he was necessarily intimately acquainted with all the foreign relations of Texas. He was, moreover, chosen by the *State* of Texas to represent her in the United States Senate. On the 19th February, 1847, he declared in his place in the Senate, "England *never* proposed the subject of slavery or of abolition to Texas; England *never* made a suggestion to Texas which, if she had pursued or accepted, would have degraded her in the eyes of the purest patriot that ever lived. Captain Elliot (British Minister in Texas) required nothing but commercial relations between England and Texas, and an interchange of her fabrics for the products of the South."* So much for the monstrous assertion that the treaty of annexation "was forced upon the Government of the United States in self-defence, in consequence of the policy adopted by Great Britain in reference to the abolition of slavery in Texas."

The treaty referred to was submitted to the Senate on the 22d April, 1844, and was REJECTED by that body by a vote of thirty-five to sixteen, Mr. Upshur's pledge to the Texan Government, that two-thirds of the Senate would approve of it, notwithstanding.

Under no circumstances could this treaty have received the consent of two-thirds of the Senate, but the greatness of the vote against it was owing to other causes than hostility to annexation. Mr. Tyler was the most unpopular President that had ever occupied the Executive Chair.

* Cong. Globe—29th Cong. 2d Sess., p. 459.

He was without personal or political influence, and his term of office was now so nearly expired, that he had but little patronage with which to secure Senatorial votes. It was clearly ascertained that the treaty could not be ratified even were all the friends of annexation to vote for it; and hence many of those friends consulted their own political views and prejudices in swelling the majority against it, and thus thwarting the aspirations of Mr. Calhoun. A presidential election was approaching, and the southern opponents of Mr. Calhoun were well content to diminish by their votes the influence his zeal in the cause of Texas was calculated to give him. Although eager for Texas, they could not vote for a treaty so *very* objectionable as that made by *Mr. Calhoun;* whereas, had its ratification depended on them, there is little doubt their votes would have been different.

CHAPTER XIV.

MORE ATTEMPTS TO IRRITATE MEXICO.

THE majority in the Senate against the Texan treaty had taught Messrs. Tyler and Calhoun the necessity of preventing, as far as possible, any new obstacle to a measure so near to their hearts. One great argument for annexation was, that the war had virtually ceased between Texas and Mexico, the latter having for years refrained from all active hostility. Suddenly the Cabinet was alarmed by some threatening proclamations issued by the Mexican authorities against Texas, couched in the usual inflated style. Past experience had shown the inability of Mexico to subdue her rebellious province, sheltered, as it was, beneath the wing of the great republic. The threats of the Mexicans were, indeed, idle words; but Mr. Tyler knew that, should the war be in fact renewed, its existence would be an argument against annexation, as that measure under such circumstances would necessarily make the United States a party to the war. It was, therefore, resolved either to induce Mexico to relinquish her design to renew hostilities, or else to goad her into war against ourselves. Hence, on the 14th October, 1844, Mr. Shannon, who had succeeded Mr. Thompson at Mexico, in obedience to instructions, presented to the Government an insolent remonstrance against the farther prosecution of the war, and the sanguinary spirit in which it was to be waged. He declared that the war was to be renewed for the purpose of defeating annexation, an object which

Mr. Tyler would not permit—dwelt upon the importance of Texas to this country, and plainly intimated that we could not permit her to be invaded, without espousing her quarrel. We can readily conceive with what intense indignation our own Government would receive a similar letter from a British Minister, insulting us for our barbarous mode of conducting the war against Mexico, threatening us with vengeance unless we made peace, and permitted the peaceful cession of California to the British crown. Mexico, feeble and exhausted, could resent the insult only in words; but they were words full of dignity, truth, and common sense. Mr. Rejon, the Mexican Secretary (October 20th, 1844), informed Shannon that he "has orders to repel the protest now addressed to his Government, and to declare that the President of the United States is much mistaken, if he supposes Mexico capable of yielding to the menace which he, *exceeding the powers given to him by the fundamental law of his nation*, has directed against it." After commenting on the conduct of the United States, he concluded, "while one power is seeking more ground to stain by the SLAVERY of an unfortunate branch of the human family, the other is endeavoring, by preserving what belongs to it, to diminish the surface which the former wants for this detestable traffic. Let the world now say, which of the two has justice and reason on its side."

This letter was received in high dudgeon by Mr. Shannon, who haughtily demanded a retraction of the Secretary's letter, on the penalty of suspending all farther intercourse till he heard from Washington. To this impertinence, Mr. Rejon replied that he was not surprised by Mr. Shannon's reluctance to discuss the conduct of his Government. "In fact, to what else can be attributed this exclusive desire to claim for himself, his nation, and his Government, that respect denied by him to the Mexican Republic and its Government, to which he has so often applied the term BARBAROUS, in his note of 14th October? Is the Government of the United States superior in dignity, or has its legislature any right to be thus wanting in respect to a Government to which it has refused the attentions due by courtesy to mere individuals? Instead of withdrawing his letter, he is ordered to reiterate his former statements."

The manly, honest rebuke administered by Rejon to President Tyler, naturally gave great offence to that gentleman; and on the 19th December, 1844, he laid the correspondence before Congress with very indignant comments on "the extraordinary and highly offensive language which the Mexican Government has thought proper to employ." But although he thought the conduct of Mexico "might well justify the United States in a resort to any measure to vindicate their national honor," he abstained, through a sincere desire to preserve peace, from recommending a resort to "measures of redress," and contented himself with urging "prompt and immediate action on the subject of annexation."

CHAPTER XV.

ELECTION OF MR. POLK.

A SUCCESSOR to Mr. Tyler was to be chosen at the close of 1844; but, when the treaty was rejected in June of that year, no political sagacity could predict upon whom the choice would fall. Mr. Tyler's wayward course, together with other causes, had greatly curtailed the power of the whigs; but there was no proof that they had lost their ascendency.

In many instances the slaveholders had boldly declared, that no candidate opposed to annexation, should receive their vote. This sentiment was uttered in the formal resolves of their popular meetings, and reiterated by the slave press. Mr. Clay was the whig candidate; and to his influence at the South was added the cordial and unanimous support of the whigs at the North; under his auspices the party anticipated a decided victory. The democratic party presented a much less imposing front than its rival. Its prominent candidate was Mr. Van Buren who, as well as Mr. Clay, had expressed a cautious qualified opinion adverse to annexation *at the present time*, and under existing circumstances; but neither had ventured to hint an objection to the extension of slavery. The democratic nominating convention met at Baltimore late in May, and gave Mr. Van Buren a majority of its votes, as the democratic candidate for the Presidency. But the Southern members insisted and finally succeeded, that a majority of *two-thirds* should be necessary to a nomination.

The two-third rule of course made those members masters of the Convention; and it was soon found that no candidate could be selected except the nominee of the slaveholders. Mr. Van Buren was rejected; and the northern democracy were compelled to accept Mr. Polk in his room. The qualifications which procured for this gentleman the honor of a nomination, were doubtless his devotion to the cause of slavery, his vituperation of the abolitionists and a recent printed letter in which he advocated the IMMEDIATE ANNEXATION OF TEXAS.

The Convention having thus been compelled to nominate Mr. Polk, the triumph of the democratic party, and its possession of power and office, of course depended on his election. To secure that election, the party were necessarily compelled to adopt as their own the policy avowed by their candidate. Hence it became expedient for the Convention, as the representatives of the whole democratic party, to insist upon the *immediate annexation of Texas*, and to enter the contest with these ominous words inscribed on their banners. Many of the party presses at the North had been loud in their denunciations of the Texan plot; and in the northern legislatures, democrats had vied with the whigs in passing resolutions condemning annexation. But the council of Baltimore was deemed infallible in matters of faith; and forthwith the democracy of the North united with the slaveholders of the South in their efforts to extend the curse of human bondage. Mr. Polk received a majority of the electoral votes, but not of the popular suffrage by which the Electors had been chosen.

CHAPTER XVI.

ANNEXATION BY JOINT RESOLUTION.

UNTIL the refusal of the Senate to ratify Mr. Tyler's treaty, no other mode of annexation than by treaty had been imagined. Texas claimed to be an independent nation, and had been acknowledged as such by the United States, France, and Great Britain. But contracts between independent nations are *treaties*, and the constitution intrusts the power of making treaties to the President and two-thirds of the Senate. Of all contracts between two nations, none can be more important and solemn than that which surrenders the sovereignty and domains of the one to the other. All the territory which had been added to the United States, had been acquired by treaty. Hence, when Texas contemplated annexation, she proposed doing it by treaty; and Messrs. Tyler, Upshur, and Calhoun, all concurred at a later date in inviting Texas to enter the confederacy by the operation of a treaty. But the slaveholders were reminded by the recent occurrences, that it required a majority of two-thirds of the Senate to annex a foreign territory in accordance with the provisions of the Constitution; and that, as half of the Senators represented free States, such a majority was at present unattainable. Necessity is the mother of invention; and the truth of the aphorism now received a remarkable illustration. It was suddenly discovered, that what could not be effected by treaty, could as well be performed by a joint resolution of the two houses of Congress. Such a resolution required only a bare majority in each branch. In this way treaties for the future, might be dispensed with whenever the Senate was found uncomplying; and the foreign intercourse of the nation might be regulated, disputed boundaries settled, and even the conditions of peace determined, by joint resolution. To whom is to be attributed this ingenious device for setting aside the Constitution, smothering the oaths taken to support it, and usurping the treaty-making power, is not known; but Mr. Tyler has the credit of first announcing the discovery to the public. Mortified and irritated by the rejection of his treaty, he immediately appealed to the House of Repretatives, laying the dishonored document before them, and hinting that it was possible to effect annexation by other means than a treaty. But Mr. Tyler had so utterly annihilated the respect and confidence he had once enjoyed, that his influence was nugatory for good or for evil. The annexation of Texas was indeed effected, but it was effected by other influences than those wielded by himself or by Mr. Calhoun.

The administration of Mr. Tyler was to close, and that of Mr. Polk to commence, on the 4th March, 1845. The vote againt the annexation treaty the preceding June, had convinced the partisans of Texas, of the impossibility of effecting their favorite object in a constitutional mode, and the friends of human liberty congratulated themselves that the danger was passed. The election, however, of Mr. Polk, by identifying the democracy of the North with the policy of the South, revived the hopes, and invigorated the efforts of the friends of Texas. The patronage of the government had now for the next four years been placed at the disposal of an avowed and zealous advocate of annexation. Under these circumstances, it was determined to make a new effort to secure Texas, regardless of the Constitution. Nor was the expectation very unreasonable, that a majority of the very Senate that had treated Tyler with contumely, as he was sinking below the horizon, might do homage to the rising sun.

Mr. Polk was to be sworn into office on the 4th March; and this circumstance afforded an excuse for the arrival at the Capitol some weeks earlier, of the dispenser of the nation's patronage. His presence is well understood to have exerted a powerful influence on the votes subsequently given. On the 1st March, 1845, the famous joint resolutions, for the annexation of Texas as one of the States of the Federal Union, were finally passed after a severe and doubtful struggle.

One of the most extraordinary incidents of this most extraordinary and calamitous legislation, was the very peculiar tenderness of conscience evinced by certain southern Senators. The Lower House had passed a simple resolution of annexation by a majority of twenty-two. But some of the Senators, although rabid for Texas, were troubled by the oath they had taken to support the Constitution, and they did not well know how to reconcile that oath with the trickery by which it was intended to nullify the treaty-making power. They were happily relieved by the addition of another resolution virtually giving to the President the option of effecting annexation by resolution *or by treaty*. This ingenious device of authorizing the President to respect or contemn at pleasure the requirements of the Constitution, and throwing upon him the responsibility of the choice, relieved the scruples of these conscientious gentlemen, and enabled them almost at the very last hour, by the change of their votes, to carry the question of annexation, in the Senate, by a majority of *two*. Should this strange expedient for satisfying constitutional scruples seem insufficient for the momentous effects ascribed to it, possibly a more satisfactory cause may be found in a declaration made in a southern paper during the debate, "We rejoice that those *deserting democrats* who oppose this vital measure which Mr. Polk so anxiously desires to be settled at this session, WILL HAVE NOTHING TO EXPECT FROM HIS ADMINISTRATION." As Mr. Polk was at this time at Washington, it is not unreasonable to believe that the editor of the *Richmond Enquirer,* was not the sole confidant of his intention to withhold office from every member who voted against annexation.

One of the gentlemen whose scruples threatened to defeat annexation—but who, on his conscience becoming enlightened, voted for the measure, and thus ensured it a majority in the Senate—was subsequently appointed by Mr. Polk to a foreign mission.

No time was lost by Mr. Tyler in making the choice offered to him by the joint resolutions. On the 3rd March, a few hours before his term of office expired, he despatched a messenger to the American agent in Texas, with a letter from Mr. Calhoun, instructing him to propose the *resolution* of annexation to the acceptance of the Texan Government, very sensibly objecting to annexation by treaty, because a treaty "must be submitted to the Senate for its ratification, and run the hazard of receiving the votes *of two-thirds* of the members present, which could hardly be expected if we are to judge *from recent experience.*"* On the 4th July, Texas consented to

* The late Chancellor Kent, of New York, was at this time unquestionably the most eminent Jurist in America. He thus wrote to a member of Congress:—"I acknowledge your speech of January last on the Annexation of Texas. I have perused it with much satisfaction; and I deem it perfectly conclusive, that the Annexation of Texas, by *concurrent resolution of Congress,* was unwarrantable, and *a usurpation of the treaty-making power;* in every view, violent, unjust, unconstitutional, and most pernicious and unprincipled, and will lead to the ruin of the Union."

be annexed, and the 22nd of the ensuing December, she was formally received as a State into the Federal Union.

Independent of the violence done to the cause of morality in the *mode* by which annexation was effected, and in the *motive* by which it was prompted, the measure itself was a gross and palpable violation of the neutral obligations of the United States. It is freely admitted that Texas was at the time an independent State, and as such had a right to form a union with the Federal Republic. But Texas was at war with Mexico; and we have seen that Mr. Tyler not merely acknowledged the existence of the war, but, *after* his Treaty of Annexation had been rejected, officially remonstrated with Mexico on the *barbarous* manner in which that power intended to prosecute hostilities. It is impossible to deny that a neutral nation, forming an alliance offensive and defensive with another at the time engaged in war, by that very act becomes herself a belligerent. But annexation was an alliance, in the strongest sense, both offensive and defensive. So sensible was the Administration of this fact, that, as we shall see hereafter, a land and naval force was prepared to *defend* Texas against the meditated assault of Mexico. If after the commencement of hostilities between Mexico and the United States, England or France had accepted a cession of California from Mexico, the acceptance itself would have been tantamount to a declaration of war against this country. Had a fleet and army been sent from Europe to protect Mexico from our invasion, would the fact that Mexico was an independent nation have satisfied us that we had no cause for complaint at such an interference? By the laws of nations, annexation was an act of war against Mexico.

Eight years before this event, the Rev. Dr. Channing, of Boston, in a publication against the scheme which he well knew was entertained by the Administration—of adding Texas to the Union—uttered the following fearful prediction, which has now for the most part become history :—"By this act (annexation) our country will enter on a career of encroachment and crime, and will merit the punishment and woe of aggravated wrong-doing. The seizure of Texas will not stand alone. It will be linked, by an iron necessity, to LONG-CONTINUED DEEDS OF RAPINE AND BLOOD. Ages may not see the catastrophy of the tragedy the first scene of which we are so ready to enact. Texas is a country conquered by our citizens, and the annexation of it to our Union will be but the beginning of conquests, which, unless arrested and beaten back by Providence, will stop only at the Isthmus of Darien. Henceforth we must cease to cry—Peace, peace. Our Eagle will whet, not gorge, his appetite on his first victim, and will snuff a more tempting quarry, more alluring blood, in every new region which opens *southward*."

CHAPTER XVII.

ANNEXATION OF CALIFORNIA DESIGNED BY MR. POLK.

IMMEDIATELY after the final vote on the annexation of Texas had been taken in the Senate, a senator from Florida arose in his place, and introduced a resolution declaring it expedient for the President to open negotiations for the cession of the Island of Cuba to the United States. No action was called for; the sole object of the resolution being to familiarize the public mind with devices for the acquirement of slave territory. The addition of Texas operated but as blood to the famished wolf; and the appetite for Mexican provinces, instead of being satiated, was stimulated to a ravenous ferocity. Texas had been gained virtually under Mr. Tyler's administration, and there is reason to believe that Mr. Polk was resolved that *his* should be signalized by the annexation of California. This province had long excited the cupidity of the slaveholders, and great efforts were now made to stimulate public opinion into unison with the designs of the President. The newspapers teemed with articles on the fertility of California, its vast importance to the United States, and, as a matter of course, the secret designs of Great Britain to appropriate it to herself, either by force or by treaty. The reader will recollect the premature seizure and *annexation for ever* of California by Commodore Jones: he will also call to mind that, at an earlier period, fruitless efforts had been made to purchase the province, whole or in part. Already many of our restless wandering adventurers had penetrated into that distant territory; and the opinion had been extensively propagated, that it was a region too rich and too convenient to be left in possession of the Mexicans. The Mexican Government, taught wisdom by the result of Texan colonization, made an order expelling American citizens from California. Our Minister protested; and the ordinance was so modified as to include all foreigners deemed dangerous to the public peace. But against this Mr. Calhoun, then Secretary of State, ordered a new protest.

Let us now attend to the confessions of our Minister, Mr. Thompson: "Near the end of December, 1843, I received information that the Government of Mexico had issued an order expelling all natives of the United States from the department of California and the adjoining departments. No attempt, however, had been made up to that time to execute the order. A similar order had been issued a few years before, including not only citizens of the United States, but British subjects also; and this order had been actually executed to the great damage and, in some instances, ruin of the persons removed. All the efforts of the English and American Ministers to procure a recision of this order were ineffectual for six months. I had the good fortune, however, after a somewhat angry correspondence, to have the order rescinded, not, however, until I resorted to the *ultima ratio* of diplomacy, AND DEMANDED MY PASSPORTS—a measure which a minister is rarely justified in resorting to without the orders of his government. I confess I was very much afraid that the passports would have been sent; but I thought that the step was justified by the circumstances, and that it would cut short a long discussion. The result showed that in this calculation I was right. The order was rescinded, and expresses sent to all the departments, the distance of some of which was two thousand miles. I confess that in taking the high ground I did, upon the order expelling our people from California, I felt some compunctious visitings; for I had been informed that a *plot had been arranged, and was about being developed by the Americans and other foreigners in that department, to re-enact the scenes of Texas.*" *

Mr. Thompson, in describing California, says: "Sugar, rice, and cotton, find there their own congenial clime"—p. 234. Of course the same motives which led to the "scenes in Texas," would prompt their re-enactment in California. We shall see hereafter that Mr. Thompson was not misinformed.

There were two modes of acquiring California — by negotiation and by war. The first was the most economical, the latter would probably be the most expeditious, but, unless *commenced* by Mexico, would be extremely hazardous to the popularity and stability of the Administration.

By blustering about our claims, swelling them to the greatest possible point of inflation, and then kindly offering to waive them all in consideration of a cession of California, and throwing in a *douceur* of a few millions, perhaps it might be possible to worry Mexico into a surrender of the province. But the result was doubtful. Mexico had been very tenacious of her soil, and had refused every bribe to part with it. War was the alternative. Mexico was just now extremely sensitive on the subject of Texas. Her Minister at Washington had demanded his passports on the passage of the joint resolutions. Mr. Shannon, after irritating the Government by his insulting demeanor, had left Mexico, and all diplomatic intercourse between the two countries was now suspended. Under such cir-

* Recollections of Mexico, p. 227-232.

cumstances, it would not be difficult to excite a war, and a war would give us California. But then a war, to be popular or even to be endured by the North, which would share its burdens but not its spoils, must be "a war by the act of Mexico."

It was obviously most expedient to try negotiation in the first instance, and, if that failed, then to bring on a war by inducing Mexico to strike the first blow. Such a war could be waged as one of *defence*, not of aggression; Mexico would of course be immediately humbled, and we might dictate the terms of peace, one of which would be the surrender of the coveted province. Subsequent events have manifested that the policy we have explained was early adopted by Mr. Polk, and maintained with unwavering pertinacity

CHAPTER XVIII.

MISSION OF MR. SLIDELL TO MEXICO.

Before an attempt could be made to acquire California by negotiation, it was necessary to restore the diplomatic intercourse between the two countries. For this purpose, the American Consul in Mexico, in compliance with instructions, addressed a letter, 13th October, 1845, to the Mexican Secretary of State, inquiring whether the Mexican Government "would receive an Envoy from the United States, entrusted with full powers *to adjust all questions in dispute between the two Governments*." Two days afterwards, the Secretary personally delivered to the Consul a reply, stating, "that although the Mexican nation is deeply injured by the United States through the acts committed by them in the Department of Texas, which belongs to this nation, my Government is disposed to receive the *Commissioner* of the United States who may come to this country with full powers to settle the *present dispute* in a peaceful, reasonable, and honorable manner, thus giving a new proof that even in the midst of its injuries and of its firm decision to exact adequate reparation for them, it does not repell with contumely the measures of reason and peace to which it is invited by its adversary." This, it will be observed, was an indirect reply to the question put by the Consul. Instead of consenting to receive an *Envoy* with full powers to adjust *all questions* in dispute, the Secretary refers expressly to the dispute about Texas, and, with a show of condescension, says that his Government will receive the *Commissioner* who may come to settle the *present dispute*. The language irresistibly refers to a Commissioner who is to offer, not to demand, reparation for a certain injury, alleged to have been committed in "the department of Texas."

Such is the fair, and indeed, the only inference to be drawn from the answer returned to the Consul. The answer was not improbably dictated by that species of cunning which politicians are so apt to mistake for wisdom. It may have been the design of the Mexican Government to use language which would hereafter permit it to reject an American *Minister*, or to refuse entering with him into negotiations on other topics than Texas, should circumstances render such a course expedient. A similar cunning was evinced by the Cabinet at Washington in its prompt acceptance of the equivocal reply of the Mexican Secretary, as a full and explicit answer to the question proposed by the Consul. Should the Envoy be received, the affair of Texas would of course be set aside as *res adjudicata*, while the alternative of California or payment of claims would be pressed upon the feeble, distracted Government of Mexico. If, however, the Envoy should be rejected on the ground, that the Government had consented to receive only a Commissioner to treat about Texas, then loud complaints of breach of faith, and of insult offered to the national honor, would prove convenient incentives to war. Mr. Polk avoiding all explanations, hurried off Mr. Slidell, of Louisiana, as Minister to Mexico, within three weeks of the meeting of Congress, and of course without waiting for the confirmation of his nomination by the Senate. The Mexican Secretary, mindful of the rudeness with which his Government had been hitherto treated by American functionaries, expressed the hope, that the person now to be sent would be one "whose dignity and prudence, and moderation, and the discreetness and reasonableness of his proposals, will tend to *calm*, as much as possible, the just irritation of the Mexicans." How far the gentleman selected by Mr. Polk endeavored to exercise a *calming* influence, will be seen in the sequel.

On the 3d of December, it was reported in Mexico, that the new Envoy had landed at Vera Cruz. On this, the Mexican Secretary sought an interview with our Consul, and begged him to induce Mr. Slidell to postpone, for the present, his appearance in the Capital, as he had not been expected before *January*, by which time the Government, having collected the opinion and consent of the departments, "it would be able to proceed in the affair with more security." The existing administration were charged by the party in opposition with being too friendly to the United States. "You know," remarked the Secretary to the Consul, "the opposition are calling us traitors for entering into this arrangement with you;" and he declared that the Government were afraid that the appearance of the Envoy at this time would produce a revolution against it, which would terminate in its destruction.* The Consul immediately advanced to meet Mr. Slidell, and at Puebla acquainted him with the wishes of the Government. Far from consulting those wishes, he pushed on to the Capital, where he arrived on Saturday, the 6th of December, and the *ensuing Monday* officially announced his arrival, and asked for an audience for the purpose of presenting his credentials as *Envoy Extraordinary and Minister Plenipotentiary* of the United States. This letter was the same day delivered by the Consul to the Mexican Secretary of State, who assured him that "he himself was well dis-

* 29th Cong., 1st Sess., Senate Documents, No. 337, p. 18.

posed to have *everything amicably arranged*, but that the opposition was strong, and opposed the Government with great violence in this measure, and that the Government had to proceed with great caution; that nothing positive could be done until the new Congress met in January." On Wednesday, the 10th December, Slidell was informed that his letter must be submitted to the Council of Government before a reply could be returned. But this gentleman would not brook delay, and on Saturday sent the Consul to inquire when an answer would be given. The Consul was told the letter had been submitted to a Committee of the Council, and that as soon as the Committee had reported, an answer would be sent; that Mr. Slidell came as a resident Minister, and not a Commissioner to treat of Texas, as was expected. The Secretary appealed to the Consul, that he himself knew "the critical situation of the Mexican Government, and that it had to proceed with great caution and circumspection in this affair; *that the Government itself was well disposed to arrange all difficulties*."

These assurances of the friendly dispositions of the Government, and their earnest solicitation for a little delay, till those dispositions could be sanctioned and supported by the Congress about to assemble, seemed to have confirmed Mr. Slidell in his resolution to *force matters to extremities*; and accordingly, without waiting for the report of the Committee, he dispatched another letter on the ensuing Monday to the Secretary, requiring to know when he might expect an answer to his first, and declaring, what was absolutely false, that "he is necessarily ignorant of the reasons which have caused so long a delay." The "long delay" was precisely *seven* days, and within that time he had been *twice* officially informed through the Consul of "the reasons" of the delay. To this letter an answer was returned, stating that the delay complained of, had arisen from certain difficulties arising from the nature of his commission, compared with the character of a negotiator to treat on the subject of Texas, whom the United States had proposed to send to Mexico; that the subject had been submitted to the Council of Government, and that the result would be communicated to him without loss of time. The *next* day, 17th December, Mr. Slidell wrote to the Government at Washington, detailing the progress of the negotiation thus far. It will be observed, that up to this date he had neither been *received*, nor *refused*, and in this very letter he remarks that "the impression here among the best informed persons is, that the President and his Cabinet are really desirous to enter frankly upon a negotiation which would terminate all their difficulties with the United States." The *day after* this letter was received at Washington, peremptory orders were sent to General Taylor to march to the Rio Grande; and this order, necessarily calculated and obviously intended to bring on a war, has been vindicated on the ground, that the Mexican Government had *refused* to treat with Mr. Slidell!

It was obvious, from what had passed, that the Mexican administration, although pacific in its feelings, was not strong in the confidence of the public, and it was naturally inferred, that it would not have the power, even should it have the disposition, to conclude a treaty for the dismemberment of the Republic by the cession of California. Hence the determination of Mr. Polk to secure by the sword what he now saw could not likely be acquired by the pen. This determination was moreover strengthened by the following information communicated in the same letter from Mr. Slidell. "The country, torn by conflicting factions, is in a state of perfect anarchy, its finances in a condition utterly desperate. I do not see where means can possibly be found to carry on the government. The annual expense of the army alone exceeds twenty-one millions of dollars, while the net revenue is not more than ten or twelve. While there is a prospect of war with the United States, no capitalist will loan money, at any rate, however onerous. Every branch of the revenue is already pledged in advance. The troops must be paid, or they will revolt." Of course from such a government, it would be easy to wrest California, and as much more as we might want.

Mr. Slidell, having, as we have seen, refused to permit the Mexican Cabinet to postpone their decision respecting his reception, till the meeting of Congress in January, that decision was communicated, to him on the 20th December. He would be received as a Commissioner to treat of the questions relating to Texas; but until that question was arranged, he could not be received as Minister plenipotentiary.

Mr. Slidell was of course very insulting in his reply. "*The annals of no civilized nation present, in so short a time, so many wanton attacks upon the rights of person and property as have been endured by the citizens of the United States from the Mexican authorities.*" It is to be apprehended that this gentleman is either very imperfectly acquainted with the annals of civilized nations, or very unscrupulous in drawing inferences from them. In the excitement of the moment, and for the sole purpose of irritation, he paraded before the Mexican Secretary, the millions demanded by the American government as compensation for "the accumulated wrongs" of its "much-injured citizens." The indebtedness of Mexico, according to Mr. Slidell was as follows, viz.:

The award under the treaty of 1839,	$2,026,139
Claims then left unsettled,	4,265,464
Claims subsequently presented,	2,200,000
	8,491,603
Credit by payments made on the award,*	303,919
Balance,	$8,187,684

We have heretofore seen that the total amount of claims presented to the board of arbitrators, was $11,850,578
The claims *afterwards* fabricated were, it seems, 2,200,000

Total claim from Mexico, $14,050,578

It may here be edifying to the reader, to interrupt our narrative for a moment, to advise him of the fate of these modest demands, under the especial guardianship of the Cabinet of Washington. The Commissioners and umpire appointed by treaty, after a judicial investigation, rejected as spnrious, or fraudulent, claims to the amount of $5,568,975. The unliquidated claims, after deducting the award made under the treaty, amounted to $6,455,464. Of these, by the treaty of peace, the American Government assumes and promises to pay such as may be found valid by its own Commissioners, *not exceeding, however,* in amount $3,250,000. This sum deducted from the balance above, leaves no less than $3,205,464, absolutely and irrevocably abandoned and repudiated by the Federal Government, while the Government of Mexico is by treaty

* It will be recollected that a convention concluded by Mr. Thompson, the interest on the whole award was to be paid on the 30th April, 1843, and the principal in twenty instalments, one every three months. The Interest was punctually paid, as were the three first instalments. The money for these payments was raised by *forced loans*, so anxious was the Mexican government to meet its engagements, notwithstanding its financial embarrassments. The measures adopted by our own government in reference to the annexation of Texas, together with the state of the Mexican treasury, delayed, and finally prevented the other payments.

stipulation released from all obligation to pay them! The sum thus abandoned, added to the sum rejected by the arbitrators and umpire, makes the very respectable amount of $8,774,439. But this amount is yet to be greatly enlarged. The unliquidated claims are those preferred at the eleventh hour, when the government was striving to exaggerate the sufferings of our citizens, for the purpose of bullying Mexico out of territory, and when it was hoped that the greater the amount of claims, the more ready would the nation be for war. The best claims were undoubtedly those first presented. We here find that of those which were investigated *five-sevenths* were found spurious. On the very unreasonable supposition that the remaining claims are not more worthless than the first, less than two millions will remain to be paid for by the government. In all human probability, one million will be more than sufficient to meet every equitable demand; and thus of the 14 millions of claims about 11 will have proved in the end to be fictitious. Of this base currency Mr. Slidell, as we have seen, took 6 millions with him to Mexico. The use he was to make of it, is thus specified in his instructions:

"Fortunately the joint resolution of Congress for annexing Texas to the United States, presents the means of *satisfying these claims*, in perfect consistency with the interests as well as the honor of both republics. It has reserved to this government the adjustment of all questions of boundary that may arise with other governments. This question of boundary may therefore be adjusted in such a manner between the two republics as to cast the burden of debt due to American claimants on their own Government, while it will do no injury to Mexico."*

* The instructions to Mr. Slidell were called for by the House of Representatives; but the President refused to communicate them. A copy, however, was surreptitiously obtained, and was published in the newspapers: its authenticity has never been questioned.

In other words, Mr. Slidell is to buy territory, and these fraudulent claims are to form part of the consideration. He is authorized to offer the claims and $5,000,000 for New Mexico, and *the claims* and $25,000,000 for both New Mexico and California. Thus we see the envoy was sent on a land-jobbing mission, armed with claims to the amount of eight millions to bully, and with twenty-five millions of dollars to bribe, the Mexicans to dismember their republic.

Mr. Polk was determined to have Mexican territory, peaceably if he could—forcibly if he must. If he could not *buy*, he intended to conquer. Hence, the moment the Cabinet learned from Slidell's letter, that he had not been immediately received, although the question of reception was still undecided, the army was ordered to the Rio Grande. A few days after the decision was made known to Slidell, the Mexican administration was changed, and Paredes, the head of the belligerent party assumed the reins of government. On this change becoming known at Washington, Slidell was ordered to present his credentials to the new Cabinet, and demand his recognition; and this very order was avowedly given to facilitate war. "On your return to the United States, energetic measures against Mexico would at once be recommended by the President, and these might fail to obtain the support of Congress, if it could be asserted that the existing Government had not refused to receive our Minister."* The demand was accordingly made, and, as was foreseen, refused, and Mr. Slidell came home.

It was, it seems, the intention of Mr. Polk, on this last refusal, to invoke Congress to declare war (take "energetic measures") on the ground that Mexico by refusing

* For the Slidell Correspondence, see Senate Documents, 29th Cong., 1 Sess.

to receive his Minister Plenipotentiary, compelled us to seek payment of our claims by the sword. On further reflection, this design was abandoned. A recommendation to commence the work of human butchery *for such a cause*, "might fail to obtain the support of Congress." It was thought more expedient *first* to provoke hostilities, and then to call on Congress to raise armies to DEFEND the country. Hence, although Congress was in Session when the President received intelligence of Mr. Slidell's final rejection, he did *not* "recommend energetic measures against Mexico," as Mr. Buchanan said he would. A course had been taken which left but little to the discretion of the Legislature. Before we proceed to describe that course, it will be necessary to examine the claim on which it was founded, viz., that the Rio Grande was the western boundary of the United States.

CHAPTER XIX.

WESTERN BOUNDARY OF TEXAS.

WHATEVER may have been the original limits of the region which ancient discoverers and geographers named Texas, the boundaries of the revolted Mexican province of that name, are no more necessarily identical with those limits, than are the boundaries of the State of Louisiana with the limits once assigned to the vast territory bearing the same name. The *State* of Texas was carved by Mexico out of her domains, and, in union with Coahuila, was entitled to a common legislature, and a representation in the Mexican Congress. In 1833, Texas, as already mentioned, dissolved her union with Coahuila, but laid no claim whatever to any portion of the territory of her late associate. The limits of the *State* of Texas were well known, and defined on maps. Its boundary commenced at the mouth of the river Nueces, in Corpus Christi bay; and followed that river to its source, thence to the line of New Mexico, near the Gaudaloupe mountains, thence easterly to the southern branch of the Colorado, and along that branch to the main stream, and with that to and along the boundary line of the United States to the Gulf of Mexico. The country between the Nueces and Rio Grande was embraced in Coahuila and the Northern district of Tamaulipas. A map of Texas, published in 1831, gives the Nueces as its southern limit; and in a description of Texas, published in the same year, by a visitant, it is said that the province is bounded by "the Nueces, which divides it from Tamaulipas and Coahuila."

In 1833, Benjamin Lundy travelled extensively in Texas and Mexico; and his diary, published since his death, contains entries which show most conclusively what was then considered by the Texans as the southern or south-western boundary:—"1833, October 11th. We proceeded this morning over some delightful plains, on a good level road. At half-past nine, we reached and crossed the river Nueces, which is the western limit of what is called Texas. Of course we are now in Coahuila."

"February 1, 1833. Laredo is a poor-looking place. It contains about 2200 inhabitants. The people look like mulattoes. They are friendly and clever, *but not one of them can speak English*. Laredo is the first settlement that I have seen in Tamaulipas." Life of Benjamin Lundy, pp. 57, 95.

In 1836, as we have seen, President Jackson laid before Congress the report of his special agent, Mr. Moffit, who was sent to Texas to acquire information for the Government. The agent reported that "the political limits of Texas proper (that is, the Mexican State of Texas), before the last revolution, were the Nueces river on the *West*," &c.

In 1837, was published a map of Texas, "compiled by Stephen F. Austin, from surveys by General Teran of the Mexican Army;" and here again we have the Nueces for its western boundary. So late as June 28th, 1845, Mr. Donaldson, American Chargé d' Affaires to Texas, declared, in an official letter, that Corpus Christi "is the most western point now occupied by Texas." The Mexican Government always insisted, that the territory on the Rio Grande, had never belonged to Texas. The Mexican commissioners appointed to treat of peace, were, by instructions, authorised to acknowledge the independence of Texas; but, to avoid mistake, it was added, "by Texas is understood the territory known by that name after the treaties of 1819, when it formed part of the State of Coahuila and Texas, and not by any means the territory between the Nueces and the Bravo, which the Congress of the pretended Texans claimed to belong to it." On the 18th March, 1846, Gen. Mejia, the commandant at Metamoras, in a proclamation announcing Taylor's invasion, to prove that the Americans intended to seize territory not included in Texas, remarked, "the limits of Texas are certain and recognised; *never have they extended* beyond the river Nueces."

It is, therefore, beyond all doubt, that no point of the Mexican *State of Texas* came in contact with the Rio Grande. In what manner, then, had the *Republic of Texas* acquired the immense extent of territory she claimed? As it came neither by purchase, nor by treaty; the title, if any, must have been conferred by the sword. On the 2d March, 1836, the Mexican State of Texas, bounded, as we have seen, by the Nueces, declared its independence. This declaration, while it changed the political relations of Texas, had no effect on its territory. On the 21st April of the same year, the victory of San Jacinto secured the separation of Texas from Mexico; but it was a victory obtained over Mexican troops in the heart of Texas, not a conquest of Mexican territory. It was a victory, however, which emboldened the Texans *to claim* for the purpose of occupying at pleasure, whatever land they thought might be convenient. We find from the official report of General Jackson's agent, laid before Congress by the President, that almost on the battle-field, "immediately after the battle of San Jacinto," it was the intention of the Texan Government "to have claimed from the Rio Grande, along the river to the 30th degree of latitude, and then West to the Pacific" !! It was, however, on reflection, thought this was more than was necessary; and so, on the 16th December of the same year, the Texan Legislature voted themselves parts of New Mexico, Coahuila, and Tamaulipas, about equal in extent to the whole of Texas itself. This additional territory is bounded by the Rio Grande, and *hence*, and in virtue of this act of the 16th December, 1836, when the Texan Government did not own or possess jurisdiction over one inch of land on the Rio Grande, Mr. Polk ordered General Taylor, 15th June, 1845, to hold himself in readiness to march his troops into Texas, where "you wlll select and occupy, on or near the Rio Grande del Norte, such a site as will consist with the health of the troops, and will be best adapted to repel invasion, and to protect what, in the *event of annexation, will* be OUR WESTERN FRONTIER."

The act of the Texan Legislature, of course, no more deprived Mexico of her right to Santa Fé, than it could have deprived us of our right to Oregon. Mr. Polk, in claiming thus early the Rio Grande as the western boundary of the United States, and ordering a military force to take possession of it, acted in his capacity of chief magistrate, and either with or without authority. As the claim he advanced to this boundary, and his measures to enforce that claim, led to hostilities, it is important to inquire how far this gentleman was authorised by the laws of his country, to involve it in the calamity of war.

It was only in the *event of annexation*, that Mr. Polk claimed the Rio Grande as the western boundary of the United States. Hence it becomes important to ascertain, if the act of annexation did indeed transfer to the United States the territories voted to itself by the Republic of Texas. The Tyler treaty of annexation was silent as to boundaries; and why? Let Mr. Calhoun, who negotiated it, answer. No sooner was the treaty signed, than the Secretary officially informed the Mexican Government, that the United States had "taken every precaution to make the terms of the treaty as little objectionable to Mexico as possible; and, among others, has left the boundary of Texas without specification, so that *what* the line of boundary should be might be an *open question*, to be fairly and fully discussed and *settled* according to the *rights* of each."

Notwithstanding this letter, it was objected to the treaty in the Senate, that the very absence of all specification of boundary might be regarded as an implied sanction of the ridiculous pretensions of Texas. Mr. Benton who, as we have seen, was one of the earliest advocates of annexation, indignantly rejected the idea, that Texas could confer upon the United States title to territory she never owned. In his speech against the ratification of the treaty, he used the following language: "I wash my hands of all attempts to dismember the Mexican Republic by seizing her dominions in New Mexico, Chihuahua, Coahuila, and Tamaulipas. The treaty, in all that relates to the boundary of the Rio Grande, is an act of unparalleled outrage on Mexico. It is the seizure of two thousand miles of her territory, without a word of explanation with her, by virtue of a treaty with Texas to which she is no party. By this declaration, the thirty thousand Mexicans in the left half of the valley of the Rio del Norte are our citizens, and standing, in the language of the President's Message, in a hostile attitude towards us, and subject to be repelled as invaders. Taos, the seat of the Custom-house, where our caravans enter their goods, is ours; Santa Fé the capital of New Mexico is ours—Governor Armijo is our Governor, and subject to be tried for treason, if he does not submit to us; twenty Mexican towns and villages,* are ours, and their peaceful inhabitants cultivating their fields and tending their flocks, are suddenly converted by a stroke of the President's pen into American citizens or American rebels.

"I therefore propose, as an additional resolution, applicable to the Rio del Norte boundary only, the one which I will read, and send to the Secretary's table, and one on which I shall at the proper time ask the vote of the Senate. This is the resolution:

"Resolved, that the incorporation of the left bank of the Rio del Norte into the American Union, by virtue of a treaty with Texas, comprehending, as the said incorporation would do, a part of the Mexican departments of New Mexico, Chihuahua, Coahuila, and Tamaulipas, would be an *act of aggression on Mexico*, for all the consequences of which the United States would stand responsible."

There can be no doubt the resolution would have passed, had not the rejection of the treaty prevented a vote being taken. Mr. Silas Wright, a distinguished democratic Senator from New York, afterwards vindicating his vote against the treaty, asserted, "I believed that the treaty, from the boundaries that must *be implied* from it, if Mexico would not treat with us, embraced a country to which Texas had no claim, over which she had never asserted jurisdiction, and which she had no right to cede."

* The following are some of the Mexican towns and settlements along the east border of the Rio Grande, which according to Mr. Polk, are on our side "the boundary line of the United States," but in which, at the time of the invasion, was not to be found one single magistrate holding a commission either from the Federal Government, or the State of Texas—viz Taos, Peuris, Grampa, Embudo, Namba, San Juan, Vitior, San Domingo, San Branilla, San Aux, San Dios, Albuquerque, San Fernanda, Valencia, Fonclara, Las Nutrias, Alamillo, San Pasqual, Christobal, Las Pepuallas, Presidio, Dolores, Loredo, and Point Isabel.

It thus appears that, in 1844, Messrs. Tyler and Calhoun admitted the boundary of the Rio Grande to be *an open question;* while Messrs. Wright and Benton, and probably a great majority of the Senate, disclaimed and repudiated all right whatever to what Mr. Polk terms "our western frontier."

On the 3rd March, 1845, Congress passed an act allowing drawback on goods exported to "Santa Fé *in Mexico.*" But according to the Texan Act of 16th December, 1836, Santa Fé was in the Republic of Texas. Here, then, we have, on the part of the Congress of the United States, a distinct repudiation of the paper boundaries set up by the victors at San Jacinto. We had, moreover, a Consul at Santa Fé, recognized not by the Texan but the Mexican Government. Yet it was *after* this act was passed, and before we had acquired a title to a foot of Texan land, that Mr. Polk took measures to seize by force of arms the territory on the Rio Grande, in case of annexation.

Falsehood is ever inconsistent with itself. Mr. Polk, in his Message, 8th December, 1846, speaking of the actual separation of Texas from Mexico previous to annexation, uses the expression, "No hostile foot finding rest within her territory for six or seven years." Yet all this time, Mexican villages east of the Rio Grande were governed by Mexican laws and magistrates, and the Secretary-at-War, in ordering General Taylor to advance to that river, warns him of the *Mexican military establishments* on this side of it. If no hostile foot had found rest in Texan territory for six or seven years, then most certainly the Rio Grande territory was not in Texas. Mr. Polk, moreover, tells Congress that, in December, 1836, a Texan law declared "the Rio Grande from its mouth to its source to be their boundary, and by the said act they extended their civil and political jurisdiction over the country up to that boundary;" and yet in this very same Message he announces to Congress that, "by rapid movements the province of New Mexico, with Santa Fé, its capital, has been *captured* without bloodshed." But Santa Fé was on the East of the Rio Grande, and far below its source, and therefore, according to the President, included within the Territory of Texas. And why was it captured if no hostile foot rested in it?

Let us now inquire with what boundaries we received Texas. The terms of the joint resolutions were, "Congress doth consent that the territory *properly included within and rightfully belonging to the Republic of Texas*, may be erected into a new State to be called the State of Texas, &c.; "said State to be formed, subject to the adjustment *by this Government* of all questions *of boundaries* that may arise *with other governments*." Here is no sanction of the act of 16th December, 1836, no claim of title founded on it, but an indirect admission that Texas has made unfounded claims, and we mean to take not what she claims, but what she rightfully owns; and this we will settle with Mexico of course by treaty, the President and Senate being "*this Government*" mentioned in the resolution. The resolutions embracing this language were officially *approved* of by Mr. Polk, immediately on his accession to the Presidency; and yet, notwithstanding they thus rejected all title to territory founded on Texan claims, reserving to the President and Senate the decision of what should be "our Western frontier," Mr. Polk resolved not merely to decide that question of his own will and pleasure, but to maintain his decision at the point of the bayonet, without any consultation with the Senate, and without waiting to discuss it with Mexico. For many years a question existed between Great Britain and the

United States, respecting the North-eastern boundary of the latter. No President assumed the responsibility of plunging the country into war by taking military possession of the disputed territory, and the question was finally settled by treaty. Mr. Polk, on his accession to the Presidency, found another and most important question of boundary pending between the same parties respecting the territory of Oregon. He expressed, in his inaugural address, the opinion, that the title of the United States to the whole of that vast region up to 54° 40′ of North latitude, was clear and unquestionable; and he refused all offers of compromise, and all reference of the question to arbitration. Yet he sent no army to defend what he declared to be our Northern frontier. On the contrary, he entered into negotiation with Great Britain, and surrendered five degrees and forty minutes of territory, which he had himself asserted belonged to us "by irrefragable facts and arguments," by a treaty which General Cass declared in the Senate was "prepared by the British Government," and which was ratified by the Senate without "the crossing of a *t*, or the dotting of an *i*, untouched and unchanged." Great Britain was a powerful nation, and Mexico a feeble one; the territory surrendered was in the North, and would for ever be free—that which was seized was in the South, and was intended to be for ever a slave region.

CHAPTER XX.

COMMENCEMENT OF WAR AGAINST MEXICO BY GENERAL TAYLOR.

Mr. Polk, having decided on war, in case California could not be had by negotiation, commenced his preparations for waging it, even before the annexation with Texas was consummated. On the 8th July, 1845, the Secretary of War wrote to Taylor, "This department is informed, that Mexico has some *military establishments* on the east side of the Rio Grande, which are, and for some time past have been, in the actual occupation of her troops. In carrying out the instructions heretofore received, you will be careful to avoid any acts of aggression, unless a state of war should exist. The Mexican forces at the posts in their possession, and which have been so, will not be disturbed so long as the relations of peace between the United States and Mexico continue." An invading army is sent into a territory in military possession of Mexico; territory which had *never* been out of her possession since its conquest from the aborigines. But no attack is to be made on the Mexican forts; let the first blow be struck by the Mexicans, and then the war will be one of *defence*, and therefore more popular. On the 6th August, Taylor is informed that the seventh regiment of infantry and three companies of dragoons have been ordered to Texas, and 10,000 muskets, and 1,000 rifles. A few days after he is told, he will have "a force of four thousand men of the *regular* army." In addition to these regulars, requisitions were made upon the Governors of Alabama, Mississippi,

Louisiana, Tennessee, and Kentucky, to furnish Taylor with as many volunteers as he might require. The Secretary of War, in thus calling for an indefinite number of troops, makes the following candid and extraordinary confession: "It is proper to observe, that the emergency rendering such assistance from the militia of your State necessary, *does not appear to have been foreseen by Congress,* and consequently no appropriation was made for paying them." Truly indeed Congress had not foreseen that Mr. Polk meant to invade Mexico, and had made no provision for the intended war.

The President having thus made, on his own responsibility, ample provision for the commencement of the war, instructed Taylor how he might bring it on in case Mexico remained passive. On the 30th August, he was told, "The assembling a large Mexican army on the borders of Texas, and crossing the Rio Grande with a considerable force, will be regarded by the Executive as *an invasion of the United States* (*!*) and the commencement of *hostilities.* An attempt to cross the river with such a force will also be considered in the same light. In case of war, either *declared or made manifest by hostile acts,* your main object will be the protection of Texas; but the pursuit of this object will not necessarily confine your action within the territory of Texas. Mexico having thus *commenced* hostilities, you may in your discretion *cross the Rio Grande,* disperse or capture the forces assembled to invade Texas, defeat the junction of troops uniting for that purpose, drive them from their positions on either side of the river, and, if deemed practicable and expedient, take and hold possession of Metamoras and other places in the country."

Thus we find the President in time of peace, and without the knowledge or expectation of Congress, ordering the invasion of a territory in the actual and exclusive possession of Mexico, a territory having Mexican villages under the authority of Mexican magistrates, a port of entry, a custom-house, and various "military establishments." Should the Mexicans, prompted by the natural dictates of patriotism and self-defence, assemble a body of troops which in General Taylor's discretion might be deemed "large," and attempt to cross the river to reinforce their military establishments, to protect their villages, to secure the collection of their customs, to watch the motions of the invading army, then General Taylor is to regard their conduct as AN INVASION OF THE UNITED STATES, and is to begin a *war of defence,* although not a Mexican shot has been fired, and is to capture the city of Metamoras, and to carry the war into the interior of Mexico.*

So confident was Mr. Polk of the success of his plan, that, as we have seen, the Governors of no less than five States were ordered to supply Taylor with an unlimited number of troops to commence the intended campaign with eclat.

The pretended apology for this most unwarrantable assumption of power in thus plunging the country into an unexpected, unprovoked, and unnecessary war, was that Texas was in danger. None were more sensible than the administration of the utter inability of Mexico to wage an offensive war against the United States. Since the commencement of the Texan rebellion, the Mexican Government had been uttering inflated threats against its revolted province, yet no hostile force had entered it since the di-

* The following from the *Union* of the 11th Sept., 1845, the official paper of the Administration, shows how well the editor understood the designs of his employers, "If Arista (the Mexican General at Metamoras), dares to carry out his braggart threats, if he ventures to cross the Rio Grande *with reinforcements to any little armed posts,* which the Mexicans may occupy on the east side of the river, General Taylor will attempt to prevent him—blood must flow—war WILL ENSUE."

sastrous conflict at San Jacinto: A vast desert extended between the Nueces and the Rio Grande; and in the district along the east of that river not one Texan dwelling was to be found. The population of the country invaded by Taylor, was exclusively Mexican. There was no human probability that Mexico, feeble, disorganized, and distracted as she was, would dare to invade Texas, now protected by the whole power of the American confederacy, when nine years before a handful of adventurers had destroyed her army, and taken captive her President. The pretence was no less absurd than false; and, had danger been indeed apprehended, there was no necessity to send an army 200 miles in *advance* of the Texan settlements, when no hostile movements of the Mexicans indicated an intention to cross the intervening desert, and enter Texas. The falsity of the pretence is evinced by a remarkable confession made by the government so late as 16th Oct., 1845. The Secretary of War, writing to Taylor, says, "The information we have, renders it probable that no serious attempts will at present be made by Mexico to invade Texas, although she continues to threaten incursions."* General Taylor, instead of proceeding immediately to the Rio Grande agreeably to his instructions, stopped at Corpus Christi at the mouth of the Nueces, the extreme point of Texas proper, and Oct. 4th, 1845, wrote to the Secretary, "Mexico having as yet made no positive declaration of war, or committed any overt act of hostilities, I do not feel at liberty under my instructions, particularly those of July 8th, to make a forward movement to the Rio Grande without authority from the war department." He alluded to his instructions to take a position on the Rio Grande to repel invasion, but

* For correspondence, &c., with Taylor, see Senate Doc., 29th Cong., 1st Sess.

to avoid acts of aggression unless an actual state of war existed. As there was no invasion to repel, and as his march into the Mexican territory in time of peace would be an act of aggression, he prudently waited for further orders.

Under these circumstances, and considering that all was now ready for commencing hostilities, the administration deemed it on the whole most prudent to wait the result of the proposed negotiation to be opened at Mexico, measures for that purpose having already been taken. If our claims could be bartered for California, it would not be necessary to compel Taylor to march to the Rio Grande. We have seen that the order to Taylor to invade the territory of the Rio Grande, the requisitions upon five States for troops, and the instructions to Taylor how and on what pretences to commence the war, and to capture Metamoras, &c., were all *previous* to the appointment of Slidell; and therefore, that the actual march to the Rio Grande and the war that ensued, were only the *resumption* of a policy that had merely been suspended to allow time to ascertain whether California could possibly be obtained by negotiation. The suspension, however, was brief. We have already noticed the avowal of Mr. Buchanan, Secretary of State, that in case of the refusal of Mexico to receive Mr. Slidell, "nothing can remain but to take the redress of the injuries of our citizens, and the insults to our Government, into our own hands," in other words, to go to war. On the 12th January, 1846, the first dispatch was received from Slidell, from which it appeared probable that, although the Government had not yet refused to receive him, it would enter into no negotiation with him, except in reference to Texas. Of course there was no hope of a cession of California; and the very *next day* peremptory orders were sent to Taylor to advance to the Rio Grande; an order unquestionably dictated by the avowed determination we have mentioned.

It seems, therefore, that the Government resolved on war *professedly* for two causes; 1st, The injuries to our citizens, all of which were estimated in dollars and cents. To collect a few millions of alleged debts, it acknowledges it willingness to commence the work of human slaughter, and that, too, at the very moment when no less than six States of the Union were indebted in the prodigious amount of $52,000,000, of which they paid neither principal nor interest. The very idea of collecting two or three millions of dollars by spending a hundred or more in murdering the debtors, is so utterly absurd and diabolical, that we must be excused from believing Mr. Buchanan when he pretends that such was the intention of the Cabinet. The second cause assigned is little less credible. The insults to our Government which were to be revenged by killing Mexicans, are the imputations of bad faith cast by their rulers upon the Government at Washington for its conduct towards Texas; imputations which, however disagreeable, were unhappily supported by facts, and which had already been most abundantly repaid with insult and injury. The acquisition of California, and the extension of slavery, afforded motives for war which the pretended causes assigned by Mr. Buchanan failed to supply.

It was not sufficient that Taylor should march to the Rio Grande; the Secretary tells him, "points *opposite* Metamoras and Mier, and the vicinity of Laredo, are suggested for your consideration." The object was to provoke a collision, and, if possible, induce the Mexicans to attack our forces; and hence the American standard was to be insultingly displayed in the immediate vicinity and in full view of these Mexican towns. It would be hard indeed if our troops, stationed in the suburbs of these three places, did not bring on a quarrel, and thus enable Mr. Polk to announce to Congress that "War existed by the act of Mexico."

General Taylor, in pursuance of orders, commenced his march into the Mexican territory. Not an American, not a Texan was to be found South of Corpus Christi. After proceeding through the desert about one hundred miles, he met "small armed parties of Mexicans who seemed disposed to avoid us."

On approaching Point Isabel, a Mexican settlement, and the site of a Mexican Custom House, he found the buildings in flames. At the same time he received a protest from the "Prefect of the Northern District of Tamaulipas" against his invasion of a territory "*which had never belonged to the Colony seized upon*" (Texas), an invasion of which no notice had been given to the Government of Mexico, and for which no reason had been assigned. The protest concluded with assuring Taylor that, so long as his army "shall remain in the terrritory of Tamaulipas, the inhabitants must, whatever professions of peace you may employ, regard you as openly committing hostilities, and for the melancholy consequences of these they who have been the invaders must be answerable in the view of the whole world." The inhabitants of Point Isabel fled before the invaders, and sought refuge in Metamoras. Taylor announced to his Government, that he considered the conflagration of Point Isabel "*as a decided evidence of hostility.*" To understand the purport of this declaration of opinion, it must be recollected that in his orders of the 13th January, 1846, he was instructed that, should Mexico assume the character of an enemy "by a declaration of war, or *any open act of hostility* towards us, you will not act *merely on the defensive.*"

On the 28th March, Taylor, without having met with the slightest opposition, planted his standard on the bank of the Rio Grande. On the 6th April he wrote home that the guns of his battery "*bear directly upon the public square of Metamoras, and within good range for demolishing the town;* their object cannot be mistaken by the *enemy;*" and he tells the Secretary of War, "the Mexicans still retain a hostile attitude, and have thrown up some works to prevent us from crossing the river."* No declaration of war had been issued on either side, and the

* During the progress of this invasion, and while the army was before Metamoras, various letters from the officers found their way into the public journals. A few extracts from these will be found instructive. "West of the Nueces the people are all Spaniards. The country is uninhabitable excepting the valley of the Rio Grande, and that contains a pretty dense population, and in no part of the country are the people more loyal to the Mexican Government."

"*Camp opposite Metamoras, April 19th,* 1846. Our situation here is an extraordinary one. Right in the enemy's country, and actually occupying their corn and cotton fields, the people of the soil leaving their homes, and we with a small handful of men marching, with colors flying, and drums beating, right under the very guns of one of their principal cities, displaying the star-spangled banner as if in defiance under their very nose, and they with an army twice our size at least, sit quietly down, and make not the least resistance, not the least effort to drive the invaders off. There is no parallel to it." Capt. Henry, the writer of this letter, seems not to have been aware that he was in the United States, and that the *people of the soil* were his fellow-citizens.

Another officer writes, 21st April, "Our flag waves over the waters of the Rio Grande, and we have a battery of eighteen-pounders that can *spot* anything in Metamoras." To understand this last operation, it must be recollected, that the city was on one bank, and the American fort on the other. Captain Henry, of the U. S. Army, in his "Campaign Sketches of the War in Mexico," says, that on the evening of the day the army reached the river opposite to Metamoras, "I walked down to the bank, and found it lined with citizens (on the other side), attracted, no doubt, by the arrival of so many strangers. Strolling along, and seeing some genteel-looking young ladies upon the bank, I took off my hat, and saluted them with 'Buena Senoritas.' The river at this point was *so narrow, that I could have thrown a stone across it.*"—p. 68.

Mexicans, although they saw their country invaded, and a battery planted within good range for demolishing the principal city in that part of their Republic, had not fired a musket, yet General Taylor chooses to style them "*the enemy*," and asserts that they retain a hostile attitude.

Five days after our arms had thus threatened and insulted Metamoras, General Ampudia reached the city with reinforcements, and immediately addressed a letter to the American General, complaining that his advance to the Rio Grande had "not only insulted but exasperated the Mexican nation," and requiring him within twenty-four hours to remove his camp, and retire beyond the Nueces; adding, "If you insist on remaining upon the soil of the department of Tamaulipas, it will clearly result that arms, and arms alone, must decide the question." As Taylor had been sent to Tamaulipas expressly to produce this very result, he took occasion of this letter to hasten the desired crisis. The Mexicans had shown a forbearance amounting almost to pusillanimity. Should this forbearance continue, and the *enemy* remain on the other side of the river, how could the war be commenced? He must wait for some pretext for crossing the river to attack them. The fact that the inhabitants of Point Isabel had fired their own houses, would hardly justify him in bombarding Metamoras. He chose therefore to consider Ampudia's notice to quit as an hostile act, but not one to be resented with powder and shot. He therefore resorted to an expedient which would compel Ampudia to fire the *first shot,* and thus, according to the wishes of the Cabinet, to make the intended war, one *of defence,* "a war by the act of Mexico." There were two American armed vessels at Brazos Santiago, and these he ordered to blockade the mouth of the Rio Grande, thus cutting off all commuication with Metamoras by sea. Soon after a vessel with a cargo of grain for the city, was prevented by the squadron from entering the river, and in consequence of the alarm excited by the blockade, flour rose, as stated in the papers, to forty dollars a barrel. Taylor, with a frankness bordering on indiscretion, thus avows his reason for ordering the blockade: "It will at any rate compel the Mexicans to withdraw their army from Metamoras where it cannot be sustained, *or to assume the offensive on this side of the river*."*

Yet in this very letter he reports that since his last of the 15th, "the relations between me and the Mexicans have not changed," that is, the Mexicans had not commenced hostilities. Notwithstanding the blockade, the Mexicans did not attack Taylor; whereupon he determined, it seems, not to remain any longer idle. Accordingly, the very day on which he informs the Secretary that the relations between himself and the Mexicans remained the same, and when not a single shot had been fired by the latter, he reports, "with a view to check the *depredations* of *small* parties of the *enemy* on this side of the river, Lieutenants Dobbins of the 3d Infantry, and Porter, 4th Infantry, were authorized by me a *few days* since to scour the country for some miles with a select party of men, and *capture* and *destroy* any such parties that they might meet. It appears they separated, and that Lieutenant Porter at the head of his own detachment surprised a Mexican camp, drove away the men, and took *possession of their horses*." In this affair, Porter and one man were killed—whether any, or how many Mexican lives were sacrificed, does not appear.

Thus it seems, that notwithstanding all the contrivances of the administration to compel the Mexicans to strike the *first* blow, it was in fact given by ourselves.

* Letter to Secretary of War, April 23, 1846.

The idea of small parties committing depredations, is a paltry apology for commencing a war. There were no Americans, no Texans, except the American army in the country, upon whom these small parties could commit depredations. What were the depredations complained of, and who were the sufferers, the General did not think proper to specify. But, moreover, the detachments were not authorized to arrest the depredators, but to *capture* and *destroy* ANY small parties they might meet, guilty or innocent. The General was instructed not to molest "the military establishments" on this side of the river; yet he resolves that any small parties from these establishments who might leave their barracks, were to be captured and destroyed. His next letter, 26th April, reports, "that a party of dragoons sent out by me on the 24th instant to watch the course of the river above on this bank, *became engaged* with a very large force of the enemy, and, after a short affair in which some sixteen were killed and wounded, appear to have been surrounded and compelled to surrender." The very peculiar phraseology used to express this battle, "became engaged," was not perhaps accidental. Did the party of dragoons gallantly attack the *very large force* of the enemy, and were they in consequence of their *rashness* taken prisoners after losing sixteen in killed and wounded? Or did the large party commence hostilities by *attacking* the dragoons? To these very natural inquiries no response is found in the General's despatch. The particulars of the case were, however, disclosed in letters from the army, and published in the newspapers. It appears that Thornton the commander of the party, discovering a *small* body of Mexicans on the summit of a rising ground, "*immediately charged upon them;*" but the main body who were on the other side of the hill, and therefore unseen, coming up, captured the assailants.* Another letter, published in the Philadelphia *Inquirer*, says, "Captain Thornton, when about twenty-five miles above the army, discovered some Mexicans on a hill, *when he immediately charged upon them.* When he got to the top of the hill, he found himself in a trap. The Mexicans were on the opposite side of the hill in a field."†

General Taylor, after mentioning the affair in the words we have given, announces to the Cabinet the attainment of the long desired result. "HOSTILITIES MAY NOW BE CONSIDERED AS COMMENCED." Upon the strength of this despatch, the President announced to Congress and the world, "MEXICO HAS PASSED THE BOUNDARY OF THE UNITED STATES, HAS INVADED OUR TERRITORY AND SHED AMERICAN BLOOD UPON THE AMERICAN SOIL. *She has proclaimed that hostilities have commenced, and that the two nations are now at war.*" How far the unqualified assertions contained in the first sentence of the passage quoted, are in accordance with truth, those who have read the preceding pages are qualified to judge for themselves. The following *facts* may tend to test the veracity of the last averment.

General Arista arrived at Metamoras on the 24th April, and finding the supplies intended for the army cut off by the blockade of the river, the great square of the city commanded by Taylor's cannon, American parties scouring the country, breaking up Mexican camps, and seizing their horses, he gave notice that he considered, as well he might, hostilities commenced, and that he should prose-

* See New Orleans *Picayune*, May 2d, 1846.

† Nearly a year *after* the commencement of the war, Thornton's official report of this affair was made public. It differs in some particulars from the newspaper accounts, but the fact of the *charge* is admitted, though under the plea of self-defence. The charge was made before the Mexicans had fired a shot.

cute them. He thus plainly disavowed *commencing* the war. How far Arista's declaration, that he considered hostilities commenced by the Americans, justifies Mr. Polk's solemn asseveration that Mexico had "proclaimed that hostilities had commenced, and that the two nations are now at war," the reader will decide. Should the notice of the 24th April, fail to establish the veracity of Mr. Polk's announcement to Congress, the friends of that gentleman call to his defence an order issued by the President of Mexico on the 18th April, more than a month after Taylor had left Corpus Christi, and commenced his invasion of the Mexican territory; "From this day," says the order, "begins our *defensive* war, and every point of our territory *attacked* or *invaded* shall be *defended*." As the invasion continued, a proclamation was issued by the Mexican President on the 24th April in which he says, "The flag of the stars waves on the left bank of the Rio Bravo del Norte, opposite to the city of Metamoras, after taking possession of the river with their ships of war. The town of Laredo was surprised by a party of their troops, and a picket of ours on the watch was disarmed. Hostilities then have *been commenced by the United States of America,* in making new conquests upon our territories within the boundaries of Tamaulipas and New Leon. *I have not the right to declare war.* It is for the august Congress of the nation, as soon as they assemble, to take into consideration all the consequences of the conflict in which we are involved. But if, during this interval the United States should without notice, attack our sea coasts on the *Texan frontier,* then it will become necessary to repel force by force, and a beginning once made by the invaders, to make fall upon them the immense responsibility of disturbing the peace of the world."

It will be observed that in no instance is the annexation

of Texas cited as an evidence of the existence of hostilities; but solely the invasion of the Rio Grande, and the acts of General Taylor connected with the invasion.

General Taylor lost no time in prosecuting the war with his utmost energy without waiting for further orders. On the 17th of May, only four days after Congress had declared, "that war existed by the act of Mexico," and of course before he had received advices that the war he had commenced had been recognized by either government, General Arista sent a flag of truce to him requesting an armistice for six weeks, giving as a reason, his wish to communicate with his own government. But General Taylor was too well acquainted with the designs of his own government to accept a proposition so much in accordance with the dictates of humanity, and which possibly might have led to the restoration of peace. The armistice was rejected; and the next day he crossed the river and took possession of the city of Metamoras.*

In the fierce strife of contending factions, the awful guilt of *commencing* an offensive and unnecessary war, will be imputed to different parties; but the punishment due to guilt so enormous will be awarded by a tribunal before which all hearts will be open, and from which no secrets will be hid.

* General Taylor, informing the War Department of his rejection of this proposal, states, that he replied to Arista, "I was receiving large reinforcements and could not now suspend operations which *I had not initiated nor provoked*—that the possession of Metamoras was a *sine qua non*." It is to be supposed that the General reconciled this extraordinary declaration to his conscience, on the principle of *qui facit per alium, facit per se*, and that, being a mere instrument, the war was initiated and provoked, not by himself, but the President.

CHAPTER XXI.

SEIZURE OF CALIFORNIA.

BEFORE proceeding to detail the part taken by Mr. Polk and Congress, on the receipt of Taylor's announcement that hostilities had commenced, we will call the attention of the reader to the early and provident measures devised to secure, as speedily as possible, the object of these hostilities, the ACQUISITION OF CALIFORNIA. On the 24th June, 1845, by order of Mr. Polk, "secret and confidential" instructions were given to Commodore Sloat, commanding the United States naval forces in the Pacific. "If you ascertain with certainty that Mexico has declared war against the United States, you will at once possess yourself of the port of Saint Francisco, and blockade and occupy such other ports as your force may permit."* This naval force consisted of five vessels, and for months it was kept on the California coast, ready to make the coveted prize at a moment's warning, and without waiting for advices from home. The Commodore with his own and another vessel were waiting at Mazatlan, at the entrance of the Gulf of California, two more were stationed off Monterey, and the fifth was at St. Francisco. So admirably had all been arranged for an immediate conquest. On the 7th June, and of course within less than four weeks after the declaration of war by Congress, the Commodore

* See documents submitted by the President, in obedience to a call from the House of Representatives, for instructions to officers in California and the Pacific, communicated Dec. 22d, 1846 App. to Cong. Globe, 2 Sess. 29 Cong., page 45

heard of Taylor's conflicts on the Rio Grande. The long expected moment had arrived, and the *next day* he weighed anchor and sailed for Monterey. On the 7th July, that place was once more, without resistance, seized by our forces, and Sloat, like his predecessor, Jones, forthwith distributed his *proclamations* in English and Spanish. Where or when they were prepared, and whether they were in manuscript or print, does not appear. *Two* days after, St. Francisco was likewise in our possession. Sloat's proclamation reflected the determination of his employers —"*Henceforward California will be a portion of the United States.*"

On landing at Monterey, the Commodore addressed a general order to his men in which he told them, "It is not only our duty to take California, but to preserve it afterwards *as a part of the United States,* at all hazards.* It is the duty of commanders to make conquests, but not to anticipate the terms of a treaty of peace. Yet here we find a naval captain solemnly proclaiming that the conquest he has made is never to be restored. He foresees and proclaims the annexation of California, without *apparently* knowing the wishes and intentions of his own government, or without speculating on the fortunes of war. On the 13th August, Pueblos des los Angelos, the capital of the province was taken, and on the 17th August, Commodore Stockton, who had succeeded Sloat, and who styled himself "Commander-in-Chief and *Governor of the Territory of California,*" announced in a proclamation, "The flag of the United States is now flying from every commanding position in the Territory, and California is entirely free from Mexican dominion. The territory of California now belongs to the United States." On the

* For the documents here quoted, see Ex. Doc. 29 Cong, 2 Sess. House of Rep., No. 4.

28th of the same month, he wrote home, "this rich and beautiful country belongs to the United States, and is FOR EVER free from Mexican dominion." All this, it must be admitted, was quick work. On the 7th July, Monterey was taken, and in six weeks the object of the war was accomplished, "the rich and beautiful country belonged to the United States." Not a life appears to have been lost in the conquest. The Mexican government had made no declaration of war, and its whole attention was engrossed by the defence of its territory on the Rio Grande. The inhabitants of California were utterly unprepared for war, and were as ignorant as Commodore Sloat himself of the action of Congress.

The rapidity with which the conquest of California was effected, was not however, entirely owing to the adroit measure of stationing armed vessels on different points of the coast, ready to make their descent the moment Taylor had succeeded in provoking hostilities on the Rio Grande. It will be recollected that the Mexican Government had been alarmed some years before at the ingress of Americans into that province, and had passed an order requiring their departure. Nor will it be forgotten that, intimidated by the bullying demeanor of Mr. Thompson, and his threat to demand his passports, the order had been revoked. The reader will call to mind that gentleman's confession of his "compunctious visitings" on the occasion, well-knowing that these foreigners were intending to re-enact the Texan game. The alarm of Mexico was well founded. The conquest of the province was prepared and facilitated by the treasonable course of the American settlers *previous* to their knowledge of the existence of the war. The history of the rebellion in California is but imperfectly known. The only information respecting it, disclosed by the Cabinet at Washington, is contained in the report of the Secretary of War, made 5th December, 1846, and from this document we gather the following narrative. In May, 1845, shortly before "the secret and confidential" instructions were given to Commodore Sloat, Captain Fremont, of the United States Army, was despatched by Government on a tour of scientific exploration beyond the Rocky Mountains. He had sixty-two men under him; but the Secretary declares that the expedition was not of a military character, and that the attendants did not belong to the army. On reaching the frontier of California, the Captain proceeded alone to Monterey to solicit permission from the Commandant, General Castro, for himself and party, to pass through a portion of the province. The desired permission was granted, but after the party had entered California, Fremont received information from *Americans,* that Castro was preparing to attack him with "a comparatively large force of *artillery, cavalry* and *infantry,* upon the pretext that, under the cover of a scientific mission, he was exciting the American settlers to revolt." This was indeed marvellous intelligence, and most marvellous means did the scientific Captain take to remove the groundless suspicions of the Californian General. Instead of making his way out of the province as fast as he could, and proceeding upon the business entrusted to him by his Government, "he took a position on a mountain overlooking Monterey at a distance of about thirty miles, *entrenched* it, raised the flag of the United States, and with his own men sixty-two in number, awaited the approach of the Commandant-General." But the Captain, however valiant, did not depend solely on his sixty-two men to resist the artillery, cavalry, and infantry of Castro; for the Secretary tells us, "*the American settlers* were ready to join him at all hazards, if he had been attacked;" and hence we discover his motive for taking a military position at a convenient distance from Monterey. This was in March, 1846. After waiting some time for the anticipated attack, but nothing occurring to furnish a pretext for commencing hostilities, he proceeded, without the slightest molestation from the Government, on his route to Oregon.

In Oregon, he was annoyed by hostile Indians, who, as the Secretary informs us, but without condescending to furnish a particle of proof, "had been excited against him by General Castro." Again the Captain received alarming intelligence, but from what source does not appear, "that General Castro, in addition to his Indian allies, was advancing against him with *artillery* and *cavalry* at the head of four or five hundred men!" He also *heard* that "the American settlers in the valley of Sacramento were comprehended in the scheme of destruction, meditated against his own party."—"Under these circumstances (continues the Secretary), he determined to turn upon his Mexican pursuers, and seek safety both for his own party and the American settlers, not merely in the defeat of Castro, BUT IN THE TOTAL OVERTHROW OF THE MEXICAN GOVERNMENT IN CALIFORNIA, AND THE ESTABLISHMENT OF AN INDEPENDENT GOVERNMENT IN THAT EXTENSIVE DEPARTMENT."

Here let us pause a moment, to reflect on the utter atrocity and profligacy of a design which the Secretary of War ostentatiously parades before the world. Admitting the truth of the ridiculous rumors said to have reached Fremont, it is very evident, that he was perfectly confident that the combined strength of his own party and that of the American settlers, was abundantly sufficient for their own protection, since he relied on it to *overturn* the Mexican authority and to establish an independent Government. He, a commissioned officer of the

United States, without any known authority from his own Government abandons the object of his mission, and returns from Oregon into California, for the express purpose of organizing a rebellion and wresting from Mexico with whom we were at peace, an "extensive department." It is certainly a remarkable coincidence, that while we had a squadron off the ports of California with orders to seize them at a moment's warning, Captain Fremont was opportunely exciting rebellion and a civil war in the interior. The Secretary himself foolishly puts the stamp of iniquity upon this adventure by declaring, "it was on the 6th of June, and before the commencement of the war between the United States and Mexico *could have been known*, that this resolution was taken, and by the 5th July it was carried into effect by a series of rapid attacks by a small body of adventurous men under the conduct of an intrepid leader." We are told that on the 11th June, a convoy of two hundred horses for Castro's camp with an officer and fourteen men, were surprised and captured by twelve of Fremont's party. On the 15th, the military post of Sanoma was also surprised and taken, with nine brass cannon, two hundred and fifty stand of muskets, and several officers and some men, with munitions of war. "Leaving a small garrison in Sanoma, Colonel Fremont went to the Sacramento to *rouse the American settlers*; but, scarcely had he arrived when an express reached him that Castro's whole force was crossing the bay to attack that place. On the morning of the 25th, he arrived with ninety riflemen from the American settlers in that valley. The enemy had not yet appeared—scouts were sent out to reconnoitre, and a party of twenty fell in with a squadron of seventy dragoons, attacked and defeated it. The country north of the Bay of San Francisco being cleared of the enemy,

Colonel Fremont returned to Sanoma on the evening of the 4th July, and on the morning of the 5th called the people together, explained to them the condition of things in the province, and *recommended an immediate declaration of independence.* The declaration was made, and *he* was selected to take the chief direction of affairs." The new-born *Republic of California* existed but for the brief period of four days, being then strangled by its parent, on receiving, as the Secretary tells us, "the gratifying intelligence" of the war with Mexico. Fremont and his followers, together with the American settlers, immediately co-operated with the naval forces, and, on the departure of Commodore Stockton, the captain of the scientific exploring party beyond the Rocky Mountains, became Governor of the AMERICAN TERRITORY OF CALIFORNIA.

Such is the account the *American Government* thought proper to give of the Californian rebellion, throwing the whole responsibility of this atrocious affair on Fremont. Fortunately for the character of that officer, transactions which the Secretary did not deem it expedient to report have since come to light. On his return to the United States, Colonel Fremont presented certain pecuniary claims growing out of the conquest of California. The subject was investigated by a committee of the Senate, and their report dissipates much of the mystery which had hitherto rested on Fremont's extraordinary conduct.*

It seems that, on the 3rd Nov., 1845, after Taylor had been ordered to the Rio Grande, and while he was waiting with the army at Corpus Christi, five States having been required to furnish him with whatever troops he might need, a messenger was despatched by the Cabinet to Fremont. This messenger was Lieutenant Gillespie of

* See Report, Senate Doc., No. 75. 30th Cong., 1st Sess.

the navy. He was sent to Vera Cruz, and thence travelled through Mexico to Mazatlan, in California, in the *disguise of a merchant.* After an interview with Commodore Sloat at Mazatlan, he proceeded to Monterey, having been intrusted at Washington with a letter of instructions to the American Consul. The contents of this letter have been withheld from the public, and no doubt for sufficient cause, since we find from Gillespie's own confession that, before landing in Mexico, *he destroyed the letter,* having first committed it to memory. This letter to the Consul he was instructed to communicate to *Fremont also.* Hence we find that Gillespie was charged with instructions of such a character, that he deemed it imprudent to carry the paper about his person, and that these instructions, although addressed to the Consul in Monterey, were equally intended for Fremont. After *reciting* to the Consul the commands from Washington, the agent penetrated into Oregon in pursuit of Fremont, and found him a little beyond the California frontier. He delivered to him a note from the Secretary of State, composed in perfect keeping with the fictitious character assumed by the bearer. It consisted of a few lines, addressed to J. C. Fremont, *Esquire,* and telling him that *Mr.* Archibald H. Gillespie, *about visiting the North-west coast of America on business,* had *requested* a letter of introduction to him; a request with which the Secretary complies, because the bearer was a gentleman of worth and respectability, and *worthy* of Mr. Fremont's *regard.* This, it must be confessed, was a novel mode of introducing an officer of the navy to another of the army. But as one party was for the time being a travelling merchant, and the other a man of science, it was proper the introduction should be adapted to the parts they were playing. Of course, the note was to accredit Gillespie as a confidential agent of the Government, and to intimate to Fremont that he was to obey the instructions *orally* communicated to him. Gillespie, in his examination before the Committee, remarked, "I was directed by Mr. Buchanan to confer with Colonel Fremont, and make known my instructions, which, as I have previously stated, were to watch over the interests of the United States, and counteract the influence of any foreign agents who might be in the country with objects prejudicial to the United States. I was also directed to show Colonel Fremont the duplicate of the despatch to Mr. Larkin, Consul at Monterey, and telling him it was the wish of the Government to conciliate the feelings of the people of California, and encourage a friendship towards the United States."

The Government, of course, knew as well as Mr. Thompson that the Californian settlers were anxious to re-enact the Texan game. It is not to be supposed that so much secrecy and pains were taken to have agents on the spot to watch over our interests, and encourage friendship towards us, without intimating the *means* to be used in effecting their object. An independent republic in California, composed of American citizens, would, should peace continue with Mexico, inevitably result in annexation: should war ensue, it would greatly facilitate the conquest of the territory.

The messenger from Washington reached Fremont on the 9th May. Immediately all his scientific pursuits were abandoned, and he and his party, together with Gillespie, hastened to the American settlements in California. These were reached on the Sacramento River in thirteen days. And now opened another scene in the plot. The gentleman "about visiting the North-west coast of America on business" proceeded down the river to Saint Francisco, off which port a United States' ship-of-war was lying, ready to seize upon the place at a moment's warning. The American commander, Gillespie tells us, "with great kindness, *promptness*, and *energy*, furnished me with all the supplies he could spare from his vessel, as also having supplied Captain Fremont with a small sum of money." What these supplies were we are not told, but may readily imagine, especially as they were sent in the ship's barge, under the command of a lieutenant. Gillespie accompanied the supplies up the river, and on the 13th rejoined Fremont. He found that the insurrection had already commenced, the settlers rising, as he *says*, "to save themselves and their crops from destruction."

On the 16th, Captain Merritt, one of the settlers, "arrived with a small escort, bringing with him General Vallejo, Colonel Salvador Vallejo, and Colonel Prudon, prisoners; a party of forty of the settlers having surprised and taken Sonoma, the first military garrison in that part of the country." Thus we see a war against the Californians was commenced after the arrrival of Fremont, and without one single act of hostility having been committed against them. Of course, we have *assertions* in abundance of the *intentions* of General Castro, the commanding officer, while the result proved his utter inability even to defend himself. Fremont and his party zealously coöperated in the war, and were presently masters of that part of the country. The force at his disposal was a battalion of 224 men, and on the 5th July he raised the standard of the Republic of California.

On a calm review of the facts before us, it is impossible to resist the conviction, that Fremont was given to understand, but in a way not to compromit the Government, that the abandonment of his exploration in Oregon for the purpose of exciting and aiding an insurrection in California, would not expose him to censure. On no other supposition would it be possible for him to escape the personal application of the principle laid down by General Jackson, that "any individual of any nation making war against the citizens of another nation, they being at peace, forfeits his allegiance, and becomes an outlaw and a pirate." If he acted, as there is little reason to doubt, as the agent of the President, and in accordance with his wishes, upon that officer rests the perfidy and turpitude of secretly instigating this rebellion and civil war, while professing friendly intentions towards Mexico, and soliciting a renewal of diplomatic intercourse with her. Had Mexico paid all our claims to the last cent, had she yielded the Valley of the Rio Grande without a murmur, and had there consequently been no war, still, Fremont's "Republic of California," like Houston's "Republic of Texas," would have become ours by "joint resolutions" of annexation, and Mr. Polk, or some other President in his words would have congratulated Congress that "This accession to our territory," like that of Texas, "has been a *bloodless* achievement. No armed force has been raised to produce the result. *The sword has had no part in the victory.*"

It is curious to observe with what wonderful *clairvoyance* the naval officers in California understood and executed their instructions, long before they were received. It appears officially* that the despatch of the 13th May, 1846, announcing the declaration of war, did not reach the Squadron till about the 28th of August; and of course up to that time these officers had been acting on their own discretion. Let us now see what instructions were sent to them *after* the war, and how exactly they had been anticipated *before* their receipt.

* Report of Secretary of Navy, 19th Dec., 1846 Appendix to Cong. Globe for 29th Cong., 2d Sess., p. 45.

On the 15th May, two days after war was declared, Commodore Sloat was directed to "consider the *most* important object to be, to *take* and *hold* possession of San Francisco." On the 19th July, San Francisco *was taken*, and the inhabitants were informed by proclamation, that "henceforth California will be a *portion of the United States.*"

The next despatch, June 8th, instructs Sloat to "take such measures as will best promote the attachment of the people of California to the United States." Sloat, in his proclamation, dated 7th July, assures the Californians that "peaceable inhabitants will enjoy the same rights and privileges as the citizens of any other portion of that territory (the United States), with all the rights and privileges they now enjoy, together with the privileges of choosing their own magistrates and other officers for the administration of justice among themselves, and the same protection will be extended to them as to *any other State* in the Union." Thus the proclamation had already *annexed* them to the United States.

On the 12th July, Sloat is told, "The object of the United States is, under its rights as a belligerent nation, to *possess itself* entirely of Upper California," and *if*,* at the

*That this hypothetical statement was mere affectation, is evident from the indiscreet disclosures of the intentions of Mr. Polk, contained in the instructions to Stockton, of 11th January, 1847: "At present it is needless, and might be injurious to the public interests, to agitate the question in California, how long those persons who have been elected for a prescribed time, will have official authority. If our right of possession shall become absolute, such an inquiry is needless. And if by treaty or otherwise, we lose the possession, those who follow us will govern the country. The President, however, anticipates no such result. On the contrary, he foresees no contingency in which the United States will *ever surrender or relinquish the possession of California.*" Of course Mr. Polk had thus early, and without consulting the Senate, determined at all hazards to make the cession of California the *sine qua non* of a treaty of peace.

conclusion of peace, "the basis of the *uti possidetis* shall be established, the Government expects through your forces to be found in actual possession of Upper California. This will bring with it the necessity of a civil administration—*Such a Government should be established under your protection.*" Sloat had retired on account of ill health, and been succeeded by Commodore Stockton who, long before the receipt of this despatch, issued a proclamation making "Known to all men," that the territory known as Upper and Lower California, is a territory of the United States, under the name of the territory of California. "I do, by these presents," continues the proclamation, "further order and decree, that the Government of the said territory of California shall be, until altered by the proper authority of the United States, constituted in manner and form as follows;" and then follows a form of Government consisting of a Governor, Secretary, Legislative Council, &c.

On the 17th August, Commodore Shubrick was sent to relieve Sloat, from whom not a word had yet been received. He was ordered to take immediate possession of Upper California, especially of the three ports of San Francisco, Monterey, and San Diego, if not already captured,—and also, "to take possession, by an inland expedition, of Pueblos de los Angelos." All four places were captured before a line was received from Washington, and Pueblos de los Angelos was taken by an inland expedition four days *before* the date of the instructions. Shubrick was farther directed that "all United States vessels and merchandize must be allowed by the local authorities of the ports of which you take possession, to *come and go free of duty;* but on foreign *vessels* and *goods* reasonable duties may be imposed." But Commodore Stockton had already anticipated this instruction two days before it was written. On the 15th August, he had imposed a duty of fifteen per cent. ad valorem on all *goods* imported from foreign ports, and a tonnage duty on *foreign* vessels of fifty cents per ton, but no duties were imposed on American vessels and merchandize.

On finding these various instructions so exactly anticipated, so minutely fulfilled by officers who had not received one line of intelligence from their government subsequent to the commencement of the war, it is impossible to resist the conviction, that the seizure of California had long before been deliberately planned, and that the intentions and wishes of the Government had been fully made known to the officers, the plan of proceeding agreed on, and the squadron stationed off the Californian ports, awaiting news from the Rio Grande as a signal for instantly seizing and securing the prize for which the war was to be commenced on the Rio Grande.

CHAPTER XXII.

DECLARATION OF WAR AGAINST MEXICO.

THE receipt of Taylor's letter of the 26th April, relating to the capture of Thornton's party which had, as we have seen, "*become engaged*" with the Mexicans by attacking them, gave the administration its first intelligence that the march to the Rio Grande had led to its intended result. The letter reached Washington on Saturday the 9th May. Its contents were speedily made known, and on *Sunday* evening a meeting of members of Congress, partisans of the President, was held, and WAR was decided on.* On *Monday* morning, the President sent a war message to Congress, which from its length† must either have been written on the day devoted by the Creator to holy rest, or else prepared some time before in anticipation of the success of Taylor's mission. In this message, after adverting in the usual style to the grievous wrongs perpetrated by Mexico upon our citizens throughout a long period of years, he closed the mournful catalogue by announcing to the representatives of the nation, "MEXICO HAS PASSED THE BOUNDARY OF THE UNITED STATES, HAS INVADED OUR TERRITORY, AND SHED AMERICAN BLOOD UPON THE AMERICAN SOIL. SHE HAS PROCLAIMED THAT HOSTILITIES HAVE COMMENCED, AND THAT THE TWO NATIONS

* Speech of C. J. Ingersoll. App. to Cong. Globe, 29th Cong., 2 Sess., p. 125.

† Occupying six pages in print.

ARE AT WAR." "I invoke," said Mr. Polk, "the prompt action of Congress to recognize the existence of the war, and to place at the disposition of the Executive the means of prosecuting the war with vigor, and thus hastening the restoration of *peace* (!)" Thus emulous was this gentleman of the blessing promised to the peace-maker.

Let us now see how this invocation to make peace by commencing with vigor the work of human slaughter, was received by the American Congress. This body was the grand inquest of the nation. The President appeared before them as a prosecuting officer, accusing the Government of Mexico of high crimes and misdemeanors, and demanding from his auditors a judgment which would be equivalent to a *sentence of death* against thousands and tens of thousands of human beings, including multitudes of their own countrymen. We might suppose that Congress, impressed with the awful responsibility thus imposed upon them, would apply themselves with calm, patient, and prayerful consideration to the duty before them; that they would rigidly scrutinize the evidence submitted to them, and most earnestly seek for expedients to rescue their own and a neighboring country from the tremendous calamities impending over them. They were informed by the President, that a party of Americans and Mexicans had "*become engaged*," and sixteen of the former had been killed and wounded. Thus a collision had occurred. But such a collision does not amount to war. A British frigate had some years since assaulted an American national ship, killed a portion of her crew, and forcibly impressed another portion. No war ensued; but explanations were given, and redress made. Still later an American steamboat was seized in our own waters by a British force, and destroyed, and one of the crew killed. Still no war ensued. An examination of the testimony submitted by Mr. Polk might possibly show, that the recent collision was accidental, or provoked on our part, or unauthorized by Mexico. Explanations, if demanded, might lead to a pacific result, and the effusion of blood be prevented. Of all crimes, the commencement of an unnecessary war is the most atrocious, the most deserving the wrath of God, and the execration of mankind.

Melancholy and humiliating is the fact, that the American Congress passed a decree which they knew would occasion wide-spread wailing and lamentation, and woe and death, with a recklessness, a precipitation, and a disregard of evidence, which no court of judicature in our land would dare to manifest in consigning to the penitentiary a man charged with petit larceny. Shocking as is such an assertion, its truth is still more so. The Message of the President was accompanied with manuscript copies of the correspondence between the Government and Mr. Slidell and General Taylor; and this correspondence contained the evidence on which he rested his momentous charges against Mexico; the testimony on which alone Congress could pronounce on the truth or falsehood of the charges. We will let one of the members relate the proceedings of the House of Representatives on Monday the 11th May, 1846, on the receipt of the message. "It was proposed by a whig member (Mr. Winthrop), that the documents accompanying the Message be read. By a strict party vote this MOTION WAS REJECTED. The House went *immediately* into a committee of the whole. The Committee rose in a very short time, and reported a bill according to the President's wishes. The previous question (preventing all debate), was called and carried, and the

House brought to a vote, without one word of explanation, proof, or argument on the amendment which asserts the existence of war by the 'act of Mexico.' On this question the vote stood—ayes 123, to 67 noes. The amendments having been gone through, and the bill engrossed, the question came, on its final passage. Again the previous question was moved and seconded; and, after some ineffectual efforts on the part of various members to enter their protest against this very preamble, the vote was forced under the *gag*, and the bill carried by ayes 174, nays 14. The whole proceeding from beginning to end occupied but a *small* portion of a single day. The previous question was applied at every step and all debate, explanation, and every attempt to get information, was put down by party votes of the dominant party."* In the Senate, the Message was referred to a Committee, which the *next* day, instead of reporting *facts*, contented themselves with reporting the bill from the House, and this was passed by a vote of 50 to 2. "We had not," said Mr. Calhoun, alluding to this precipitate action, "a particle of evidence that the Republic of Mexico had made war against the United States."† This bill declaring that war exists by the act of Mexico, placed the army and navy at the disposal of the President, provided for the employment of fifty thousand volunteers, and appropriated ten millions of dollars for the prosecution of the war. Thus was a system of human butchery commenced without argument, without examination, with-

* Speech of Mr. Pendleton of Virginia, 22d Feb. 1847. See App. to Cong. Globe, 29th Cong., 2 Sess., p 112.

† See speech, 24th Feb., 1847. Cong. Globe, 27th Feb. 1847. The preamble of an act of the Mexican Congress raising supplies, thus repudiates the idea that the war was commenced by the Republic: "The Mexican nation *finds itself* in a state of war with the United States of America."

out listening to one word of the evidence offered, and without even the pretence of a desire to avoid or delay the awful calamity.

Whatever opinion may be entertained of the lawfulness of defensive war, the moral sense of mankind, irrespective of religious creeds, condemns as most iniquitous an offensive and aggressive one. Such a war differs from murder and robbery only in the stupendous enormity and extent of the crime. The vast military power and resources confided to the President, were to be employed not in enforcing rights, not in obtaining redress for injuries. Congress disclaimed, by their acts and the preamble of their bill, all idea of *commencing* hostilities. A motion to *declare* war was rejected by an overwhelming majority. It was deemed expedient to declare, that it already *existed by the act of Mexico,* thus representing to the nation and the world, that the war was on our side purely a defensive one, undertaken to repel an invading enemy.

And what was the power that had dared to invade the United States, and by its assault had thrown this great confederacy into such imminent danger, that Congress found it necessary to provide fifty thousand troops in addition to the regular army, in such haste as not to allow them time *even to read the despatch announcing the invasion?*

The Republic of Mexico had long been the prey of military chieftains, who, in their struggles for power and the perpetual revolutions they had excited, had exhausted the resources of the country. Without money, without credit, without a single frigate, without commerce, without union, and with a feeble population of seven or eight millions, composed chiefly of Indians and mixed breeds, scattered over immense regions, and for the most part sunk in ignorance and sloth, Mexico was certainly not a very formidable enemy to the United States.* It was impossible for any Mexican force to reach us by sea; and to reach us by land, her armies would have been obliged to cross an uninhabited desert nearly two hundred miles in breadth, before they arrived at the Nueces, the boundary of Texas. The people of that revolted province had for years maintained their independence in spite of Mexico, and no doubt can be entertained that their militia were amply able to drive back any army Mexico might send into her territory. There was not a female in our country whose slumbers were broken, through apprehension of the pretended invasion of the United States. Not a Mexican soldier had trod on soil owned by an American citizen—not a shot had been fired within a hundred miles of an American dwelling.

The apparent *panic*, therefore, under which Congress voted fifty thousand additional troops for *defence*, was not real but feigned. The war, as we have seen, was not commenced to recover the amount of our claims, and procure redress of grievances, but avowedly for *defence*; a motive so palpably false and absurd, that, although officially professed by the President, and in the preamble of the Act of Congress, but one single member of Congress, it is believed, had the hardihood to urge it in justification of his vote. The *true object* of the war

* The following particulars are gathered from the work on Mexico, by Brantz Mayer:

	Population.
Indians, - - - - - - -	4,000,000
Whites, - - - - - - -	1,000,000
Negroes, - - - - - - -	6,000
All other casts, - - - - -	2,009,509
	7,015,509

Exports from Mexico in 1842, exclusive of Gold and Silver, - - - - - -	$1,500,000
National debt, - - - - - -	85,000,000

—"*Mexico as it was, and as it is.*"

was thus frankly stated by Mr. C. J. Ingersoll, as Chairman of the Committee of Foreign Relations, in a report he presented February, 1847: "Complaints of the resort to territorial conquests from Mexico are disarmed of reproach by the undeniable facts, that Mexico, by war, constrains the United States to take by conquest what, ever since the Mexican independence, every American administration *has been striving to get by purchase;* and that the executive orders, and military and naval execution of them for the achievement of conquest, have conformed not merely to the long established policy of our Government but wise principles of self-preservation indispensable to all provident Government." This official language of the report was but a repetition of sentiments advanced by the chairman, in a speech in the House, 19th January, 1847: "War as often waged," said Mr. Ingersoll, "is a theme of copious lamentation; and so it should be. But what the *old women* of both sexes are given to deplore as the calamities of war, where have they been yet felt in these hostilities with Mexico? Never was the country more prosperous, or so powerful as at present. I mean to show unanswerably that all parties in the United States, all administrations of this Government since Mexico ceased to be a Spanish Province, have united in the policy of getting from her by fair means *precisely those territories* which, and only which, she has now constrained us to take by force, though even yet we are disposed to pay for them, not by blood merely, but by money too."* In other words, if Mexico will yet consent to sell us these coveted territories—at our own price, we will cease to murder her citizens in order to acquire them. This avowal explained the extreme and apparently ludicrous solicitude expressed by Mr. Polk for peace. The

* App. to Cong. Globe, 1847, p. 125.

war being waged solely for territory, the more vigorously it was prosecuted, the sooner would Mexico be compelled to purchase peace by making the desired cession. The dismemberment of another, not the *defence* of its own country, was the object of the American Government. *Why* such dismemberment was desired, will be seen in the sequel.

The object we have assigned for the war, does not explain why of two hundred and forty members of Congress, only sixteen were found who voted against a bill containing in its preamble an assertion unsupported by proof, and appropriating great supplies for defence when no danger threatened.

Few, if any, of the Northern members had a direct interest in the conquest of California; but all were interested in the ascendency of one or the other of the two great political parties. Mr. Polk and his Cabinet were the leaders and representatives of the democratic party, and the dispensers of the vast patronage wielded by the Federal Government. To vote against the war would have been, in the democratic members, an act of rebellion against their own party, and an exclusion of themselves for the future from all participation in the favors of the administration. It would, moreover, alienate the Southern Democrats from their Northern brethren, and by the division thus occasioned would most probably, at the next elections, transfer the political power of the nation, with all its emoluments, into the hands of the rival party. Not a solitary democratic vote in either House was given against the war.

The Whig party was placed under very different circumstances. They were in the minority, and were striving to gain the seats occupied by the present incumbents. Hence it was their policy to cast the utmost odium upon the administration, and to represent its measures as unwise and dishonest, and injurious alike to the interests and the morals of the country. Hence no denunciations of the course by which the administration had involved the nation in the calamaties of war, were too violent or too unmeasured. The conduct of Mr. Polk, in particular, was all that was false, base, and wicked. The war was the *President's war ;* and the assertion, that it was the act of Mexico, a palpable falsehood. But the multitude are ever fascinated with military glory, and ever ready to enjoy the spoils of war. It was, therefore, deemed most politic to make a distinction between the war and its authors. The latter were, if possible, to be hurled from office for commencing an iniquitous war; but the patriotism of the Whig party was to be manifested in their vigorous prosecution of this same iniquitous war, for the *glory* of the nation. Had the Whigs voted against supplies after they were told that war existed, they might have been charged at the polls with dereliction to the cause of their country. It was, therefore, deemed more expedient to concur in sending fifty thousand men to rob Mexico, and murder her citizens, than to hazard the loss of votes at the approaching elections. The excuse generally made by the Whigs for supporting the war bill was, that General Taylor and his army were in danger of being destroyed or captured by the Mexicans. The excuse was not only *false,* but it was palpably ridiculous. The very despatch in which Taylor announced that hostilities had commenced, demonstrated his entire security. After stating the calls he had made on the governors of Texas and Louisiana for troops, he adds, "This will constitute an auxiliary force of nearly five thousand men, which will be necessary to prosecute the war with energy, and carry it, as it should be, into the *enemy's country.*"

So that, at the very moment he wrote, instead of being in danger of captivity, he was making preparations for advancing into Mexico, and for this purpose, he deemed *one-tenth* of the force so liberally allowed him by the Whigs, amply sufficient. *Seven* days after the fifty thousand men had been voted, Taylor, without even waiting for the five thousand for which he had called, entered the city of Metamoras, the Mexican army flying before him.

But had Taylor indeed been in danger, the Whigs well knew that his fate would be decided long before a corporal's guard raised under the act could possibly reach him. They were, moreover, told by the President himself, in his Message, that Taylor was authorized to call for and accept volunteers from no less than six of the nearest States. The Administration. foreseeing and intending the war, had already, without any authority from Congress, most amply provided for Taylor's security. Well was it said on the floor of Congress, in reply to this pitiful apology, "Compare the provisions of the bill with the object avowed of affording relief to General Taylor and his army; and what a picture does it present? The bill provides that the militia, army, and navy of the United States, together with fifty thousand volunteers, shall be placed at the disposal of the President *for the purpose of prosecuting the war to a speedy and successful termination.* Thus upon the face of the bill is its object clearly, distinctly, and explicitly set forth and declared." The assertion, therefore, made by the Whigs, that their vote was given for the protection of General Taylor, is of a similar character with that which they so bitterly denounced in the preamble of the bill, that war existed by the act of Mexico. Their apology for voting for this assertion, which they acknowledged to be a falsehood, was, that they had *first* voted against it. However consistent such an apology may be with the morals of politics, it will certainly not be deemed satisfactory by those who regard the Scriptures as the standard of ethics. The vote of the Whig members was probably the most extraordinary and humiliating exhibition of *moral cowardice* ever witnessed in the national Legislature; nor did it escape exposure and castigation. Sarcasms and reproaches, which it was impossible to elude or to answer, were showered upon the Whig members without stint by their opponents. The following is a sample of the rebukes they received: Mr. Brockenborough of Florida thus exposed the false and unhappy position in which the Whigs had placed themselves by their unscrupulous calculations of expediency—"The very term 'unjust war' involves rapine and bloodshed, robbery and murder. Every step is infamous, a crime for which the country should shroud itself in mourning. But *you* rejoice and glory in it. You send forth the poor soldier, for whom you affect such sympathy, and tell him to slay—but it is murder: to fall fighting valiantly—but it is a felon's death. You bid the American mother send forth her child at her country's call, to stain himself with crime—to return a robber, red and reeking with innocent blood. You call your soldiers heroes, and write on their monuments 'rapine, murder.' You vote swords and thanks, and medals and land, and money and pensions, for what you say is crime; and crime so black that individuals committing it, *without your sanction*, receive only ignominy, a prison, or a halter.

"*We* (democrats) believe, before God and the world, that the war is just on our part. If we err, we err after full deliberation and argument, with the best judgment Heaven has vouchsafed to us, in the belief that we are discharging a patriotic duty redounding to the honor and character of our country. If there is any infamy—any crime, it is not ours. Gentlemen claim it all. We have no *intention* of wickedness. We act throughout as we profess. But *you* declare war and denounce it as infamous, but vote all supplies, and urge its vigorous prosecution. You preach that it is murder, and boast how many Whigs there are in it—how many friends, how many constituents you have in it, who volunteered to go.

"You charge that it is a crime, and complain that more Democrats than Whigs have been appointed to carry on the villainy, and speak of the chief man in the gang (General Taylor) for the Presidency. You vote monuments to the dead—trophies, thanks, emoluments, bounties to the living—to entice people to imbrue their hands in blood—in infamy.

"If this war is unjust, gentlemen are not absolved by the cry of 'Mr. Polk's war.' *They voted for it.* Declamation against Mr. Polk will not screen them from their own denunciations of the horror, the sin, and crime, and murder, of unjust war. If crime and infamy, the record bears conviction of the *actors* upon its face, and there it will stand, indelible and imperishable, as the Republic itself. It will adhere, like the shirt of Nessus, to its authors. Like the garment Media wove for Jason, it will cleave and burn into the flesh until they perish. Enhancing the crime, they only invoke more fearful punishment upon themselves."

Rarely, indeed, has any deliberative body listened to sarcasm so withering, or invective so powerful and so just.

Still the *leaders* of the Whig party in Congress clung with fearless tenacity to a policy which, although immoral, they believed to be advantageous. They continued through the whole existence of the war to denounce it as unjust, wicked, and unconstitutional, but nevertheless evinced their patriotism, by voting the supplies required by the

President for ensuring a criminal triumph. It is, however, due to the party at large to acknowledge, that its submission, especially at the North, to this policy of its leaders, was partial and reluctant. The *American Review*, a very able journal devoted to the interests of the party, thus honorably confessed and condemned the motives which actuated the Whig members of Congress who voted for the war: "The vote for fifty thousand volunteers and ten millions of dollars was all but unanimous. The resolution asking for these means were preceded by a *lying* preamble, which imputed the war to the act of Mexico. The resolution, preamble and all, was eagerly swallowed. So much more solicitous seemed even the *Whigs* about *personal popularity*, which might be jeoparded by what would be represented as an abandonment of the cause of a gallant but beleaguered army, in refusing or delaying to vote for this bill, than for the cause of TRUTH and RIGHT."

The Whig Legislature of Massachusetts emphatically rebuked the course pursued by some of the Whig representatives from that State in Congress, by adopting a resolution declaring: "That such a war of conquest, so hateful in its objects, so wanton, unjust, and unconstitutional in its origin and character, must be regarded as a war against freedom, against humanity, against justice, against the Union, and against the free States; and that a regard for the true interests and highest honor of the country, not less than the impulses of Christian duty, should arouse all good citizens to join in efforts to *arrest this war*, and in every just way aiding the country to retire from the position of aggression which it now occupies towards a weak, distracted neighbor and sister Republic."

That only sixteen members out of two hundred and forty should have voted against the war, while a very large minority admitted its injustice, and the falsehood of the assertion that it had been commenced by Mexico, is a melancholy proof that moral courage and independence were not characteristics of the American Congress of 1846. And yet these qualities invariably attract confidence, esteem, and influence, even from those against whom they are exercised. "I admire," said one of the leaders of the war party, "I admire the sincerity, I reverence the consistency of the immortal FOURTEEN (in the House of Representatives) who voted against the declaration of war. Their judgment was convinced that the war was wrong, and they voted as their judgment dictated. They violated the laws neither of God nor of man. But he who denounces the war as unjust, and yet votes for it, violates God's holy law and every principle of ethics." Let the names of these honest, consistent men, who feared God more than man, and looked rather to the Day of Judgment than to the day of election, be borne upon the affectionate remembrance of the Christian community. They were:

SENATE.*

Thomas Clayton, ...	Delaware.
John Davis, ...	Massachusetts.

HOUSE OF REPRESENTATIVES.

John Quincy Adams, . . .	Massachusetts.
George Ashmun, ...	Massachusetts.
Joseph Grinnell, ...	Massachusetts.
Charles Hudson, ...	Massachusetts.
Daniel P. King, ...	Massachusetts.
Henry Y. Cranston, . . .	Rhode Island.
Erastus D. Culver, ...	New York.

* It is due to justice to mention, that Mr. Corwin, a Senator from Ohio, afterwards publicly condemned and regretted the vote he had given for the war.

Luther Severance, ...	Maine.
John Strahan, ...	Pennsylvania.
Columbus Delano, . . .	Ohio.
Joseph M. Root, ...	Ohio.
Daniel R. Tilden, . . .	Ohio.
Joseph Vance, ...	Ohio.
Joshua R. Giddings, . .	Ohio.

CHAPTER XXIII.

THE WAR PROSECUTED FOR CONQUEST.

In utter disregard of the multiplied proofs to the contrary, Mr. Polk thought it expedient, in his Message to Congress of the 8th December, 1846, to hazard the extraordinary assertion, "THE WAR HAS NOT BEEN WAGED WITH A VIEW TO CONQUEST"! He added, "But having been commenced by Mexico, it has been carried into the enemy's country, and will be there vigorously prosecuted, with a view to obtain an honorable peace, and thereby secure ample indemnity for the expenses of the war, as well as to our much-injured citizens, who hold large pecuniary demands against Mexico." We have seen Mr. Polk's early and persevering efforts to secure California, and his official declaration, in the instructions to Stockton, that he could foresee *no contingency* in which the United States would ever surrender or relinquish that province. What abuse of language can be greater than to fight for territory with the declared intention of holding it for ever, and yet to pretend that we fight not for conquest but indemnity? But, independent of this most wretched quibbling about a word, let us pause for a moment to consider the avowal made by the President of the United States to a Christian people. It is no longer pretended that the war is one of defence. We are, it seems, to continue fighting till we are *paid* for our trouble in slaughtering. We killed Mexicans on the Rio Grande; but, receiving no pay, we bombarded Vera Cruz, and killed more. This swelled our demand for compensation. Not receiving it, we marched hundreds of miles to the City of Mexico, and killed some thousands more. This added another and a heavy item to our bill; and thus we were to proceed, spreading misery and death, till we were fully *indemnified* for the money, and trouble, and blood, we had expended in filling a sister Republic with wailing, and lamentation, and woe. The idea of thus killing other people, and sacrificing the lives of our own citizens, for the purpose of *getting pay for fighting*, is original with Mr. Polk; at least, he finds no precedent for such policy in the history of his own country. Our revolutionary fathers rejoiced to lay down their arms the moment the object for which they had been taken was accomplished. Not a voice was heard recommending a continuance of hostilities till Great Britain indemnified us for fighting her the last seven years. In 1815, we again rejoiced in making peace with Great Britain, without asking any indemnity for killing Englishmen, capturing British vessels, and carrying the war into Canada. It is only poor, feeble, exhausted Mexico, who must bleed on, till she pays us for letting blood.

But we are to continue the work of slaughter, not only till we are paid for our powder and shot, &c., but also till Mexico discharges a debt of a few millions, which she is said to owe certain of our citizens. And thus, at a day when it is deemed inhuman even to imprison an insolvent, Mr. Polk recommends that Mexican bonds shall be steeped in human gore, and that we shall proceed to collect our debts by murdering the debtors. And all this to indemnify our "much-injured citizens." But how will Mr. Polk indemnify the vast multitude of women and children whom his policy has made widows and orphans? What tariff will he establish for broken hearts and blasted hopes? What indemnity would he claim from Mexico for all the crimes and blasphemies, for all the horrors of the hospital and the battle-field, for all the desolation and misery in this life, and in that which is to come, engendered by the war?

In justice to Mr. Polk, we acquit him of the horrible atrocity of wishing to continue the slaughter of the Mexicans for compensation for the cost of killing them, and of the consummate folly of expending a hundred millions of dollars in collecting three or four of alleged debt. Politicians often think it wise to conceal their real motives by assigning false ones. The war was to be continued, not to obtain a reimbursement of its expenses, not to collect a paltry debt, but solely for CONQUEST. We have already seen that it was the President's determination to annex California to the Union. Let us now listen to a few of the frank avowals of the partisans of the war in Congress.

Mr. STANTON, of Tennessee, declared that, "The annexation of California to the United States, was the great measure of the age."*

Mr. BEDINGER, of Virginia—"Was this to be a war of conquest? He answered, yes; trusting in Heaven, and on the valor of their arms, this *should* be a war of CONQUEST."†

Mr. SEVIER, of Arkansas, speaking of the territories to be acquired from Mexico, observed, "He supposed no Senator would think that they ought to be less than New Mexico and Upper California. He did not suppose that a treaty of peace with less than this would ever pass that body."‡

Mr. GILES, of Maryland—"I take it for granted, that we shall gain territory, and must gain territory, before we

* Cong. Globe, 10th Dec., 1846, p. 23.
† Cong. Globe, 6th Jan., 1847, p. 126.
‡ Cong. Globe, 2d Feb., 1847, p. 306.

shut the gates of the temple of Janus. We must have it. Every consideration of national policy calls upon us to secure it. We must march right out from ocean to ocean. We must fulfil what the American poet has said of us, from one end of this confederacy to the other,

> 'The broad Pacific chafes our strand,
> We hear the wide Atlantic roar.'

We must march from Texas straight to the Pacific ocean, and be bounded only by its roaring wave. We must admit no other government to any partition of this great territory. It is the destiny of the white race, it is the destiny of the Anglo-Saxon race; and, if they fail to perform it, they will not come up to that high position which Providence, in his mighty government has assigned them."*

In January, 1847, a resolution was offered in the House of Representatives, declaring that the war "is not waged with a view to conquest;" but the House was too candid to endorse the words of the President, and rejected the resolution. In the same Session, it also rejected, by a vote of 126 to 76, the following amendment proposed to the supply bill, viz.; "Provided farther, that these appropriations are made with no view of sanctioning any prosecution of the existing war with Mexico for the acquisition of territory to form new States to be added to the Union, or for the dismemberment of Mexico."

These disclaimers of all intention of making conquests came from the Whigs, who were unmeasured in their denunciations of Mr. Polk's obvious policy.

In his next message of December, 1847, that gentleman adroitly revenged himself upon his opponents, by reminding Congress, that only sixteen members had voted against the war; and that Congress, including, of course, the Whig members with the exception of the sixteen, "*could not*

* Cong. Globe, 11th Feb., 1847, p. 387.

have meant, when in May, 1846, they appropriated ten millions of dollars, and authorized the President to employ the military and naval forces of the United States, and to accept the services of FIFTY THOUSAND volunteers to enable him to prosecute the war; and when at their last Session, and *after* our army had invaded Mexico, they made additional appropriations, and authorized the raising of additional troops for the same purpose—that no indemnity was to be obtained from Mexico at the conclusion of the war." It was impossible for the Whigs to elude the force of this sarcasm. If the war "was not waged with a view to conquest," with what view did *they* vote for an army of fifty thousand men?

Puerile as is the distinction made by Mr. Polk between *conquest* and *territorial indemnity,* it appears from his own showing, that it is a distinction without a difference; a mere quibble on words. The President, informing Congress what territories he had claimed of Mexico as conditions of peace, remarks, "as the territory to be acquired by the boundary proposed, might be estimated to be of *greater value than a fair equivalent* for our just demands, our Commissioner was authorized to stipulate for the payment of such additional *pecuniary consideration* as was deemed reasonable." Here we see that Mr. Polk meant to take more territory, than he even pretends we are entitled to for indemnification. And how did he mean to acquire it? By conquest? Oh no, but by a forced sale, negotiated by a Commissioner at the head of a victorious army, ready to enter the city of Mexico; and for this surplus territory he would pay such a price as *he* deemed reasonable, and, if the Mexicans refused to make the bargain on his terms, they refused at the peril of their lives, and the loss of their capital; their blood was to flow, till they accepted, for territory to which we had no *just* claims, the price we might please to pay.

CHAPTER XXIV.

EXTENT OF TERRITORY REQUIRED FROM MEXICO.

WE have already admitted that Mr. Polk's frequent and earnest asseverations of his desire for peace were sincere, because in his mind the term *peace* included the acquisition of all the territory he wanted. The peace he desired, was not a just, and therefore an honorable one, but a bold, rapacious spoliation. If we use strong terms, it is because they are warranted by strong facts. After we had obtained military occupation of the country on the Rio Grande and all the sea-ports on the Atlantic and Pacific; after the Mexican armies had been routed in three general engagements; after the efforts of the Mexicans had failed to protect their capital, and General Scott was ready to enter its gates, peace was again offered Mexico. In the time, place, and terms of this offer, we can see no indication of generosity, no desire for justice, no feeling of honor. Mexico, utterly prostrated, could obviously make no successful resistance, and it was certainly within the power of the United States to take military possession not merely of the capital, but of every city and strong place in the republic. Such, however, was not the desire or the interest of the Administration, or of the country. To hold the entire of Mexico by force of arms, would occasion an expenditure of treasure and an imposition of taxes which would soon hurl Mr. Polk and his partisans from office. Nor would a continuance of the war give us that quit-claim to the coveted territories which was required, to enable us to convert them with facility into slaveholding States with a representation in Congress. The *object of the war* could be most advantageously obtained by a treaty of peace, giving us undisputed possession of New Mexico and California. Hence the desire for peace; and the prostrate condition of Mexico induced the hope that she would be compelled to make the cession we demanded. And what was that cession? Why, all the territory between the Nueces and the Rio Grande, together with the whole of New Mexico, and all California, both Upper and Lower! An inspection of the map of Mexico will show that these demands, *exclusive* of Texas proper, are estimated at upwards of eight hundred thousand square miles, while the whole area of the Republic is supposed to contain one million six hundred thousand. Thus did Mr. Polk seek for a "just and honorable peace" in the seizure of one half of Mexico!*

Such was the territorial indemnity we attempted to extort from a vanquished and almost unresisting enemy. Napoleon, in the career of conquest, never indulged in wilder rapacity. Mexico, humbled and disabled, offered to cede all Texas proper, beyond the Nueces, and all of New Mexico and California North of the 37th degree of latitude; an extent of territory equal to nine States of the size of New York! It is true, that in the Mexican *projet* of a treaty containing this proposed cession, there was a stipulation for compensation for injuries done by the American troops, a mere matter of discussion, but not represented as a *sine qua non.* The negotiation was broken off not on account of that or other exceptionable proposals, but because Mexico refused to cede the whole of New

* These estimates are taken from an official statement of the areas of the different provinces, published by the Mexican Government, and attached to Disturnell's map of Mexico.

Mexico and California. Mr. Polk, in his Message to Congress, declared, "the boundary of the Rio Grande, and the cession of the States of New Mexico and *Upper* California constituted an ULTIMATUM which our Commissioner was under no circumstances to yield." It may seem strange that Mr. Polk refused to accept the proffered cession. The solution is easy, and will be given in the subsequent chapter.

CHAPTER XXV.

MOTIVE FOR ACQUIRING TERRITORY.—THE WILMOT PROVISO.

The possessions of the United States extended from the Atlantic to the Pacific, and from the 49th to the 30th degree of latitude. Independent of the thirty States, comprising the Federal Union, the national territories embraced 1,335,398 square miles—an area equal to about half of all Europe. The American Republic, anterior to the Mexican war, possessed one of the largest regions in the world under one Government, and at the same time one of the most thinly inhabited. It will not, therefore, be pretended, that additional territory was required for the convenience of our population. It is said a port was wanted on the Pacific. The portion of California north of the 37th degree of latitude, which Mexico offered to cede, contains the harbor of St. Francisco, the best and most capacious on the Pacific. Mr. Polk had officially declared, that our title to the whole of Oregon was "clear and unquestionable;" yet, with the consent of southern Senators, he surrendered to Great Britain no less than 5° 40′ of what he insisted was territory belonging to the United States. Why give away northern territory which is ours, and lavish blood and treasure for the conquest of southern territory to which we have no title? It was known, that from natural and other causes, slavery would be for ever excluded from the territory yielded to Great Britain, but would find in California and New Mexico a genial soil and climate; and that these States, when subdivided and annexed, would give to the slaveholding interest a predominating and resistless influence in the Federal Government.

Were other proofs wanting of the real object of the war, it might be found in the avowals of the southern press: "We trust," said the *Charleston Patriot*, "that our southern representatives will remember that this is a SOUTHERN WAR." Said the *Charleston Courier*: "Every battle fought in Mexico, and every dollar spent there, but insures the acquisition of territory which must *widen the field of southern enterprize and power for the future.* And the final result will be to adjust the whole balance of power in the Confederacy, so as to give us the control over the operations of the Government in all time to come."

The *Federal Union*, a Georgia paper in the interest of the administration, remarked, "The Whigs of the North oppose the war, because its legitimate effect is, as they contend, the extension of southern territory, and of southern slavery. It is true, this is a war in which the South is more immediately interested. Its vast expenditures must be made within her limits. During its continuance, New York, the great emporium of commerce, must be shorn in part of her greatness. Exchange, usually in her favor, must now be reversed, and in favor of New Orleans, where the supplies are furnished for the army. Let the SOUTH now be true to herself, and the days of her vassalage are gone, and gone for ever."

Said the *Mobile Herald*: "The natural tendency of the slaves under our humane policy is to increase. The effect follows that, if we have no outlet for them, no soil to put them on, they will be huddled within the extreme southern limits of the Union." After showing that insubordination, and loss of profit, would result from a too crowded slave population, the editor proceeds, "These evils may be avoided by taking new territory in the direction of Mexico. The profitable existence of slavery is by no means incompatible with a more temperate region, but it is incompatible with a very dense population. We need *plenty of soil* to render *it profitable.*"

As the war was waged only for territory, Mr. Polk was anxious to secure its object as speedily as possible; and, thinking it probable that money judiciously distributed in Mexico might hasten the cession of California, recommended to Congress, August 8th, 1846, an appropriation of two millions of dollars, to be placed at his disposal, for the purpose of facilitating *a peace.* The very proposal utterly destroyed the pretext upon which he first justified the war, that it was one of defence. "Millions for defence, not a cent for tribute," was once the proud rallying cry of the Republic. Now he proposed two millions to *buy a peace.* Had it not been known that the money was to be employed in gaining *territory,* the very proposition would have excited universal abhorrence and indignation. A bill granting the desired sum was introduced into the Lower House, but to the extreme mortification and alarm of the administration, and the pro-slavery party, was passed with a proviso offered by Mr. Wilmot, excluding slavery from all territory that might be ceded by Mexico. The bill was reported to the Senate on the last day of the Session, and, for want of time, no question was taken upon it. At the ensuing Session, Mr. Polk asked for three millions for the same purpose, and a law was passed appropriating this sum "to enable the President to conclude a treaty of peace, *limits and boundaries,* with the Republic of Mexico, to be used by him in the event that said treaty, when signed by the authorized *agents* of the two Governments, and duly ratified by *Mexico,* shall call for the same, or any part thereof." It will be observed that the law contemplated not merely a treaty of peace, but of *limits and boundaries*, in other words, a treaty ceding California and New Mexico. The condition of the appropriation is unexampled in the history of diplomacy. The money is to be paid not when the treaty is consummated, but as soon as Mexico consents to the terms Mr. Polk may demand. Mr. Tyler found that a contract entered into by the authorized agents of two Governments, did not constitute a treaty without the ratification of the Senate; but, in this most extraordinary law, such a ratification is wholly disregarded. As soon as Mexico binds herself to cede territory, the money is to be paid, never to be returned, whether the Senate reject or confirm the bargain. Never before, probably, did a civilized nation stipulate to perform in advance, a condition required by an unratified and therefore unobligatory treaty. Viewing the appropriation in the least offensive light, it is an offer to pay the consideration money of a purchase in advance, whether the title-deed may prove valid or not, with permission to retain the money, although the deed should be refused. There must have been some weighty reason for this procedure. The credit of the United States was not so low, that it was necessary to pay in advance. Louisiana and Florida had been purchased by treaty; but the consideration money in neither case had been paid before the treaties were ratified. The departure in the present case from the ordinary course of negotiation was caused by the burning desire to acquire additional slave territory.

The war was expensive, and might prove hazardous to the popularity of the administration. Mr. Polk had no wish to kill Mexicans, provided they would surrender their lands. It was hoped our invasion, and the fearful array of fifty thousand men, would have instantly frightened the enemy into the desired cession of her territories; but, in the language of the administration presses, Mexico was "mulish," was "obstinate." It was thought a large sum of money, judiciously distributed, might be more successful than intimidation had proved. The Mexican leaders were supposed to be mercenary; the army was known to be necessitous. Three millions distributed among the officers and soldiers, either secretly as bribes, or openly under color of an instalment in advance for the purchase of territory, might induce the Mexican Congress through military coercion, to consent to the dismemberment of the Republic. This payment in advance of so large a sum, might be useful, also, in compelling the American Senate to ratify the treaty. If they declined, the money paid would be lost, and the responsibility of sacrificing the people's money would rest upon the Senators, who should dare to vote against the treaty. The attempt to re-annex the Wilmot proviso to this bill, and the long debate it occasioned, rent asunder the transparent veil with which the pro-slavery party had attempted to conceal the true object of the war, and provoked the southern members into unusual frankness.

The northern Democrats had long justified the character given to them, of being "the natural allies" of the slaveholders. Anti-slavery sentiments had recently made rapid progress at the north, and the tone of the elections in various States, warned them that their devotion to slavery, was undermining their own power. The grant of three millions, afforded them an opportunity of strengthening their waning popularity at home, without, as they contended, dissolving an alliance, from which they had derived so many pecuniary and political advantages. As Democrats, they were bound to support the war, and to give the President the appropriation he had asked for. But to this appropriation, they attached the Wilmot proviso. This now famous proviso was in these terms: "Provided always, that there shall be neither slavery nor involuntary servitude, in any *territory* on the continent of America, which shall hereafter be acquired by or annexed to the United States by virtue of this appropriation, or in any other manner whatsoever, except for crimes whereof the party shall have been duly convicted." To this was added a provision for the return of fugitive slaves found in such territory. In this attempt to prevent the extension of slavery, the northern Democrats endeavored to shelter themselves from the reproaches of their southern friends by calling their proposal "the Thomas Jefferson proviso,"* its language being copied from the ordinance for the Government of the North-Western territory, originally drafted by Mr. Jefferson, in 1784.† The northern Whigs gave the proviso their cordial support. It may, however, be asked with what propriety they could vote for an appropriation even with the proviso, which they themselves contended, was to be used for the purposes of bribery and corruption. To this question they gave a far more satisfactory answer, than they ever returned to the question why they voted for a war which they denounced as iniquitous. Mr. Stewart of Pennsylvania, thus ably vindicated the policy and duty of voting for the appropriation with *the proviso*: "As a friend of peace, present and prospective, I am in favor of this proviso. The object of this war being the acquisition of southern territory, as long as there is a hope of accomplishing this object, there will be no peace. Put an end to this hope; and you at once put an end to the war, by defeating its object. The moment the President finds this proviso accompanying this grant of money, he

* Speech of Mr. Brinkerhoff, Feb. 10, 1847. Cong. Globe.
† See Journal of Congress, April 19, 1784.

will be for making peace, and so will all the South. They want no *restricted* territory. If the restriction is imposed, and the territory acquired is to be *free*, from that moment the President would pay Mexico to keep her territory, rather than bring it in on such conditions. I am for the proviso, therefore, because it will bring us PEACE. Impose this restriction, and Mr. Polk will say he wants no territory, the South will say they want none; we say, agreed, we want none. Then, if Mexico is to lose no territory, she will be for peace; and, if we are to acquire none, what are we fighting for? Then impose this restriction, and the war will be promptly ended to the great benefit and joy of both Republics."

The avowals of southern members, the messages of southern Governors, the action of southern Legislatures, and the language held by slaveholders assembled in popular meetings, all bear witness to the wisdom, foresight, and truth, of Mr. Stewart's remarks.

The alarm and irritation of the south caused by the introduction of the proviso, was greatly augmented by the circumstance of its originating with the northern democracy; with that party which had heretofore cheerfully sacrificed the right of petition, and the freedom of debate, and had consented to the annexation of Texas, through subserviency to southern interests. The slaveholders felt that they were now in their utmost need deserted by the friends, who had hitherto professed devotion to their cause.* In their exasperation they, for the

* In 1843, Mr. Buchanan, Senator from Pennsylvania, opposed the ratification of the treaty with Great Britain settling the North-East boundary, because it did not provide compensation for certain slaves liberated in the West Indies. He remarked: "All christendom is leagued against the South, upon the question of domestic slavery. They have no other allies to sustain their constitutional rights, except the DEMOCRACY OF THE NORTH. In my own State, we inscribe upon our party banners *hostility to abolition*. It is there one of the cardinal principles of the democratic party."

first time, avowed the real object of the war to be, the conquest of territory for the extension of slavery.

Mr. SEDDON, of Virginia, declared the proviso a "gross and offensive proposition, outraging the whole scope and spirit of the Constitution. The South never would, never could *prosecute conquests* which were to be made the instruments of direct attack upon her institutions. She never would acquiesce in the acquisition of territory from which her sons, *with their property,* were to be wholly excluded. In contrast with the effects of that law (the proviso), the question of the prosecution of the war, of the acquisition of the most extensive territories, shrinks into insignificance. It is to involve the *momentous issue of the Union of these States.*"

Mr. DARGAN, of Alabama, was exceedingly frank: "Say to the South that they are only fighting to make FREE TERRITORY, that it *is only for this* that the brave men of Carolina, Georgia, and Alabama, are periling their lives; and they will demand the settlement of this question *now,* preliminary *to any further prosecution of the war.*"

Said Mr. LEAKE, of Virginia: "If the present attempt to impose limitation with respect to the EXTENSION OF SLAVERY should be persisted in, and should prevail, the South must stand in self-defence; for they could not and would not submit to it."

Mr. TIBBATTS, of Kentucky, was equally frank with Mr. Dargan: "If the people of the South are to be told that in acquiring territory, for which their blood is to be spilled and their treasures expended, they are realizing benefits for others in which they are to have no share, and that they are, in effect, to be excluded from territory which their own blood and treasure have helped to win, then I am against *keeping one foot of Mexican territory*—I am opposed to *carrying on this war on such terms.*"

Mr. CALHOUN, in great excitement, exclaimed: "I am a Southern man and a slaveholder, a kind and merciful one I trust, and none the worse for being a slaveholder. I say for one I would rather meet any extremity upon earth than give up one inch of our equality—one inch of what belongs to us as members of this great Republic. What! acknowledge our inferiority! The surrender of life is nothing to sinking down into acknowledged inferiority."

Yet this kind and merciful slaveholder had devoted the energies of his life to keeping in acknowledged inferiority, ignorance, and degradation, millions of his fellow-men and fellow-countrymen, and was at this very moment opposing an effort to prevent immense regions being peopled with beasts of burden in human form.

Mr. BAGBY, of Alabama, averred, "If the time should come when this principle was to be acted upon, that no more territory was to be acquired lest *Southern institutions* should exist in such territory, he would say, AWAY WITH THE UNION." This gentleman, the more effectually to secure the object of the war, introduced into the Senate a resolution declaring that, "If territory is hereafter acquired by the United States, either by treaty or conquest, it shall not be competent for the treaty-making power or Congress to exclude SLAVERY from such territory, either by treaty, stipulation, or by act of Congress."

Mr. BUTLER, of South Carolina, "Would, before God, warn gentlemen, if the South was to be regarded and treated with inequality, they would tear up the instrument (the Constitution) to which they had subscribed in good faith."

Mr. KAUFFMAN, of Texas, declared "Should the proposed amendment be adopted, *all hopes of acquiring territory in that quarter are gone for ever.* The South would never consent, under such a state of things, to add any territory to what we now possess."

Mr. Thompson, of Mississippi, denouncing the proviso, affirmed that its passage would be the dissolution of the Union.

Mr. Mangum, of North Carolina: "There are now three millions of slaves penned up in the slave States, and they are an increasing population, increasing faster than the whites. *And are the slaves to be always confined to their prison States?*"

Thus we find from their own avowals that the acquisition of slave territory was the *sine qua non* on which the slaveholders would continue the war; and that for such acquisition they were ready, if necessary, to dissolve the Union. Hence, the honor of the nation, the grievances of the claimants, the shedding of American blood upon American soil, were hollow, and false pretexts for the war, its true and sole object being the extension of human bondage.

To the confessions of the slaveholders may be added the following decisive testimony of General Cass, then a member of the Senate, given in a private letter of 19th February, 1847, but which found its way into the newspapers: "The Wilmot Proviso will not pass the Senate. It would be death to the war—*death to all hopes of getting an acre of territory*—death to the Administration, and death to the Democratic party."

The reference made by the slaveholders to the Missouri compromise, and their alleged willingness to apply that compromise to the conquered territories, utterly stultified their argument against the constitutionality of the Proviso. If Congress had a right to exclude Slavery from territory purchased of France, and conquered from Mexico, *north* of 36° 30, they had surely an equal right to exclude it from every part of New Mexico and California. By the Constitution, Congress is constituted the Legislature of the territories, and of course possesses the same power over slavery in them, that a State legislature does within its own jurisdiction.

The bill appropriating three millions of dollars was, after a severe struggle, carried in the House of Representatives, with the Proviso, by 115 to 106. In the Senate, the Proviso was stricken out 31 to 21. The whole influence of the Government, and all the appliances of party discipline, were now put in requisition to induce the House to concur with the Senate, and the Proviso was finally rejected, 102 to 97. It will be observed that the total vote on the adoption of the Proviso was 221, and on its rejection 199. Of course no less than 22 members found it convenient to be absent at this important crisis, and SIX who had supported the Proviso found motives for changing their votes.

The Proviso had indeed been rejected for the present, but it might be renewed at the next session; and, even should it fail in the Senate, yet a treaty, ceding an immense territory to be consecrated to slavery, might not command in that body the vote of two-thirds necessary to its ratification. The very possibility of thus losing the prize for which the war was commenced, exasperated and alarmed the South, and vigorous efforts were made to induce the North to abandon the position it had taken in behalf of human liberty, by the usual threats of dissolving the Union, and by appeals to the interests of selfish politicians. Many of the governors of the slaveholding States brought the subject before their respective Legislatures. The Governor of Virginia, in his Message, remarked that it was "unquestionably true that, if our slaves *were restricted to our present limits*, they would greatly diminish in value, and thus seriously impair the fortunes of their owners. The South never can consent to be confined to prescribed limits. She wants and *must have space*, if consistent with honor and propriety."

The Governor of South Carolina objected to the restriction as tending to diminish the political influence of the South, in the Federal Government, and insisted on strenuous resistance. The Legislature of Virginia, setting at defiance the power of Congress, "Resolved unanimously, that under no circumstances will this body recognize, as binding, any enactment of the Federal Government which has for its object the prohibition of slavery, in any territory, to be acquired either by conquest or treaty." The Legislature of Georgia resolved, "That any territory acquired by the arms of the United States, or by treaty with a foreign power, becomes the common property of the several States composing this confederacy; and whilst it so continues, it is the right of each citizen of each and every State, to reside with his property of every description, within such territory."

The Legislature of Alabama "Resolved, That under no circumstances will this body recognize as binding, any enactment of the Federal Government which has for its object the prohibition of slavery in any territory, to be acquired either by conquest or treaty, *south of the line of the Missouri compromise*."

A public meeting in Richmond, Virginia, declared not only the right of slaveholders to carry their slaves into all territories hereafter to be acquired *south* of 36° 30', "but also that we will, by all peaceable means, and this failing, by ARMS, if necessary, sustain such of our fellow-citizens as may elect to settle within such territory hereafter acquired, in the maintenance of their rights thus to settle, and take with them their SLAVES."

A meeting in Charleston, S. C., declared it would be dishonorable and debasing to submit to the prohibition of slavery, "*beyond what is already yielded by the Missouri compromise.*"

But it was not enough to threaten the North with a dissolution of the union, and with civil war. These are evils which, when they occur, will not fall exclusively upon the people of the free States. It was thought advisable to threaten the *politicians* of the North with the loss of political power and emolument—a menace far more influential than any other. A Presidential election was approaching, and northern aspirants were warned that no opponent to the extension of slavery should receive the votes of the South. A similar warning had secured the annexation of Texas, and the election of Mr. Polk.

The Legislature of Georgia "Resolved, that the people of Georgia, at the ensuing Presidential election, should not and will not support any man for the Presidency or Vice-Presidency, *who favors the principle of the Wilmot proviso.*" The determination thus officially announced, was reiterated by various meetings and on various occasions, and had a sensible and immediate effect in cooling the zeal of northern politicians in behalf of the proviso. General Taylor was a cotton planter, and the owner of numerous slaves; and the popularity he had acquired by his victories, pointed him out as a most available southern candidate. He was accordingly early nominated, and his interests were so thoroughly identified with slavery, that it was deemed unnecessary to demand from him any pledge of opposition to the Wilmot proviso. Said the *Richmond Whig*:—"Why ask pledges of him on the subject of slavery, when the fact that his whole estate consists of land and negroes, and that when they go, he must be a beggar, is the very strongest pledge he could possibly give?"

The frankness and determination of the southern Whigs left to their northern brethern the alternative of uniting with them in raising General Taylor to the Presidency, or of resigning to their political opponents the favors of official patronage. They adopted the former, and General Taylor received the nomination of the party.

The northern Democrats claimed a candidate selected from among themselves. The claim was allowed by their southern brethren, *on condition* of a satisfactory pledge against the Wilmot proviso. Four prominent northern Democrats entered the lists, to bid against each other for the votes of the slaveholders. General Cass's bid was accepted, and he was duly nominated, having declared the proviso unconstitutional.

Notwithstanding the hostility of the South to the proviso, they anticipated the possibility of being compelled to yield to the North, so far as to renew the Missouri compromise, and to consent to the exclusion of slavery north of 36° 30'—and here we find a solution of Mr. Polk's rejection of the cession proposed by Mexico. Great and valuable as was that cession, it was chiefly *north* of the compromise line, leaving space for scarcely more than two *slave* States. The territory offered was not far enough south to secure the object of the war, and hostilities were to be continued for conquests, *below* the Missouri line.

In August, 1847, negotiations were opened for peace, and Mr. Trist was appointed by the President to conduct them on the part of the United States. The Mexican Commissioners were instructed to procure a stipulation, by which "The United States shall engage not to permit slavery in that part of the territory which they may acquire by treaty." It is to be presumed that Mr. Trist was well acquainted with the views of the Cabinet at Washington, on this subject. In an official despatch to the Secretary of State, of 4th September, 1847, he thus describes his conference with the Mexican Commissioners, on this point of their instructions:—"In the course of their remarks on this subject (exclusion of slavery), I was told that, if it were proposed to the people of the United States to part with a portion of their territory, in order that the INQUISITION should be therein established, the proposal could not excite stronger feelings of abhorrence than those awakened in Mexico, by the prospect of the introduction of slavery in any territory parted with by her.

"I concluded by assuring them that the *bare mention* of the subject in any treaty to which the United States was a party, was an absolute impossibility: that no President of the United States would dare to present any such treaty to the Senate; and that, if it were in their power to offer me the whole territory described in our project, increased ten-fold in value, and in addition to that, *covered a foot thick all over with pure gold, upon* THE SINGLE CONDITION THAT SLAVERY SHOULD BE EXCLUDED therefrom, I could not entertain the offer for a moment, nor think even of communicating it to Washington."

CHAPTER XXVI.

UNWORTHY EXPEDIENTS FOR FACILITATING CONQUESTS.

General Santa Anna had been one of the ablest and most popular of the Mexican chieftains. A political revolution had deprived him of power, and driven him into exile—and he had taken refuge in Havana. Shortly before the commencement of hostilities, an officer of the United States navy was despatched to that city. The object of his mission has not been officially disclosed; but it was asserted in the newspapers, and generally believed, that it was to confer with the Mexican General. An American squadron, in *anticipation* of the war, had for some time been stationed off Vera Cruz, and *the very day war was declared,* "private and confidential"* orders were sent to the commander not to obstruct the return of Santa Anna to Mexico. The distinguished exile, it was well-known, had wrongs to resent; and it was no doubt taken for granted, and perhaps expressly stipulated, that, being indebted to Mr. Polk for the opportunity of wreaking his vengeance, he would foment an insurrection, kindle the flames of civil war, recover his former power, and exercise it in concluding a peace with the United States,

* "United States Navy Department,
May 13th, 1846.

"*Commodore.*—If Santa Anna endeavors to enter the Mexican ports, you will allow him to pass freely.

"Respectfully yours,
"GEORGE BANCROFT."

"Commodore David Conner,
Commanding Home Squadron."

by the cession of California. He did return through favor of Mr. Polk's order,* and, as was expected, effected a revolution, and assumed the reins of Government; and, by his wonderful energy and perseverance in behalf of his country, rebuked the artifice of the American President.

To aid in fomenting the civil dissensions which, it was hoped, would result from Santa Anna's sudden appearance in Mexico, General Taylor was required to distribute a proclamation prepared for him at Washington. In this strange document, the General is made to tell the Mexicans, "Your Government is in the hands of tyrants and usurpers. They have abolished your State Governments; they have overthrown your Federal Constitution; they have deprived you of the right of suffrage, destroyed the liberty of the press, despoiled you of your arms, and reduced you to a state of absolute dependence upon the power of a military dictator. We come to obtain indemnity for the past, and security for the future. *We come to overthrow the tyrants who have destroyed your liberties, but we come to make no war upon the people of Mexico,* nor upon any form of free Government they may choose for themselves. It is our wish to see you liberated from despots, *to drive back the savage Camanches,* to prevent the renewal of their assaults, and *to compel them to restore to you from captivity your long-lost wives and children!*" Not satisfied with forcing General Taylor to distribute this mendacious proclamation as his own act, he was expressly instructed (9th July, 1846), to pursue a course of deceit and fraud. He was directed by the Secretary of War, "to take occasions to send officers to the head-quarters of the enemy for the military purposes real or *ostensible*

* Commodore Conner announcing to the Secretary of the Navy the arrival of Santa Anna at Vera Cruz, added: "I have allowed him to enter without molestation."

which are of ordinary occurrence between armies, and in which opportunity may be taken to speak of the war itself as only carried on to obtain justice, and that we had much rather procure that by negotiation than by fighting." Here, we may observe, is an awkward admission, that the war is not a *defensive* but an aggressive one. Again: "A discreet officer who understands Spanish, and who can be employed in the intercourse so usual between armies, can be your *confidential agent* on such occasions, and can *mask* his real under his *ostensible object of a military interview.* You will readily comprehend that in a country so divided into races, classes, and parties as Mexico is, and with so many local divisions among individuals, there must be great room for operating on the minds and feelings of large portions of the inhabitants, and inducing them to *wish success to our invasion,* which has no desire to injure their country, and which, in overthrowing their oppressors, may benefit themselves. Between the Spaniards, who monopolize the wealth and power of the country, and the mixed Indian race who bear its burdens, there must be jealousy and animosity. The same feelings must exist between the *the lower and higher orders of the clergy,* the latter of whom have the dignities and revenues, while the former have poverty and labor. In all this field of division, in all these elements of social, political, personal and local discord, there must be openings to reach the interests, passions, or principles, of some of the parties, and thereby conciliate their good will, and make them co-operators with us in bringing about an honorable and a speedy peace. The management of these *delicate movements,* are confided to your discretion."

There is no evidence that General Taylor ever engaged in these "delicate movements." He bravely fought the

Mexicans; but there is no reason to believe that he ever condescended to corrupt them.

It was very true that Mr. Polk would rather acquire territory by negotiation than by fighting; and hence it was his aim to disqualify the Mexicans from fighting, by promoting treason and rebellion; and hence Taylor was instructed to encourage the *departments* to declare themselves independent of the central Government. Hence also Commodore Sloat was instructed (June 8th, 1846), "to encourage the people of that region (California), to enter into relations of amity with our country." Hence, General Kearney, four days after entering Santa Fé, informed the inhabitants by proclamation (22d August, 1846), that it was the "wish and intention of the United States, to provide for New Mexico a free Government, with the least possible delay, similar to those in the United States." He moreover required those who had in loyalty to their country "left their homes, and taken arms against the troops of the United States, to return forthwith to them, or else they will be considered as enemies and TRAITORS, subjecting their persons to punishment, and their property to seizure and confiscation." But these Mexicans who were to be punished as traitors for resisting the invaders of their soil, owed the same allegiance to their Government, as the General did to his. To remove this difficulty, the Brigadier assumed the prerogative once exercised by the Papal See. "The undersigned," continued the proclamation, "hereby ABSOLVES all persons residing within the boundary of New Mexico, from all further allegiance to the Republic of Mexico, and hereby CLAIMS them as citizens of the United States."

The absolution and the claim were of equal validity. The General had been instructed to establish a temporary civil Government, "therein abolishing all *arbitrary re-*

strictions" and well knowing the ultimate purpose for which his conquest was made, he ordained that the right of suffrage in New Mexico, should be exercised by "every *free* male," thus preparing the inhabitants for the arbitrary restrictions of the peculiar institution to be hereafter introduced. From Santa Fé, this gentleman proceeded to California, and there again assumed the powers of the Roman Pontiff and the American Congress. Addressing the Californians in a proclamation of 1st March, 1847, he declares: "The undersigned, by these presents, ABSOLVES all the inhabitants of California, of any further allegiance to the Republic of Mexico, and regards them as CITIZENS OF THE UNITED STATES." Not content with wielding the attributes of ecclesiastical and civil sovereignty, he assumes those of a prophet: "The stars and stripes now float over California; and, as long as the sun shall shed his light, they will continue to wave over her, and over the natives of the country, and over those who shall seek a domicile in her bosom; and under the protection of this flag, agriculture must advance, and the arts and sciences will flourish like seed in a fertile soil. Americans and Californians, form henceforth ONE PEOPLE."

CHAPTER XXVII.

CONDUCT OF AMERICAN OFFICERS IN MEXICO.

WAR, being always waged for the immediate purpose of inflicting misery and death, necessarily calls into action the malignant passions of our nature. It is impossible that those who are contriving the ruin and death of their enemies, should exercise towards them that love, and kindness, and forgiveness enjoined by Christianity. Hence the profession of arms has a strong tendency to blunt the sensibilities of the soldier, and to render him callous to the sufferings of his victim. Military glory, which is the prize that stimulates the ambition of the soldier, founded, as it is upon his bravery, skill, and success in destroying his enemy, and totally disconnected from all reference to the *justice* of the cause in which his victories are achieved—has necessarily an unhappy influence in perverting the moral sense. In those qualities which twine the laurel around the brows of the warrior, there is no one element of moral goodness; nothing which has not been often exhibited by the most depraved of mankind. It has been well said, that when the soldier has vigorously assaulted the enemy, when though repulsed he returns to the conflict, when being wounded he continues to brandish his sword till his grasp relaxes in death, and he falls on the field "covered with glory," he has attained to the moral rank of a bull-dog. Hence the thirst for military fame, by diverting the mind from the contemplation and pursuit of objects really virtuous, renders the soldier peculiarly exposed to the allurements of vice. His ordinary life, moreover, is on various accounts unfavorable to the cultivation of those benevolent and virtuous affections which adorn and bless society. Banished from the softening and humanizing influences of domestic associations, exiled from wife and children, without other occupations than the monotonous routine of the camp or the barrack, and with no companions but such as are subjected to similar privations, both his mind and his heart are left without wholesome aliment. It is true that the army has had its saints; some good men have passed through its furnace without the smell of fire on their garments, but the attention excited by their wonderful deliverance attests the greatness of the peril they escaped.

The officers of an army are, with few exceptions, far superior in education and refinement to the privates, and are therefore rarely guilty of that vulgar motiveless ferocity which too often marks the conduct of the common soldier. Nevertheless, it would be unreasonable to expect, that their education and refinement should generally shield their hearts from the indurating influence of their profession.

The foregoing remarks are, it is believed, founded on the acknowledged principles of human nature; they are most abundantly verified by all military history; and the conduct to which we will now call the attention of the reader, proves that they are applicable to American, as well as to other armies.

During the horrible bombardment of Vera Cruz, and after a day of indiscriminate slaughter of men, women, and children, the French, Spanish, and English Consuls in the city, addressed on the evening of the 24th March, 1847, a joint note to General Scott asking a suspension of hostilities for a time "sufficient to enable their respective compatriots to leave the place with their women and children, as well as the Mexican women and children." How far the emergency of the case justified this application, may be learned from the report of the chief of the artillery, made the same evening to the General—"We have been restrained from the want of shells from throwing more than *one every five minutes during the day;*" he adds that a *full supply* would be sent to the batteries that night for the ensuing day. The next day the 25th, General Scott sent to the consuls a peremptory refusal of their request—the neutrals might have left the place previous to the bombardment; and as to the Mexican women and children, his summons to the city had been disregarded, and now no truce would be allowed apart from surrender. Some excuse for this stern denial of mercy to foreigners, and to innocent women and children, might have been found if the capture of the city would have been hazarded by the intermission for a few hours of the fiery deluge which was overwhelming it. But Scott well knew that he had it in his power to reduce the whole city to one mass of ruins. So also, had a reinforcement of Mexicans been approaching, a motive would have existed for compelling a surrender before their arrival; but the beleaguered city had no hopes of relief, and the position and force of the American army precluded the possibility of succor. Scott's army, moreover, were so safely ensconced in their entrenchments, that he had no reason to fear, that the boon that was asked would prove injurious to the assailants; since in his operations against the castle and city, his total loss, out of 10,000 men, did not exceed sixty-five killed and wounded. *Before* replying to the Consuls, he wrote to the Secretary of War the same day, "ALL THE BATTERIES ARE IN AWFUL ACTIVITY this morning. The effect is no doubt very great, and I think the city cannot hold out *beyond to-day.*" Hence, by his own confession, and by the fact that the city did surrender on the 26th, the slaughter of women and children occasioned by the awful activity of his batteries during the whole of the 25th, there being then a "full supply" of shells, was utterly unnecessary. To the horrors of this bombardment we may advert hereafter, and at present only offer the following as a commentary on General Scott's refusal: "I heard a great many heart-rending tales which were told by the survivors with breaking hearts; but I have neither the inclination nor the time to repeat them. One, however, I will name. A *French* family were quietly seated in their parlor the evening (night of the 25th), previous to the hoisting the white flag, when a shell from one of our mortars penetrated the building, and exploded in the room, killing the MOTHER AND FOUR CHILDREN, and wounding the residue."*

Truly, indeed, said Sir Harry Smith, in a speech at a late military dinner in London, "It must be confessed, gentlemen, that ours is a damnable profession."

The refusal of General Taylor to accede to the request of the Mexican General for an armistice, before he knew that either Government had recognized the war he had commenced, has been already mentioned. During the attack on Monterey, the Governor sent a flag of truce to the General, stating that "thousands of victims who, from indigence and want, find themselves now in the theatre of war, and who would be uselessly sacrificed, claim the rights which, in all times and in all countries, humanity extends." He asked that orders might be given that families might be respected, or else that a reasonable time might be granted them to leave the city. The General refused to permit any to leave the city; and, however much we may

* Letter published in the Alton *Telegraph.*

lament his decision, it must be acknowledged, that owing to the circumstances in which he was placed, his refusal is not open to the same animadversions as that of Scott.

It is an impulse of our nature to regard scenes of suffering and of cruelty with aversion; but war, by the importance it attaches to victory, renders such scenes sources of pleasure, when their subjects are enemies. General Lane, in his despatch (22d October, 1847), thus describes his night attack upon Allixco: "I ordered the artillery to be posted on a hill near the town, and overlooking it, and open its fire. Now ensued one of the *most beautiful sights conceivable.* Every gun was served with the utmost rapidity, and the crash of the walls and the roofs of the houses when struck by our shot and shells, was mingled with the roar of our artillery. *The bright light of the moon* enabled us to direct our shots to the most thickly populated part of the town."

This beautiful scene, so gratifying to the taste of General Lane, was most horrible to the inhabitants of this little town. The morning sun beheld, amid the ruined dwellings and encumbered streets, *two hundred and nineteen* mangled corpses, while three hundred of its men, women, and children, were suffering from wounds. "After searching the next morning," says the General, with wonderful coolness, "for arms and ammunition, and disposing of what was found, I commenced my return." As he makes no other allusion to the result of his search, we infer he had no reason to be proud of the trophies acquired by this beautiful moonlight massacre.

Several of the general orders, issued by American officers in Mexico, are palpably unjust, and exhibit a painful disregard for human life. Of this nature is the following given by Colonel Gates at Tampico, Nov. 29, 1847: "As the guerilleros or armed enemies are employed by orders to rob all persons who may be engaged in the lawful purpose of trading with the inhabitants of this town, instructions have been given to all officers of the United States army or navy within this department, to take or KILL every person of that character found so employed against the peace of the community." Tampico was occupied by a detachment of the invading army. For Mexicans to supply the place, while so occupied, with provisions and the necessaries of life, would indeed be doing what Mr. Polk charged upon the Whigs, "giving aid and comfort to the enemy." The guerillas, or armed militia, had therefore a perfect right by the laws of war to seize and confiscate all supplies on their way to the enemy. It was doing no more than was constantly done by the Americans in the Revolution, when their cities were occupied by the invader. These "armed enemies" might indeed be killed in battle; but Colonel Gates's order has no reference to *fighting*. In the plenitude of his power, he gives every naval and military *officer* the option of capturing or slaying any armed Mexican who may be found attempting to intercept supplies for Tampico.

Unhappily the conduct of Colonel Gates was sanctioned by high authority. The Commander-in-Chief, seated in the conquered Capital of the Republic, issued an order on the 12th December, 1847, which adds no honor to his character as a man or a soldier. The baggage trains of the army had often been attacked by guerillas, in the long route between Vera Cruz and the city of Mexico, and the General now attempted to keep open his communication with Vera Cruz, from which place alone he could receive ammunition, &c., by a system of severity towards those who had scarcely any other method left of annoying the invaders. The preamble to his order betrays not only his object, but his consciousness that some apology was needed for his sanguinary decree. "The highways used, or about to be used by the American troops, being still infested in many parts by those atrocious bands called guerillas and rancheros who, *under instructions from the late Mexican authorities*, continue to violate every rule of warfare observed by civilized nations, it has become necessary to announce to all, the views and instructions of General Head Quarters on the subject." We are then informed, "No quarter will be given to known murderers or robbers, whether guerillas or rancheros, and whether serving under Mexican commissions or not." Offenders of this character "accidentally falling into the hands of American troops, will be *momentarily* held as prisoners, that is, not put to death without due solemnity." This due solemnity is to be the sentence of three or more officers who are to sentence to death or lashes, on proof that the prisoner belonged to any gang of murderers or robbers, or had murdered or robbed any one belonging to or following the American army. By murder, is here obviously meant, killing any of the guard accompanying a baggage train, and by robbery, carrying away any property belong- to the enemies of Mexico.

The vigor displayed in these orders by "General Head Quarters" was far surpassed by one of his subalterns. Colonel Hughes, civil and military Governor of Jalapa, on the 10th December, 1847, issued the following order, viz: "All persons who may in *any way attempt* to prevent supplies from reaching this port, will be sent to a military Commission for trial, and if convicted of *that offence*, will be SHOT." Here we find a capital offence which is not alleged to be either robbery or murder. Any Mexican, priest or layman, who by persuasion or force, or in any other way, attempts to prevent his countrymen from committing the crime of furnishing supplies to the enemy, is to be SHOT—to be put to death in cool blood by American soldiers, at the command of an American officer! We greatly doubt whether the history of modern warfare records an order so utterly at variance with the plainest dictates of patriotism, justice, and humanity.

We now turn to another melancholy but forcible illustration of the remarks in the commencement of this chapter. A large number of Irish emigrants to the United States bore arms in the invading army. These men were, of course, mere mercenaries. They fought, as others of their countrymen have labored on our canals and railroads, for money. They knew and cared nothing about the claims of "our much-injured citizens," nor did they trouble themselves about "our western boundary." On reaching Mexico, they discovered that they had been hired by heretics to slaughter brethren of their own church. The Mexicans, moreover, published appeals addressed directly to their consciences, in which was set forth, in strong language, the sin they were committing in fighting against men who had never injured them, and who were united with them in a common faith; and liberal offers were made of land and money, if they would abandon the American standard. A portion of the emigrants accepted the invitation; and it is reasonable to suppose that they were influenced both by religious and by pecuniary motives. Upwards of fifty of these men were taken prisoners in battle. They had unquestionably committed a crime in violating their pledged faith, and by the ordinary rules of war, were justly liable to punishment. A few of these men escaped death on account of some technical objections, and a few others on account of some unspecified mitigating circumstances; but a general order of the 22d of September, 1847, contained the appalling announcement: "After every effort of the General-in-Chief to save, by judicious discrimination, as many of these miserable convicts as possible, FIFTY of them have paid for their treachery by an ignominious death upon the gallows."

We have here a most extraordinary confession. The Commander of a victorious army acknowledges his inability to rescue from death one of these fifty men. Instances have occurred of whole regiments going over to the enemy on the field of battle. In such a case would General Scott feel himself *constrained* to hang a thousand men, if again in his power? Was he ignorant, that where large numbers had rendered themselves amenable to punishment, where policy demanded an example, and where humanity forbade a general slaughter, others had resorted to decimation and the lot? The death of five or ten of these men, and the corporal punishment of the rest, would have answered the sternest demands of military policy. It seems that the execution of thirty out of the fifty was intrusted to a Colonel Harney. According to the newspapers, he had them brought out with halters around their necks, and arranged them under one common gibbet in sight of the Mexican fortress of Chepultepec, which the American troops were about to storm. He then told them that they should live till they saw the American flag raised upon the battlements. The fortress was carried, the flag at last appeared, and the doomed men expired. This act of Harney's has been characterized by a foreign writer, as "a refinement of cruelty, and a fiendish prolongation at once of the ecstacies of revenge and the agonies of despair."

Desertion is a crime which, in military ethics, it is lawful for each party to encourage and reward in the other, but to denounce as atrocious, and to punish with death, when committed against itself. General Scott, in his orders, spoke of the Irish deserters as "deluded wretches —miserable convicts." Says the correspondent of the

New Orleans Picayune, "The clergy of San Angel pleaded hard to save the lives of these men, but in vain. General Twiggs told them that to Ampudia, Arista, and Santa Anna did these men owe their deaths, for they stooped to the low business of soliciting desertion from our ranks, and had succeeded in seducing from duty and allegiance the poor wretches who had to pay so dearly for their crimes." This was in September. On the 13th of the *next* month, we have an official despatch to General Scott, from Colonel Childs, dated at Puebla, in which he says, "I should be unjust to myself, and the SPY COMPANY under Captain Pedro Aria, if I did not call the attention of the General-in-Chief to their invaluable services. From them I received the most accurate information of the movements of the enemy, and the designs of the citizens; through them I was enabled to apprehend several officers and citizens in their nightly meetings, to consummate their plans for raising the populace. The Spy Company *fought gallantly,* and are now so compromised, that they must leave the country when our army retires." Says the *New Orleans Picayune,* "The Mexican Spy Company is described as a rough-looking set of men. They fight with ropes about their necks, as the saying is, and therefore they fight gallantly. We understand that we have altogether about 450 of this description of men in our pay." Thus it appears, we had in our army a corps of Mexican scoundrels—and, as the newspapers state, organized and taken into pay by order of General Scott himself. These men joined the invaders of their native land—betrayed their fellow-citizens into the hands of a foreign enemy—went with that enemy into the battle, and *gallantly* aided them in slaughtering their neighbors and countrymen, and all this for *pay!* "They fight with ropes about their necks." Should any of them be hereafter suspended by these ropes, may they not be told that they owe their death to the General, who "stooped to the low business of seducing them from duty and allegiance?" Fifty Irish deserters are hanged as miserable convicts; but a gang of 450 Mexican spies, traitors, and murderers, are recommended by an American Colonel to the attention of the Commander-in-Chief, for their "invaluable services." Such are the honor and morality of war.

In May, 1848, during the armistice, and while negotiations for peace were pending, a party of American officers and soldiers, ten in number, were arrested for the crime of burglary and murder, committed in the city of Mexico. It was probably owing to the peculiarly disgraceful character of the outrage, and its perpetration during a suspension of hostilities, that it was deemed expedient to institute a judicial inquiry. Four lieutenants, two corporals, and one private were tried and convicted by a court-martial, and sentenced to be hung. A fifth officer "belonging to one of the old infantry regiments," is said to have been implicated in the affair, but he eluded arrest. On the conclusion of the peace, all the culprits were pardoned by the commanding officer, and set at liberty. It is not surprising that so large an assembly of men as an army, should include some thieves and murderers. This case is important only because, with multitudes of others, it tends to dispel the popular illusion, that there is some mysterious undefined connection between gallantry and honor, and that a brave soldier must be both honest and merciful. One of these four officers was, it seems, a graduate of the West Point military academy; and of another, a newspaper says, "It is a fact worthy of notice, that Lieutenant Hare was one of the most valiant spirits of the army, during 'the battles of the valley,' and that on account of his unconquerable courage, he was selected by the commanding officer to command one of the 'forlorn hopes,' at the storming of the Castle of Chapultepec. He was allowed to select fifteen men to accompany him. and out of these fifteen, only five escaped the deadly fire of the enemy; and the Lieutenant conducted himself throughout with the utmost coolness and high-toned courage." And yet his brother-officers who composed the court-martial, adjudged him to be a thief and a murderer.

CHAPTER XXVIII.

THE AMERICAN ARMY IN MEXICO.

The remarks already made respecting the general immoral tendency of the military profession, are of course more peculiarly applicable to the rank and file of an army. A prudent, intelligent, industrious, pious recruit is a prodigy. The great mass of all armies, it is well known, is collected from the ignorant, reckless, and vicious. When such men are brought into close contact with each other, and at the same time removed from the restraining influences of domestic life and social observation, their vicious propensities are of course strengthened by mutual example and countenance. Discipline may prevent the commission of some gross crimes, but can in no degree improve, or even guard the moral character.

If it be, indeed, true, that the profession of a soldier is peculiarly hazardous to his well-being, exposing him and those within his influence, to crime in this world, and to misery in the next, we discover a new item of the awful responsibility which rests upon those who involve their country in war. In our contest with Mexico, 80,000 or more Americans, and probably three times as many Mexicans, have been exposed to the moral and physical injuries of military service. Could we follow the survivors on their return to their homes, what a mass of wretchedness should we discover, caused by the habits they had acquired, and the moral contamination of their example. All experience bears witness to the fidelity of the picture drawn long since, of the discharged recruit, who

—— "His three years of heroship expired,
Returns indignant to the slighted plough.
He hates the field in which no fife or drum
Attends him;—drives his cattle to a march,
And sighs for the smart comrades he has left.
'Twere well, if his external change were all;
But with his clumsy port, the wretch has lost
His ignorance and harmless manners too.
To swear, to game, to drink, to show at home
By lewdness, idleness, and Sabbath-breach,
The great proficiency he has made abroad:
To astonish and to grieve his gazing friends;
To break some maiden's and his mother's heart—
To be a pest, where he was useful once,
Are his sole aim, and all his glory now."

There is little reason for believing that American soldiers are more or less addicted than others to vice and outrage. The conduct of the soldier is governed more by discipline than by national character. A large portion of the American force in Mexico consisted of a class improperly called *volunteers*, since, where there is no conscription, every enlistment is voluntary. These volunteers, being enlisted for a short period, and being permitted to choose their officers, their discipline was probably less perfect than that of the regular army; and hence it is, that the journals of the day have teemed with accounts of their atrocities.

Of the 50,000 volunteers called into service, none perhaps have afforded a more instructive commentary on military patriotism and morality than the MASSACHUSETTS REGIMENT. These men belonged to a State surpassed by none for the intelligence, industry, and orderly deportment of its citizens. They had, moreover, responded to the official assurance of the Governor of the State, that it was the dictate of patriotism and humanity to save blood and money by volunteering to shoot Mexicans.* Passing by, therefore, the conduct of volunteers from other States, we shall confine our notice to these reputed descendants of the Puritans.† Although nothing has been heard of their martial achievements, a few extracts from the journals of the day will prove that they have attracted a large share of the public attention.

"For some days past, a strife has existed between a portion of the officers of the MASSACHUSETTS REGIMENT on the one side, and nearly all the privates on the other. That eternal disturber of order, *John Barleycorn*, 'stirred up the muss.' The officers alleged that the privates drank to intoxication, became disorderly and unfit for duty; and to put a stop to the evil, they advised closing the coffee-houses. The privates, on the other hand, say they drank to no greater excess than did the officers in question. The war thus commenced raged fiercely with various success. At one time, we thought the men defeated, from the number of prisoners we saw marched off; but they managed to escape, and in turn swung up the leader of their enemies as high as Haman—*i. e.*, his effigy. The guards were dismissed from the postern, the defences put up to keep out the Mexicans, levelled to the earth, and the deuce played generally."—*Metamoras Flag.*

"Major Abbott, by sundry acts, has made himself

* "Whatever," says the Proclamation calling for volunteers, "may be the difference of opinion as to the origin or necessity of the war, the constitutional authorities of the country have declared that war with a foreign country does exist. It is alike the dictate of PATRIOTISM and HUMANITY, that every means honorable to ourselves and just to our enemy should be employed to bring said war to a speedy and successful termination, and thus *abbreviate its calamities and save the sacrifice of human life and the wasting of public treasures.*" The best comment we can make on the *logic* and *morality* of this gubernatorial *dictum* is to exhibit the character of the men who obeyed the *dictates of patriotism and humanity*, as officially explained.

† The author deems it just to say, that he has heard it asserted that many of these volunteers were foreigners.

odious among the Americans in this place. They hoot him whenever he passes them, and last night they went so far as to hang him in effigy. He had three privates whipped last night."—*Letter from Metamoras, N. O. Bee.*

"ESCAPED. — The MASSACHUSETTS VOLUNTEER, who some week or two since stabbed to death with a bayonet the partner of Mr. Sinclair of our city, because he refused to give him what he had not—a glass of intoxicating fluid —escaped from the guard-house a few nights since. It is thought the sentinels on duty permitted him to escape." —*Metamoras Flag.*

Another paper mentions that three MASSACHUSETTS VOLUNTEERS had deserted, and a fourth had been marched through the streets of Metamoras encased in a whisky cask with the word "drunkard" written on it.

The *New Orleans Delta* announces the arrival at that city of "a select lot of murderers, thieves, and villains of every dye," sent home by order of General Taylor, including "three MASSACHUSETTS VOLUNTEERS."

"ANOTHER MANLY ACT.—On Wednesday evening last, after nightfall, several MASSACHUSETTS VOLUNTEERS entered the dwelling of a Mexican near the Upper Plaza, and demanded whisky. A female who officiated remarked that she kept nothing but beer. After some remonstrance, one of the gentlemen drew a bayonet, which he wore in his belt, and stabbed the woman to the heart."—*Metamoras Flag.*

It appears from the report of the Secretary of War,* that the deserters from this regiment, up to 31st Dec., 1847, numbered 105.

"Head Quarters, Vera Cruz, 15th October, 1846.

"The following named men (*sixty-five* in number) of 1st Regiment MASSACHUSETTS Infantry, being incorrigibly

* Ex. Doc., 1st Sess., 30th Cong., No. 62, p. 72.

mutinous and insubordinate, will of course prove cowards in the hour of danger, and they cannot of course be permitted to march with the column of the army. They are disarmed and detached from the Regiment, and will report to Brevet Major Bachus, for such duty in the Castle of San Juan De Ulloa, as may be performed by soldiers who are found unworthy to carry arms, and are a disgrace and a nuisance to the army.

"By order of Brig. Gen. CUSHING."

The following notices of these men, on their *return*, are taken from the periodicals of the day. A Boston paper says: "More than *one-third* of these, though *never in a battle*, were dead or missing before their return." The Editor of the Buffalo *Commercial Advertiser*, through which city they passed, says: "We spent some hours in conversation with these poor fellows, endeavoring to understand the meaning of such overwhelming squalor, want, and misery; for we do not exaggerate when we say, that we never beheld its parallel except at the Irish emigrant sheds in Canada last summer. The condition of these poor creatures was outrageously offensive to every human sense, as well physical as *moral*." Another editor, after their arrival in Boston, remarked: "A more pitiable set of human beings we scarcely ever saw—with unshaven beards, unshorn hair, ragged and dirty clothes of all shapes, fashions, colors, and conditions, pale and sunken faces, and a careless, unambitious saunter. They were truly objects of pity." A Boston editor, after visiting their quarters, exclaims: "We must confess that the condition of the men struck us with astonishment; it was wretched beyond conception. Rags and dirt were to be seen in abundance. Scarcely a man had a whole pair of pantaloons on, and none a second shirt. Without any offence to the soldiers, we must candidly confess, they are not fit to be seen in the streets of Boston."

To form a comprehensive view of the evils of war, and of the tremendous responsibility of those who commence it, we must consider its various and complicated assaults upon human happiness and virtue. The miseries we have inflicted upon Mexico will form the subject of a future chapter. We will now advert to the retributive justice thus far meted out to the immediate agents by whom those miseries have been inflicted.

The groans of the conquerors themselves are usually drowned in the shouts of victory, and the glare of the illumination fails to reveal the horrors of the battle-field, or the more prolonged agonies of the hospital. Eighty thousand American soldiers, abandoning the comforts of home and the pursuits of ordinary life, have been subjected to all the privations, sufferings, and evil influences of military service in a foreign land. When we recollect their long marches, some of them of a thousand miles under a burning sun, and not unfrequently exposed to the deadly *vomito*, we may readily believe that many lives have been lost through disease and casualties as well as in battle. Owing to the imbecility and ignorance of the Mexicans, the American *loss in the field* has been astonishingly small, not exceeding 5000 in killed and wounded in twenty-eight battles, as appears from official reports. But who can count the number who have died in military hospitals, and of others who, worn down by disease and vice, have found a premature grave in their own country? From very partial reports from some of our military hospitals in Mexico, it appears that the deaths *exceed* those that occurred on the field of battle.

A New Orleans paper, noticing the return of the Tennessee Regiment to that city, remarks: "Just one year ago there passed through our streets as noble and splendid a body of men as ever went forth to battle. They were about nine hundred strong. On Friday last, the whole of this gallant regiment arrived in our city. It numbers just *three hundred and fifty*—about one-third the force with which it left; and this loss it has sustained in a twelve months' campaign! It has lost on an average fifty men a-month."

Of the Second Regiment of Mississippi Rifles, one hundred and sixty-seven died of disease. Said Mr. Hudson in Congress: "Our late associate, Colonel Baker, declared in his speech on this floor, that of his regiment about one hundred had left their bones in the Valley of the Rio Grande, and that about two hundred more, worn down by hardships, and emaciated by disease, had been dismissed to perish by the way, or to find their graves with their friends at home; that all this mortality had taken place in about *six* months, and that this regiment had never seen the foe. He also informed us, that what was true of his regiment was generally true of other regiments of volunteers. We are informed by the answer of the Adjutant-General to a resolution of this House, that in a period of from sixty to ninety days after the volunteers had joined the army in the field, their numbers were reduced by disease six hundred and thirty-seven, and by discharges, in consequence of sickness and disability, between *two and three thousand*. This estimate does *not* include the sick which remain with the army." *

"I call the attention of this body and of the country to the immense sacrifice of human life now making to carry on this war. The official documents before us show that twenty-three thousand nine hundred and ninety-eight

* Speech, Feb. 13, 1847. App. to Cong. Globe, p. 869.

officers and men entered the service during the first eight months of this war; that fifteen thousand four hundred and eighty-six remained in service at the close of that time; that three hundred and thirty-one had deserted; that two thousand two hundred and two had been discharged, leaving FIVE THOUSAND NINE HUNDRED AND NINETEEN unaccounted for."*

The Rev. Mr. McCarty, a chaplain in the army, wrote from the city of Mexico: "I have now in the regular army eleven hospitals to visit, with one in the Quartermaster's department, which requires a great deal of my time. The number on the sick report in this city exceeds *three thousand* men!" "We all know," said Mr. R. Johnson in the Senate, "that at the commencement of the last Session of Congress, there were actually buried on the banks of the Rio Grande, of those who had died of disease, twenty-five hundred men."† Col. Childs, in his official report, 13th Oct., 1847, states that on taking command of Puebla, the hospitals were "filled with 1,800 sick." A New Orleans paper, noticing the return of the 3d and 4th Tennessee regiments, says that they lost 360 by death, although neither regiment had been in action. The same paper declares, that of 419 men composing the Georgia battalion, 220 died in Mexico.

We could fill sheets with extracts from the public journals, giving mournful details of the ravages of disease in our Mexican army. Let the following from a southern paper, and an advocate for the war, suffice. "At Perote there were 2,600 American graves, all victims of disease, and at the city of Mexico the deaths were most of the time 1,000 a-month. The first regiment that went out from Mississippi buried 155 men on the banks of the Rio

* Speech of Mr. Giddings, Feb. 3, 1847. Cong. Globe, p. 405
† Cong. Globe, Dec. 30, 1847.

Grande before it went into battle, and finally brought back less than half of its number. Two regiments from Pennsylvania went out 1,800 strong, and came home with about 600. Two regiments from Tennessee without being in any battle, lost 300 men. Capt. Naylor, of Pennsylvania, took down a company of 104 men, and brought back 17. He went into the battle of Contreras with 33, and came out of it with 19. But the most frightful instance of mortality was in the Georgia battalion. It went to Mexico 419 strong; about 230 actually died; a large number were discharged with ruined constitutions, many of them doubtless gone long since to their graves, and thus the battalion was reduced to 34 men fit for duty! On one parade when a certain company, once mustering more than 100 men, was called, the call was answered by a single private, its only living representative. From officers of many other regiments we have received details very similar to the above, which may be taken as a pretty fair average of the losses in the volunteer regiments—the regulars did not suffer to the same extent."

Mr. CLAY in a public speech, estimated the loss of our countrymen in the first eighteen months of the war as equal to *one half* the whole loss sustained in our seven years' revolutionary struggle!

Mr. CALHOUN declared on the floor of Congress that the mortality of our troops could not be less than twenty per cent.

If then we estimate the total mortality of our troops including those slain and such as afterwards died of their wounds, and those who have expired in Mexico and at home of diseases contracted in camp, at TWENTY THOUSAND, we shall be in little danger of exaggerating the amount. If we next turn our regards to the wives and children and relatives of these twenty thousand, we find a still expanding multitude upon whom the war has brought lamentation and woe.

Once more follow in imagination the survivors, on their return home. Mark the germinating seeds of moral and physical disease implanted by war in their constitutions, and about to bear bitter and deadly fruits.

In that approaching day when the Judge of quick and dead shall make inquisition for blood, those who have kindled the flames of war, will be called to justify the numberless and immeasurable evils both spiritual and temporal they have inflicted upon their fellow-men, upon their enemies as well as upon their own countrymen.

CHAPTER XXIX.

SUFFERINGS INFLICTED ON MEXICO BY THE WAR.

THE extreme feebleness of Mexico, arising from the ignorance and superstition of her inhabitants, was aggravated by the vast extent of her territories. This great extent, by rendering it difficult to collect a formidable force at any extreme point, rendered her whole frontier accessible to the invader. In about four months after the commencement of hostilities northern Mexico, from Tampico on the Atlantic to St. Diego on the Pacific, was a conquered country.

The smallness of the forces by which the various conquests were effected, attests the helplessness of the Mexicans, and the vigor of their enemies. In a little more than twelve months, the American standard waved over the famous castle of Vera Cruz, and the capital of the Republic was garrisoned by American troops. From that capital a corps of one thousand men could probably have traversed the Republic in every direction, through a hostile, but almost unresisting population. After the capture of Thornton's party, which General Taylor announced as the commencement of hostilities, not a battle, not a skirmish occurred in which the Mexicans were not defeated, no matter how vast their superiority in numbers. The ancient promise, "ten shall chase a thousand," seemed to be verified in the marvellous success of the American arms.* In ordinary cases, an invading army is neces-

* In the battle of Brazito, the American force under Col. Doniphan was less than five hundred; that of the enemy, 1200

sarily confined to a narrow track, and is restrained by fear of the enemy from dividing itself into detachments. But the unhappy Mexicans found the invaders spreading themselves over the country in every direction, and small parties taking possession of populous towns. We may easily imagine the innumerable and horrible insults and excesses endured by the Mexicans, from a victorious and scornful enemy, conscious alike of his power and his impunity, and far removed from the restraint, however feeble, of public opinion.

Unaware of the vast superiority of their enemy in all the dread machinery of war, the Mexicans unhappily hazarded the bombardment of Vera Cruz. Three thousand shells, each weighing ninety pounds were, it is said, thrown into that devoted city, besides about the same number of round shot. For more than three days did this horrible tempest beat upon Vera Cruz. "The darkness of the night was illuminated with the blazing shells circling through the air. The roar of artillery, and the heavy fall of descending shot, were heard through the streets of the

The Americans lost not a single man, and had but seven slightly wounded; the Mexicans were utterly routed, with a loss of 193 killed and wounded.

The result of the battle of Sacramento is thus described in an official report: "The first shadows cast by the moon, found the American army camped upon the battle-field, after having in a contest of four hours annihilated a force *six* times their number, and driven the enemy from four positions of great natural strength, fortified by thirty-six forts and redoubts, having taken *four* times their strength in artillery, the whole transportation, food, and ammunition of the Mexicans, and performed a march of twenty miles without water." Col. Doniphan tells us, "The field was literally covered with the dead and wounded from our artillery, and the unerring fire of our riflemen. Night put a stop to the carnage." The Mexicans had nineteen pieces of cannon, and were sheltered by forts and redoubts, while the Americans advanced to the attack on an open plain. The victors, in a fight of four hours, had *one* man killed, and eight wounded. Triumphs over *such* enemies, afford little cause for military pride.

besieged city. The roofs of buildings were on fire, the domes of churches reverberated with fearful explosions."

This splendid scene, and the consequences accompanying it, must have been viewed with high satisfaction, by

"The foe to all happiness human."

An officer of the navy, in an account written a few days after, says: "The bombardment lasted three days and a half. The city was greatly injured, the shells and round shot striking all over the town. One part near a small battery was utterly destroyed; and from the stench in the neighborhood, it is to be feared that the bodies of very many poor women and children, are buried in the ruins. I was in the Governor's palace, a very fine building, occupying one side of the Plaza, and was looking into a very handsome room where it was evident a shell had struck, when a Mexican gentleman came up and offered to show me over the house. I followed him, and directly we came to what had evidently been a superb room, but then almost entirely torn to pieces. He pointed to a place beside the door which was blown out—"there," said he, "sat a lady and her two children, they were killed by the shell which has wrought the injury you see."

Another officer says, that during the bombardment, "many of our officers at night crawled up close to the walls to hear, and represented the screeching, crying, and lament of the women and children, and wounded, as being dreadful."

A visitor, immediately after the surrender, tells us: "A shell struck the Charity Hospital where the sick inmates were lying, and killed twenty-three." Says Mr. Kendall, an eye-witness: "The city, or at least the northern part of it, has been torn all to pieces—the destruction is dreadful. It is impossible to get at the loss of the Mexicans by the bombardment; yet it is certain that *women, children, and non-combatants,* have suffered the most. The National Palace on the Plaza, had *five* shells burst within it; one of which, killed a woman and two children lying asleep in the kitchen."

"I rode to the town," says another writer, "to see what effect our shells had on it. I was prepared to see much destruction, but was perfectly amazed. The town is on its south-westerly side almost destroyed. The citizens of Vera Cruz say, the bombs did the most injury. They would fall on the houses, their weight carrying them from roof to cellar, and then burst, opening the houses from top to bottom, and killing all within."

Mr. Hine, thus describes his visit, the day of the surrender. "Scarcely a house did I pass, that did not show some great rent made by the bursting of our bomb-shells. During my peregrinations, I came to a lofty and noble mansion in which a terrible bomb had exploded, and laid the whole front of the house in ruins. While I was examining the awful havoc created, a beautiful girl of some seventeen came to the door, and invited me into the house. She pointed to the furniture of the mansion torn into fragments, and the piles of rubbish lying around, and informed me, while her beautiful eyes filled with tears, that the bomb had destroyed her *father, mother, brother, and two little sisters,* and that she was now left in the world alone!

"During the afternoon, I visited the hospital. Here lay upon truckle-beds, the mangled creatures who had been wounded during the bombardment. In one corner was a poor decrepid, bed-ridden woman, her head white with the sorrows of seventy years. One of her withered arms had been blown off by a fragment of a shell. In another place might be seen mangled creatures of both sexes, bruised and disfigured by the falling of the houses, and the bursting of shells. On the stone floor lay a little child in a complete state of nudity, with one of its poor legs cut off just above the knee! Not even this abode of wretchedness had been exempted from the accursed scourge of war. A bomb had descended through the roof, and, after landing on the floor, exploded, sending some twenty already mangled wretches, to the "'sleep that knows no waking.'"

The following is an extract from a *Mexican* account, written amid the ruins of the city. "The enemy, in accordance with his character, selected a barbarous mode of assassinating the unoffending and defenceless citizens, by a bombardment of the city in the most horrible manner, throwing into it four thousand one hundred bombs, and an innumerable number of balls of the largest size; directing his shots to the powder magazine, to the quarter of hospitals of charity, to the hospitals for the wounded, and to the points he set on fire, where it was believed the public authorities would assemble with persons to put it out; to the baker's houses designated by their chimneys, and during the night raining over the entire city, bombs, whose height was perfectly graduated with the time of explosion, that they might ignite in falling, and thus cause the maximum of destruction. His first victims were women and children, followed by whole families, perishing from the effects of the explosions, or under the ruins of their dwellings.

"At the second day of the bombardment, we were without bread or meat, reduced to a ration of beans, eaten at midnight beneath a shower of fire. By this time, all the buildings from La Mercede to the Paeraguia, were reduced to ashes, and the impassable streets filled with ruins and projectiles. The third day the enemy alternately scattered their shot, and now every spot was a place of danger. The principal bake-houses no longer existed—no provisions were to be had."

The details we have given of this bombardment, afford us some intimations of the sufferings occasioned by the assaults upon the cities of Monterey and Mexico.* We enter into no particulars of the battles fought in Mexico. Every battle-field is necessarily one of horrors; but, as the sufferers are those who came there to inflict upon others the very fate of which they are themselves the victims, they claim and excite less of our sympathy than the mothers and their mangled infants of Vera Cruz, whose shrieks of agony swelled the triumphal shout which greeted the American General.

In all our conflicts in Mexico, the slaughter of the enemy has been tremendously aggravated, by their natural and military imbecility. Mr. Thompson, our former Minister, in his work on Mexico, remarks: "I do not think that the Mexican men have much more strength than our women. They are generally of diminutive stature, and wholly unaccustomed to labor or exercise of any sort. What must be the *murderous* inequality between a corps of American cavalry, and an equal number of Mexicans?" He regards the superiority of Americans to Mexicans as "five to one at least in individual combats, and more than twice that in battle." Hence it is, that the Mexican loss in battle has been prodigious. It is

* A letter from a Mexican published in the newspapers, says: "In some cases whole blocks were destroyed, and a great number of men, *women, and children*, klled and wounded. The picture was awful. One deafening roar filled our ears—one cloud of smoke met our eyes, now and then filled with flame; and amid it all, we could hear the shrieks of the wounded and dying. Altogether, we cannot count our killed, wounded, and missing, at less than four thousand, among whom are many women and children."

impossible to ascertain the amount of that loss with any precision, but there is little hazard in asserting that the action of Congress in May, 1846, has consigned *fifty thousand Mexicans to a premature grave,* and ten times that number to poverty and wretchedness.

In the vast number of falsehoods of which this war has been so prolific, may be included the general unqualified eulogiums passed by its advocates upon the *hnmanity* of the American soldiery. We are not aware of any peculiar trait in our national character, that would render our soldiers remarkable for meekness and forbearance, or that would necessarily counteract that arrogance and selfishness which are the natural fruits of a bloody trade, and of military superiority. But national vanity is ever ready to believe a flattering lie, and demagogues equally ready to offer incense to every popular delusion. It is our object *to tell the truth,* and by so doing, to exhibit the odious and execrable character of war. American soldiers are like other soldiers, just what war, and discipline or the want of it, may make them. Human nature is the same in every land, and its evil propensities are equally developed under similar circumstances. It would have been an anomaly in the history of mankind, if soldiers, flushed with victory and scattered over a conquered country, and holding the vanquished in utter contempt, had not been guilty of great atrocities. It would be but cumbering our pages to detail the various instances of cruelty and oppression perpetrated by our troops, which have found their way into the public prints. A few specimens, selected from journals supporting the war, and therefore not disposed to throw unjust odium on the American army, will suffice to prove that our assertions on this point are not unsupported by facts:

"*Buena Vista, August* 20.—A ranger is missed, search

is made for him by his comrades, his body is perhaps found, perhaps not. The nearest Mexicans to the vicinity of his disappearance are required to account for him. They will not, or cannot. The bowie knife is called for, and deliberately every male Mexican in that rancho is speedily done for, guilty or not guilty. But this is not enough to make an offset for the life of a Texan. Another rancho receives the fearful visit, and again blood flows."

"*Camargo, January* 8, 1847.—Assassinations, riots, robberies, &c., are so frequent that they do not excite much attention. Nine-tenths of the Americans here think it a meritorious act to kill or rob a Mexican."

In Camp, Walnut Springs (*near Monterey*), *April* 25, 1847.—"You have published accounts of the disgraceful outrage perpetrated before the battle of Buena Vista, and will be no less shocked to learn that an equally sickening scene of outrageous barbarity has been perpetrated in this region by persons calling themselves Americans. It appears that near a little town called Guadaloupe, an American was shot two or three weeks ago; and his companions and friends determined to revenge his death. Accordingly a party of a dozen or twenty men visited the place and deliberately murdered twenty-four Mexicans."

The correspondent of the *Louisville Republican* writing from *Aqua Nueva*, after mentioning that the body of a murdered Arkansas volunteer had been found, says, "The Arkansas men vowed vengeance deep and sure. Yesterday morning a number of them, some thirty persons, went to the foot of the mountain two miles off, to an arrego which is washed in the sides of the mountain, to which the 'pisanos' of Aqua Nueva had fled upon our approach, and soon commenced an indiscriminate and bloody massacre of the poor creatures who had thus fled to the mountains and fastnesses for security. A number of our regiment being out of camp, I proposed to Colonel Bissell to mount our horses and ride to the scene of carnage, where I knew, from the dark intimations of the night before, that blood was running freely. We had turned out as rapidly as possible, but owing to the thick chapperels, the work of death was over before we reached the horrible scene, and the perpetrators were returning to the camp glutted with revenge. God knows how many of the unarmed peasantry have been sacrificed to atone for the blood of poor Colquit. The Arkansas regiment say not less than thirty have been killed."

This anonymous account of the massacre is sustained by the following order of General Taylor:—"The Commanding General regrets most deeply that circumstances *again* impose upon him the duty of issuing orders upon the subject of marauding and maltreating the Mexicans. Such deeds as have recently been perpetrated by a portion of the Arkansas cavalry cast indelible disgrace upon our arms, and the reputation of our country. The General had hoped that he might be able, in a short time, to resume offensive operations; but if orders, discipline, and all the dictates of humanity are set at defiance, it is vain to expect anything but disaster and defeat. The men who cowardly *put to death unoffending Mexicans* are not those who will sustain the honor of our arms in the day of trial."

If the General meant to intimate that cruelty and bravery are incompatible, he is contradicted by the unanimous testimony of all military history.

The correspondent of the *Charleston Mercury,* writing from Monterey after its capture, says, "As at Metamoras, murder, robbery, and rape, were committed in the broad light of day; and, as if desirous to signalize themselves at Monterey by some new act of atrocity they burned many of the thatched huts of the poor peasants. It is thought that more than one hundred of the inhabitants were murdered in cold blood."

It is not to be supposed that where human life is thus atrociously sacrificed with impunity, the decencies of society and the rights of property will be respected. A correspondent of the *New Orleans Picayune* writes from Ceralvo: "On arriving at Mier, we learned that the second regiment of Indiana Troops had committed, the day before, outrages against the citizens of the most disgraceful character, stealing, or rather robbing, insulting the women, breaking into houses, and other feats of similar character. Recently the people here have received treatment from men stationed here, that *negroes* in a state of insurrection would hardly be guilty of. The women have been repeatedly violated (almost an every day affair), houses broken open, and insults of every kind have been offered to those whom we were bound to protect."

The correspondent of the *St. Louis Republican,* writing from Santa Fé, Aug. 12, 1846, says, "I regret to say, nearly the whole territory has been subject to violence, outrage, and oppression, by the volunteer soldiery against all alike without distinction."

When we reflect how extensively Mexico has been traversed by our troops, we cannot doubt that a prodigious amount of property has been most wantonly destroyed. We are told by one of the letters describing a Mexican defeat, "Captain Morier followed up his advantage with decision, pursued the enemy, and *devastated* the valley of the Moro, burning everything in his path. The people, terrified, fled to the mountains where death in the shape of starvation awaits them." "Between Metamoras and Monterey," says another, "nearly all the ranchos and towns are destroyed."

General Scott, when about marching from Jalapa, upon Mexico, issued an order which is a singular illustration of military morality. He tells his army that it can no longer receive supplies from Vera Cruz, but must trust for them to the resources of the country—that the people must be paid for provisions, or "they will withhold, conceal, or destroy them. The people moreover must be conciliated, soothed and well-treated by every officer and man of this army, and by its followers." This preamble is succeeded by a declaration almost avowedly prompted by the fact, that supplies could no longer be brought from Vera Cruz: "Whoever maltreats unoffending Mexicans, takes without pay, or wantonly destroys their property, of any kind whatsoever, will prolong this war, waste the means present and future of subsisting our men and animals, as they successively advance into the interior, or return to our water depot (Vera Cruz); and no army can possibly drag after it to any considerable distance, no matter what the season of the year, the heavy articles of breadstuff, meat, and forage. Those, *therefore*, who rob, plunder, or destroy the houses, fences, cattle, poultry, grain, fields, gardens or property of any kind along the line of our operations, are plainly the enemies of this army. The General-in-Chief would infinitely prefer that the few who commit such outrages would desert at once and fight against us. Then it would be easy to shoot them down, or capture and hang them."

Military discipline confines to the commanding officer the prerogative of plundering the enemy, and he would no doubt wish to protect it from encroachment at all times. On the present occasion the General thought proper to dissuade the army from indulging their larcenous propensities, not from motives of justice and humanity, but *the difficulty of procuring supplies!*

This same General, in an order issued at Vera Cruz, 1st April, 1847, declared that "many undoubted atrocities have been committed in this neighborhood by a few worthless soldiers, both regulars and volunteers." The army was about marching into the interior, and to conciliate the inhabitants, and remove the unfavorable impressions made by these "atrocities," he issued a proclamation promising protection to the Mexicans, and telling them, that for outrages committed upon them, several Americans had already been punished by fine and imprisonment, and one "has been hung by the neck." "Is not this," said he, "a proof of good faith and energetic discipline?" The General did not tell the Mexicans how very cheap a sacrifice he had offered to propitiate them. The one "hung by the neck," was a NEGRO, and hence no military popularity was lost by his execution, and being a *free* negro, no *property* was destroyed. We have no evidence that during the whole war, a single *soldier* was punished with death for any outrage committed on Mexicans, however atrocious.

General Taylor, in a despatch to the War Department, 16th June, 1847, remarks, "I deeply regret to report that many of the twelve months' volunteers, in their route hence to the lower Rio Grande, have committed extensive depredations and outrages upon the peaceable inhabitants. *There is scarcely a form of crime that has not been reported to me as committed by them.*"

A great number of Mexican towns were captured and held by our forces. We may judge, from a single example, what kind of municipal government has most probably been exercised by our officers. Twelve months after the capture of Monterey, its social condition was thus described by Colonel Tibbats, in an official proclamation: "The undersigned, by virtue of an order of the commanding

General, has assumed the office of military and civil Governor of Monterey. Finding the command assigned to him, virtually without law or order, and infested with robbers, murderers, gamblers, vagrants, and other evil disposed persons, the worst of criminals going free, unscathed of justice, and rapine and even murder stalking abroad in open day without fear of punishment, insomuch that the peaceable inhabitants thereof have no protection either of person or property," &c.

The following official declaration is of a character that forbids us to doubt, that the oppression of the Mexicans has been most aggravated. General Kearney, writing to the War Department, 15th March, 1847, in reference to some insurrectionary movements, says: "The Californians are now quiet, and I shall endeavor to keep them so by mild and gentle treatment. Had they received such treatment from the time our flag was hoisted in July last, I believe there would have been but little or no resistance on their part. *They have been most cruelly and shamefully abused* by our own people, by volunteers (American emigrants) residing in this part of the country, and on the Sacramento. *Had they not resisted, they would have been unworthy of the name of men.*"*

To the individual sufferings arising from military violence, has been added that general suffering in which the whole Mexican population has participated, necessarily

* We do not know the particulars here referred to; but the following item from the news of the day gives us some intimation of the spirit manifested by the conquerors. "Lieuts. Beal, Talbot and others, left San Diego February 25th, bringing important intelligence. At Taos, the Court had condemned a large number of the insurgents. Eleven had been hung, and many whipped. Six were hung the day Lieut. Talbot passed through Taos. These executions created great excitement among the Mexicans, and efforts were making to stimulate insurrection, and raise volunteers for a rebellion."

resulting from the annihilation of their commerce. Every seaport of the Republic, whether on the Atlantic or Pacific, has been occupied by American forces. Hence, the Mexicans have been denied the privilege of exchanging their surplus productions for the necessaries and conveniences they had been accustomed to receive from foreign countries. Not a Mexican vessel floated on the ocean; of course, all imports and exports were in the hands of foreigners, and subjected to such duties as the invaders thought proper to impose. Those duties, moreover, instead of being appropriated as heretofore to the common good, were seized by the conqueror for his own use. Nor was his rapacity to be thus satiated. The ordinary municipal taxes became his spoil. Thus, for example, a *Captain* commanding in the city of Metamoras, issued his rescript requiring "the owners of all stores, groceries, billiard-tables, hotels, eating-houses, brick-yards, gambling-houses, cock-pits, and manufactories of liquors," to pay *at his office*, each month the taxes on their respective establishments. The Commander-in-Chief thought proper personally to direct and control the squeezing process. On the 15th December, 1847, General Scott issued an order beginning with the portentous announcement: "This army is about to spread itself over and occupy the Republic of Mexico, until the latter shall sue for peace *in terms acceptable to the Government of the United States.*" He then proceeds to decree that, "On the occupation of the principal point or points in any State, the payment to the Federal Government of this Republic of all taxes or dues of whatever name or kind, heretofore, say in the year 1844, payable or collected by that Government, is absolutely prohibited, as all such taxes or dues will be demanded of the proper civil authorities for the support of the army of occupation." Thus were duties on imports and exports, municipal, and all other taxes authorized by Mexico in time of peace and prosperity, to be extorted by a foreign army from the miserable impoverished people. One would have supposed that such exactions might have satisfied the Americans. But no—Mr. Polk had, from the moment he commenced the war, been sighing for PEACE. General Scott had, indeed, conquered Mexico, but he had not conquered a peace; and an organized system of plunder was to effect what his troops and bombs had failed to accomplish. Hence, a second order was issued on the 31st December, 1847, from Head Quarters, imposing on several of the Mexican States a contribution amounting to A MILLION OF DOLLARS. The following is an extract from this order: "On the failure of any State to pay its assessment, its functionaries, as above, will be *seized and imprisoned, and their property seized, registered, reported, and converted to the use of the occupation*, in strict accordance to the general regulations of this army. No resignation or abdication of office, by any of the said Mexican functionaries, shall excuse any of them from the above penalties. If the foregoing measures should fail to enforce the regular payment as above from any State, the commanding officer of the United States forces within the same, will immediately proceed to collect in money or kind from the *wealthier inhabitants* (other than neutral friends) *within his reach*, the amount of the assessment due from the State."*

This was the same General who, in his proclamation addressed "to the Mexican nation," from Jalapa, May 11th, 1847, assured them, that "The army of the United States respects, and WILL ALWAYS respect, private pro-

* It is but justice to General Scott to mention, that he acted in accordance with instructions from Mr. Polk, who, without any authority from Congress, assumed the power of imposing taxes and collecting duties in Mexico.

perty." He who directed officers of the United States forces, when assessments on Mexican States are not paid, to proceed to collect them from the *wealthier* inhabitants, is the same Commander-in-Chief who, in his order of the preceding April, wished that such of his soldiers as stole poultry, grain, &c., from the Mexicans, would desert at once, as then it would be easy to shoot them down, or to capture and hang them. Among other devices for extorting money, in connexion with the promised regeneration of the Mexicans, was the official allowance of THREE GAMING-HOUSES in the Capital, in consideration of the annual sum of *eighteen thousand dollars*, payable in monthly instalments.*

We can understand why Mr. Polk and his southern partisans deemed it expedient to acquire Mexican territory at any cost of blood, treasure, and happiness; but surely we may ask of northern Democrats and northern Whigs, why have *you* brought pillage, desolation, and death upon the people of Mexico? What offence had they committed which, in the sight of God, can justify such horrible retribution at *your* hands? Why have *you*, who have no interest in the extension of human bondage, fought the battles, not of freedom, but of *slavery?* When summoned, as you will shortly will be, before that dread tribunal, which, in another world, takes cognizance of every act committed in this, on what plea do you expect to vindicate that stupendous mass of human misery and human wickedness which *your* agency has helped to accumulate?

* It appears from the Report of the Secretary of the Treasury (Dec., 1848), that the sum of $3,844,000 was in these various ways extorted from the Mexicans. The value of property destroyed in the city of Mexico, has been estimated at four millions. The total annihilation of Mexican property, caused by the invasion, no arithmetic can compute.

Mr. Root, of Ohio, one of the "immortal fourteen," in a speech delivered *after* the triumph of our arms, and the acquisition of the "indemnity" demanded by Mr. Polk, thus expressed himself on the floor of Congress:—"But where shall the widow look for indemnity? Where shall the mother, made childless by this war, look for her indemnity? Where shall the orphan children, whose fathers have fallen in battle, or by disease in that distant land, look for their indemnity? Can any of these new acquisitions, under this treaty, indemnify them? It does seem to me, sir, that in all this bloody business, the men who have been most active in it, have regarded this war only in relation to the effect it is likely to have on *future elections*, and they have not once thought how it will be regarded by the Judge of all. And when I think of these things, I thank my God, humbly thank him, that He gave me the nerve and the firmness to stand up here in my place, and say "no" first, and "no" last, and "no" at all times, on every measure designed for the prosecution of this accursed war. And, sir, I rejoice that, when I approach the last agony of earth, whatever other guilt may press me, none of the victims of this war can meet me and say,—

'Let my fate sit heavy on thy soul to-morrow.'"

CHAPTER XXX.

COST OF THE WAR TO THE UNITED STATES.

ONE of the professed objects of the war, after the pretence of repelling invasion had been abandoned, was the indemnification of "our much-injured citizens," that is, the collection of a few millions of alleged debt. Our fleet and army were employed to collect this debt, and according to Mr. Polk, the costs of collection were to be added to the sum due. We not only gave judgment in our own cause, but taxed our own costs. Those costs, as nearly as can be ascertained, will, when finally settled, exceed ONE HUNDRED MILLIONS OF DOLLARS. In civil life, the very attempt to compel a debtor to pay a bill of costs twenty times the amount of the debt claimed, would be deemed scandalous extortion. How far the determination of a powerful government, to extort such a bill from a feeble, exhausted State by slaughter and devastation, is divested of criminality on account of its *national* character, is a question embarrassing only to those who have persuaded themselves that statesmen and politicians are under the jurisdiction of a peculiar and relaxed morality. The idea that reparation is due to Mexico for a ruthless invasion, the devastation of her cities, the plunder of her provinces, the slaughter of thousands and tens of thousands of her people, has been advanced, only to be denounced as *unpatriotic,* if not treasonable.

We have levied upon Mexican territory, for the hundred

millions we have spent in attempting to collect a paltry debt, which, after all, we have remitted by the treaty of peace. Mr. Polk declared his determination to prosecute the war till "full indemnity" had been obtained; but he failed to tell us by what moral arithmetic he ascertained what number of square miles of slave territory will afford a "full indemnity" for the misery, falsehood, and crime engendered by his war.

Many a successful plaintiff has found, to his mortification, that he has impoverished his adversary without enriching himself, and that the fruits of his victory have been pocketed by the agents he employed. A similar discovery may be in reserve for the American people. The question what *they* have gained by the war, will in time force itself upon their attention. To this inquiry, no other answer can be returned than GLORY AND TERRITORY.

Before we proceed to investigate the true value of these spoils of victory, let us dwell a moment on their pecuniary costs.

The direct expenditures in waging this war, from the departure of Taylor from Corpus Christi, to the exchange of the ratifications of the treaty of peace, cannot, at the most moderate estimate, be less than - - - - - - - - -	$100,000,000
The money to be paid Mexico, for ceding the required territories, and thus saving us the cost of protracted hostilities, is - - - - -	15,000,000
The cost of the army from the conclusion of the war, to its disbandment, including its transportation home, say - - - - - -	2,000,000
The extra pay for three months to all soldiers who had been engaged in the war, allowed by act of Congress, estimated at - - - - -	3,000,000
Every soldier, or his heir, is entitled to 160 acres of land, or in lieu thereof, at his option, $100. Supposing only 75,000 claims to be presented, and to be paid in land, the value of the	

land, at the price fixed by Congress would be $15,000,000. But to avoid the semblanee of exaggeration, we will suppose these claims commuted at $100 each, making - - -	7,500,000
The award under the treaty of 1839, due by Mexioo, and assumed by treaty of peace, with interest, - - - - - - - -	2,000,000
The Government has also assumed. by treaty, the payment of such unliquidated claims against Mexico as may be found *valid*, not exceeding $3,250,000, out of $6,455,462 demanded. Should none but *valid* claims be allowed, the sum to be paid may amount to - - - - -	500,000
Making the total cost, in money, of new territory, - - - - - - - -	$130,000,000

The above estimate, it is believed, is very moderate, and much below the estimates usually made. But let it be recollected, that it is an estimate only of the *direct* expenditures of the Federal Government, for the acquisition of the coveted territories.

For nearly two years, at least 140,000 men, as soldiers, teamsters, artificers, &c., have been diverted from productive industry, and engaged in occupations, adding nothing to the real wealth of the country, or the comfort, happiness, and morality of its citizens. The time and labor of these men have therefore been literally wasted, and consequently what they would have added to the common stock in time of peace, is to be included in the cost of the war. Many of these individuals have, moreover, been brought to an untimely grave, and probably a still greater number disqualified for future usefulness by vice and disease. The operations of commerce have, moreover, been deranged, and enterprize paralyzed by a monetary pressure, occasioned by a drain of specie from our great cities, to be expended in Mexico—and wide-spread bankruptcy only prevented, by an unusual and accidental demand for our bread-stuffs in Europe. When all these facts are taken into consideration, and when we recollect that interest is to be paid during many future years, on the money borrowed, and that large drafts are yet to be made on the treasury for pensions and for indemnities for private losses and injuries, it will not be thought extravagant to assume, that the *indirect* cost of the war will be little, if any less than the sum actually expended for its prosecution.

Dr. Franklin, long since remarked, that nothing was ever acquired by war that might not have been obtained at a less cost by purchase. For the territory of Louisiana, even more extensive and greatly more valuable than that we have wrested from Mexico, we paid $15,000,000. For Texas we offered $5,000,000, and at a previous day we had offered only $1,000,000 for Texas, with a portion of California.

Mr. Polk would have shrunk from offering fifty millions for the very land which he has now bought at such a vast amount of blood and treasure. It is impossible to resist the conviction that, by honest negotiation, we might have become the masters of these territories without crime, without human butchery, and at a far less cost in money than the sum we have paid.

The mighty sum we have exchanged for glory and territory, has added not one cent. to the productive capital of the country, nor brought one new comfort or convenience within reach of its population.

For all useful practical purposes, this amount of the nation's capital has been annihilated. But it is easy to imagine how such a sum might have been expended in modes resulting in a prodigious augmentation of the resources of the nation, and the virtue and enjoyments of the people. Such a sum might have spread a net-work of railroads and telegraphic wires over the country, uniting in bonds of interest and intercourse the remotest inhabitants of our vast empire. It would have opened through Oregon a channel by which the commerce of India and China would in a few days have reached every portion of our Confederacy. Or it might have given security and facility to our magnificent inland navigation, and formed safe and capacious harbors on our mediterranean seas. Or it might have carried science and useful knowledge to the inmates of every dwelling in our Republic; and in various ways have been made conducive to the diffusion of virtue and religion. The mere interest of this sum is vastly greater than is annually contributed by Christendom to evangelize the world. The disposal of this treasure was a talent which, in the providence of God, was entrusted to our rulers: whether the use they have made of it proves them to have been good and faithful servants will be declared on that day in which they shall give an account of their stewardship.

We should, however, take a most erroneous and limited view of the cost of this war to the United States, were we to confine our estimates to the millions which have been expended in its prosecution, or to the personal sufferings it has occasioned. Before we can sum up the total cost, we must add to the blood, the groans, the treasure, we have bartered for victory and conquest, the political and moral evils the war has bequeathed to the nation—evils as extensive as the bounds of the Republic, and whose effects upon the happiness of individuals will continue to be felt when time shall be no more.

CHAPTER XXXI.

POLITICAL EVILS OF THE WAR.

ALL war is necessarily unfavorable in its tendencies to the liberties and prosperity of a State, even when waged for the defence or recovery of freedom. The burthens it imposes, the arbitrary authority it confers, and the dispositions it fosters, are all adverse to popular rights. These tendencies are, of course, controlled and modified by circumstances. The late war, having been carried on wholly without the limits of our own country, did not inflict upon our citizens those violations of right and those oppressive exactions which are ever experienced on the theatre of hostilities. It has nevertheless shown itself a dangerous foe to constitutional liberty.

We have seen in the preceding pages that most provident and ample preparations were made for the commencement of the war on the Rio Grande, and for the seizure of California, not only without the sanction, but even without the knowledge of Congress. It is utterly impossible that Congress would have issued, or the people have tolerated, a declaration of war against Mexico, either to compel her to pay our alleged claims, or to withdraw her troops and magistrates from her villages on the Rio Grande. Hence, it was deemed necessary first to provoke a collision, and *then* to appeal to Congress to defend the country from invasion! The war, therefore, although recognized and prosecuted by Congress *after* its commencement, was in fact and in truth begun in consequence of orders issued by the President on his own responsibility, and not in pursuance of any constitutional or legal authority. He had, indeed, as Commander-in-Chief, a right to direct the movements of the troops, but not in such a manner as necessarily and designedly to involve the country in war. Most truly, therefore, did the House of Representatives declare that the war had been unconstitutionally begun by the President.

Yet has this usurpation of power, leading to the sacrifice of thousands of lives and millions of treasure, been unvisited with punishment. The offence has found an apology in the triumphs to which it has led; and thus a sanction has been given to a precedent, that invests the President of the Republic with the royal prerogative of bringing upon the nation the calamities of war.

Nor is this the only instance, in which the President in his own person has exercised powers belonging only to the legislative branch of the Government. Although not permitted by the Constitution to appoint of his own will and pleasure, a single officer, or to take from the treasury a single cent, he established a system of tariffs and internal taxation in Mexico, appointing a horde of collectors, and accumulating at his own disposal, all the revenue that could be extorted at the point of the bayonet, from the miserable and impoverished Mexicans; and all this without the slightest warrant from Congress.*

* "I am under a deep conviction, that the President has no right whatever, to impose taxes internal and external on the people of Mexico. It is an act without the authority of the Constitution or laws, and eminently dangerous to the country. If the President can exercise, in Mexico, a power expressly given to Congress, which he cannot exercise in the United States, I would ask where is the limit to his power in Mexico? Has he also the power of making appropriations of money collected in Mexico, without the sanction of Congress? *This he has already done.* Has he the power to apply the money to whatever purposes he may think proper, and, among others, to raise a military force in Mexico, without the sanction of Congress? *This*

He has also, by his sovereign will and pleasure, established civil Governments in New Mexico and California, appointed Governors, organized courts of justice, commissioned magistrates, &c., without even consulting Congress, and with no law whatever authorizing the exercise of these high prerogatives, or providing for the salaries of the numerous civil officers he has seen fit to appoint. It appears from the Report of the Secretary of War, Dec. 4, 1847, that the duties collected in California, "have been applied towards the support of the civil Government." Thus has the President, of his own will and pleasure, not only appointed officers, but paid them salaries at his discretion. Thus have a people, jealous of their liberties permitted, in the delirium of victory and conquest, their chief magistrate to assume over vast regions the most unlimited and despotic authority, grasping at once the sword and the purse. Henceforth it is to be part of our theory of Government, that during war, the President of the United States is released from all constitutional restrictions, so far as he acts without the limits of the country, and that he is wholly beyond the control of Congress. The immense power and patronage thus conferred on the President by a state of war, may hereafter prove a strong inducement with that officer to plunge his country into hostilities, and to postpone the return of peace.

The course pursued by Congress has apparently been directed by the principle, that when the country has once

also he has already done"—*Speech of Mr Calhoun in Senate, March* 1848.

"Is the establishment of a code of customs in Mexico, an act of war, or derived from war, *or an act of legislation?* Why, clearly it is the latter I want to know how the President of the United States can overturn the revenue law of Mexico, and establish a new one in its stead, any more than he can overturn the law of the descent of property, the law of inheritance, the criminal code, or any other portion of Mexican law?"—*Mr. Webster's Speech in Senate, March*, 1848.

been involved in war, no matter by what means, or for what objects, it is the duty of the representatives of the people to afford to the President every facility he demands for its prosecution, however wicked or injurious it may be.

Not only has the public mind become accustomed to executive usurpation, but it has lost, in its admiration of military success, that jealousy of military power, which is a most powerful safeguard of republican liberty. We have been utterly heedless of the melancholy example exhibited by Mexico herself, of the disastrous influence of a thirst for martial renown. The astonishing facility with which that country was overrun and prostrated by our troops, cannot be accounted for solely by the paralyzing effect of the Mexican church on the progress of science and civilization. Ever since her independence, Mexico has fostered a military spirit; but it was a spirit that consumed her very vitals. The resources of the State were squandered on the army, and the army through its generals governed the State. The blessings of peace were despised, and the citizens, instead of combining for the common welfare, were divided into partisans of rival Generals. Revolution succeeded revolution in rapid succession, one chieftain supplanting another. A civilian was scarcely ever placed at the head of the State, the reins of government being almost invariably committed to hands that grasped the sword. The history of the Republic of Mexico has been a history of military insurrections and usurpations. Even when invaded by a foreign enemy, military factions and rival chiefs paralyzed the strength of the nation, and rendered her an easy prey. All the records of the past bear witness to the fact, that popular Generals have been the chief destroyers of Republics. Yet the American people, deaf to the warnings of history, have apparently become infatuated with military glory, and have recently given, various indications of their preference for men who have served their country in the field, over such as have merely labored to advance her prosperity and happiness, by cultivating the arts of peace.

The arbitrary spirit engendered by war, and the idea which it fosters, that all rights and interests must yield to the public safety, are both necessarily hostile in their tendency, to the free expression of opinion adverse to its prosecution. It is not surprisng that the authors of the Mexican war—a war so open to animadversion, and waged for purposes so sectional and odious—should wish to discourage all investigation into its true character; and all efforts to thwart the accomplishment of its object. No *law* could silence the press, nor arrest debate in Congress, nor discussion among the people. But the hope seems to have been indulged, that *public opinion* might be so directed, as to produce what legislation could not effect. On the popularity of the war might depend not merely its successful prosecution, and the consequent acquisition of the coveted territories, but the predominance of the democratic party, and the continued possession of power and emoluments by the present incumbents of office. Hence Mr. Polk, in his first Message after the commencement of hostilities, attempted to intimidate his opponents by insinuating that they were treacherous to the cause of their country. "The war," said he, "has been represented as unjust and unnecessary, and as one of aggression on our part upon a weak and injured enemy. Such erroneous views, though entertained by *but few*, have been widely and extensively circulated, not only at home, but have been spread throughout Mexico, and the whole world. A more effectual means could not have been devised to encourage the enemy, and protract the war, than to advocate and adhere to their cause, and thus give them '*aid and comfort.*' It is a source of national pride and exultation, that the great body of the people have thrown no such obstacles in the way of the Government in prosecuting the war successfully, but have have shown themselves to be eminently patriotic, and ready to vindicate their country's honor and interests at any sacrifice."

Here we have a most arrogant impeachment, by the first magistrate of the Union, of the patriotism of such of his fellow-citizens, including no small portion of the very Congress he was addressing, who in the exercise of the very rights guaranteed to them by the Constitution of their country, ventured to express the opinion, that the war in which he had involved the nation, was unjust, unnecessary, and aggressive. Mr. Polk did not deem it prudent to denounce in plain terms, the opponents to his measures as TRAITORS to their country, and meriting an ignominious death, but preferred doing it by *implication;* and hence applied to all such as pronounced his war unjust, unnecessary, and aggressive, the technical terms, "giving aid and comfort" to enemies, used by the Constitution of the United States (Art. III. Sect. 1), in defining the crime of TREASON. If this gentleman did indeed believe, that a conscientious opposition to an existing war, is inconsistent with patriotism, and equivalent to the crime of giving aid and comfort to the enemy, he is ignorant not merely of the first principles of ethics, but of the course pursued by some of the most illustrious statesmen and patriots who have adorned the pages of modern history.

What said Lord Chatham, the celebrated Prime Minister of England, who had led his nation to victory and power, and whose memory is embalmed in the grateful remembrance of his countrymen? This great man during the American war, declared in Parliament, "If I were an

American, as I am an Englishman, while a foreign troop was landed in my country, I would never lay down my arms—never—never—never." Fox even refused to concur in a vote of thanks to officers for the victories they had achieved, in what he believed, to be an unjust war. Numerous distinguished members of the British Parliament were active and persevering in their opposition to the war. So again, the war waged by Great Britain against the French Republic, was freely denounced as unjust and unnecessary, by statesmen high in the confidence of the nation. The recent war against China, frequently called the Opium War, was sternly denounced by a large portion of the British public as most iniquitous. At a public meeting in London, at which a British peer, the Earl of Stanhope, presided, it was resolved: "That this meeting deeply laments that the moral and religious feelings of the country should be outraged, the character of Christianity disgraced in the eyes of the world, and this kingdom involved in war with upwards of three hundred and fifty millions of people, in consequence of British subjects introducing opium into China, in direct and known violation of the laws of that Empire." The meeting concurred in a petition to Parliament, for an immediate peace, and ordered that their proceedings should be translated into the Chinese language, and *forwarded to the Emperor of China.* Yet no Minister of the Crown, no member of Parliament, ventured to denounce this Constitutional expression of opinion as treasonable. In our own country we have seen men of the purest character, the most unquestionable patriotism, opposing the war of 1812 with Great Britain, as unnecessary, impolitic, and unjust. No Constitutional monarch in Europe would venture to impeach the patriotism and loyalty of those, who, in a mode sanctioned by the fundamental laws of the Empire, opposed the measures of his Government.

The system of denunciation commenced in the Message, was zealously and rudely pursued by the official journal. The following article appeared in the *Washington Union*, soon after the date of the Message.

"A WAR-REGISTER. TIMELY PROPOSITION.—It has been suggested, that the cause of the country may be promoted by the opening of a war-register in every city, town, and village, for the purpose of preserving an authentic record of the TORYISM which may be displayed by individuals, during the continuance of the present war. In this register, it is proposed to record the names of such persons as make themselves zealous in pleading the cause of the enemy, and oppose the war into which the people and the Government of the United States have been forced by Mexican aggression, insult, and robbery. Besides the *names* of the individuals who pronounce against the justice of our cause, such *sentiments* as are particularly odious, should be placed on the register. Where an individual expresses sympathy for the enemy, or wishes the death of the President, or the downfall of the National Administration as a punishment for having engaged in the war, the sentiments of the TORY should be registered in his own language as nearly as possible. All statements intended for entry on the record, should be verified by the name of the witness or contributor."

The wickedness of this article, is not concealed by the absurdity of its pretended proposition. Its evident design was to intimidate the opponents of the war, by exciting against them demonstrations of popular violence. It is a call from the Government organ upon the demagogues of the day, to stifle by brute force, all open denunciation of the war. Confiding in the countenance and patronage of the executive and his partisans, the editor of this paper assumed a dictatorship over the proceedings of Congress, rebuking either House with vulgar insolence whenever it declined an immediate compliance with the wishes of the President. Such members as voted against granting further supplies, were stigmatized as *Mexican Whigs.* At last, a vote of the Senate displeasing to the Administration, was announced as "ANOTHER MEXICAN VICTORY." Happily the purpose intended was not effected. Indignation, and not intimidation, was the result; and the President's editor was, by a formal resolution, "for having uttered a public libel on the Senate," excluded from the privilege of admission to the floor of the Senate, a courtesy that had hitherto been shown him. The course pursued by this journal merits attention only from its being the acknowledged organ of the executive, and from its obvious accordance with the spirit and design of Mr. Polk's official denunciation of the *opponents to the war.* Many of the officers of the army, following the hints given by the President and his organ, professed to be exceedingly scandalized by the objections made to the war. General Twiggs, in particular, was so regardless of decency as to give, at a public dinner in Mexico, the toast, "Honor to the citizen-soldier who steps forward to battle for his country. Shame to the KNAVES at home, who give aid and comfort to our enemies." A Colonel Wynkoop, wrote from Mexico: "We here can see no difference between the men, who, in 1776, succored the British, and those, who, in 1847 give arguments and sympathy to the Mexicans." Another Colonel of the name of Morgan, declared in a public speech: "All who will advocate the withholding of supplies, or withdrawing our armies, disguise their sentiments however they may, under whatever artful plea they choose, are TRAITORS AT HEART."*

These various attempts to suppress the freedom of debate and discussion, only reiterate the lesson universally taught by history, that war, in its spirit is hostile to civil liberty. Had the war been a popular one, had the masses been maddened by defeat, had they been thirsting for the blood of their enemies, the efforts of the President and his partisans to direct their fury upon a feeble minority whom they were taught to regard as traitors, would not have been fruitless, and the American, like the French Republic, would have had her annals disgraced by a *Reign of Terror*.

But happily the assertion of the President, that the war was regarded as unjust and unnecessary, and as one of aggression "*by but few*," was of equal veracity with many other of his declarations. This assertion was made in his Message of December, 1846, at which time his party had a very large majority in the House of Representatives. The next December, a new House of Representatives, elected in the interim, assembled; and this new House, "fresh from the people," Resolved: "that the war was unnecessarily and unconstitutionally begun by the President of the United States."

But although we have successfully maintained the liberty of speech and of the press, the sanction given by the war to executive usurpations, and the thirst for conquest and glory, which it has stimulated, are destined to exert a durable and disastrous influence on the Republic. There are also other political evils resulting from the war, which merit consideration. The nation, which at the commencement of hostilities was free from debt, is now burthened with a load of pecuniary obligations. To

* We quote these military ebullitions, from the Newspapers of the day.

relieve ourselves of this load, it will be necessary for many years, to impose heavy duties upon imports; and these duties are in fact, taxes upon the necessaries and comforts of life ; not the less real for being indirect and unperceived by the consumers. Our national vanity is flattered by the fact, that the certificates of our debt are now selling in Europe. It seems not to be recollected that our debt is thus transferred to foreigners, who, instead of our own citizens, are hereafter to receive from the national treasury, both principle and interest. Great Britain could not support, for a single year, the payment even of the interest of her debt, did it not find its way into the pockets of her own subjects, whence it is again returned in taxes to the Government. Just in proportion as our debt is due abroad, the more onerous is it to ourselves.

When we reflect on the vast extent given to our Empire by the recent conquests—the peculiar character of the conquered people who are to be invested with the privileges of American citizens—the bitter sectional feelings already engendered by the question respecting the extension of slavery over these regions—the diversity of interests that will exist between the Atlantic and Pacific States, and the perpetual struggle for mastery which must prevail between a powerful yeomanry, depending on their own industry, and a landed aristocracy supported by some millions of serfs, surely we have cause to apprehend much irritation, civil dissensions, and the ultimate disruption of the Union.

We presume not to lift the veil that conceals the future; but if the declaration, that "Wherewithal a man sinneth, by the same also shall he be punished," be applicable to nations as well as to individuals, we cannot doubt that the conquests which now swell our national pride will prove scourges to humble it.

CHAPTER XXXII.

MORAL EVILS OF THE WAR.

THE malignant as well as the benevolent affections of our nature are strengthened by exercise. A volunteer, describing in a letter his sensations on first going into battle, mentions that on discharging his musket, he was harassed with the fear that he might possibly kill somebody; but that after a while he became as eager as others in the work of death.

From the commencement of hostilities, the public was almost daily served by the newspapers with details of battles, and bombardments, and mangled corpses, and all the varieties of human suffering caused by war:

> "Boys and girls,
> And women, that would groan to see a child
> Pull off an insect's leg, all read of war—
> The best amusement of our morning meal:
> And all are learned, fluent, absolute,
> And technical, in victories and defeats,
> And all the dainty terms for fratricide;
> Terms which we trundle smoothly o'er our tongues,
> Like mere abstractions—empty sounds, to which
> We give no feeling and attach no form.
> As if the soldier died without a wound—
> As if the fibres of this godlike frame
> Were gored without a pang—as if the wretch
> Who fell in battle, doing bloody deeds,
> Pass'd off to Heaven, translated, and not killed—
> As though he had no wife to pine for him,
> No God to judge."

This constant familiarity with human suffering, instead of awakening sympathy, has roused into action the vilest passions of our nature. We have been taught to ring our bells, and illuminate our windows, and let off fireworks, as manifestations of our joy, when we have heard of great ruin, and devastation, and misery, and death, inflicted by our troops upon a people who never injured us, who never fired a shot on our soil, and who were utterly incapable of acting on the offensive against us.* Nor was our exultation at the flow of Mexican blood repressed by the recollection that American blood flowed with it. Our neighbors, and friends, and countrymen, by thousands, fell in battle, or wasted in the noisome hospital—but their sufferings excited almost as little thought and compassion as those of the Mexicans. The nation had gained glory,

* Says an able writer: "American gentlemen, husbands and fathers, send an army to collect a debt from some Mexican chieftains by bombarding Vera Cruz. By day and by night the awful storm of bomb-shells is rained down upon the devoted city. *Christian* gentlemen guide these guns, and kindle these fires of hell. Mothers and daughters fly shrieking through the streets, and their mangled limbs are buried beneath the ruins of their dwellings. These shells explode in infant nurseries, by the bedside of languishing disease, in parlors of refinement and piety. Ladies have limb torn from limb by the balls which American gentlemen fire. A large party of ladies, in the terror of that awful bombardment, fly to the cellar of one of the most costly stone mansions, hoping there to find refuge from these engines of destruction which have demolished many of their dwellings, and by a bloody death bereaved them of many of their dearest friends. The thunders of the bombardment, the crash of the explosions of bomb-shells, the shrieks of the dying, pierce the darkness of the cellar, and excite to a frenzy of terror the trembling females there. A shell falls upon the roof of the house, descends into the cellar, and explodes; and the limbs of these mothers and maidens, mangled and gory, are driven into the walls. And this is *honorable* warfare—this is *Christian* warfare—and the result of such scenes is the subject for civic rejoicing, bonfires, and illuminations! And respectable men, humane men, men who sit at the table of Jesus Christ as his disciples, who publish papers to guide the world to Christian feelings and practices, consider this a very suitable way of collecting debts."

and would gain land; and politicians seemed anxious to gain popularity by rivalling each other in exulting shouts. Alas, in very many instances those shouts proceeded from the same lips which denounced the war as unconstitutional, unjust, and a national crime!

The struggles between the convictions of conscience and the aspirations for popular favor, led others besides the Whigs into strange and almost ludicrous contradictions.

We have heard much of late years, from a certain class of philanthropists, of the inviolability of human life; and societies have been organized for the abolition of capital punishment. Life was a boon granted by the Deity, which could rightfully be taken only by the Giver. All this was very well, as applied to American felons; but to extend it to Mexican men, women, and children, guiltless of crime, was, of course, to give "aid and comfort" to the enemy. Hence was seen, in one of our largest cities, the singular spectacle of a president of an anti-capital-punishment society presiding over a large and ferocious war meeting. The president of another similar society, a prominent politician, accepted and discharged the very consistent duty of presenting a complimentary sword to a popular general.

That portion of the public press which supported the war has, in many instances, been instrumental in diffusing throughout the community most impious and ferocious sentiments. It was, of course, the policy of the dominant party to excite the passions of the people against Mexico, to encourage admiration for military prowess, and to repress all compassion for those we were slaughtering and plundering. Hence, many of the war journals apparently labored to pervert the moral sense of the community, and to insult and ridicule those religious feelings which were naturally shocked by the character and events of the war.

A few quotations will illustrate these remarks. Mr. Polk, as we have seen, while devastating Mexico, was at all times sighing for peace. His presses teemed with the most brutal plans for "conquering peace."

"We must now," said one of them, "destroy the city of Mexico, level it with the earth on which it stands, serve Puebla, Perote, Jalapa, Saltillo, and Monterey in the same way, and then increase our demands till we insist on the perpetual possession of the Castle of Juan d'Ulua, as a key to the commerce of the Gulf of Mexico. This course would save hundreds of lives. Occupy all the seaports on the Gulf and the Pacific for revenue for the payment of the expenses of the war. Such a course would compel the Mexicans to sue for peace."

Said another: "Unless we distress the Mexicans, carry destruction and loss of life to every fireside, and make them feel a rod of iron, they will not respect us." Mr. Polk's own organ, the official *Union*, declared: "Our work of subjugation and conquest must go on rapidly and with augmented force, and, as far as possible, at the expense of Mexico herself. Henceforth, we must seek PEACE, and compel it by inflicting on our enemies all the evils of war."

These barbarous sentiments, which were rife through the land, were aggravated in atrocity by the lying pretext on which they were urged. We, an invading foe, were to murder by wholesale, and level cities to the earth, to procure a peace that was ours the moment we ceased to assail the Mexicans. Did we choose to recal our armies, we well knew our enemy had no means of revenging the wrong we had done her. Mexico was fighting solely in self-defence, and the only peace we desired, the only peace we were ready to conquer, was the cession of the territory for which we had commenced the war.

Not only were the general precepts of justice and humanity thus set at defiance, but pains seemed to be taken to attract public admiration for such acts of ferocity and impiety as were calculated to nourish the war spirit. A silly child of eleven years was said to have written a letter to one of the Generals, asking to be employed against the Mexicans, and boasting that he had money enough to buy a *pair of pistols and a dagger;* and the epistle of this little boy was paraded in the papers, headed "THE RIGHT KIND OF SPIRIT." Anecdotes of officers, which, if true, could not fail to disgust all who reverence the awful realities of Christianity, have been loudly trumpeted as instances of American patriotism and heroism. Thus we have had an account of a captain mortally wounded, and just expiring. "The whole of his lower jaw, with a part of his tongue and palate, is shot away by a grape shot; he communicated his thoughts by writing on a slate. He does not desire to live. He concluded an answer to some inquiries concerning the battle of the 9th, by writing '*we gave the Mexicans hell!*'" These words so peculiarly horrible, as uttered by a dying man, became with a certain class a slang phrase, and to give the Mexicans *hell*, seemed to be the glorious privilege, as well as duty, of American Christians. A Mississippi paper adopted it, with a blasphemous addition:—"By some mistake a piece of poetry headed 'Song of the Sword,'* appears on our first page. It seems that in our absence, when, it may be, the boys were out of copy, this song was selected to fill up a place. We never saw it till it was too late to make the correction. It does not

* An English poem on war, having no allusion to this country.

express our sentiments. It is *Whiggish*, and very bad poetry withal. We go for giving the Mexicans HELL, whether Christ be our guide or not."

Under the caption, "NOBLE EXPLOIT," we are told of a soldier mortally wounded, remonstrating against being carried off the field, exclaiming, "he was a dead man, and damned if he did not want to kill some of them."

Some comment having been excited by certain profane expressions, untruly we hope, alleged to have escaped from General Taylor, in the heat of battle, a New Orleans paper replied: "It is a paltry affectation in any one who knows the General, to pretend to be shocked at what was related of him at Buena Vista. It is a mere sham for the benefit of puritanical souls, who do their damning after a more economical formulary, than is generally used in the field. The words came out of General Taylor's mouth, and were no doubt as acceptable to heaven as the roaring of the cannon which belched forth death, and strewed the earth with slaughter."

The few instances we have cited (and they might be multiplied indefinitely), indicate the baneful influences to which public opinion has been exposed, through the efforts to create and maintain a war spirit in the community.

The Church has, in some few cases, united in this unholy work of corrupting public opinion. The pulpit has occasionally uttered its benedictions on the Mexican invasion; and ministers of Christ, by joining in military funeral pageants, have given the sanction of the religion they professed, to the cause in which the deceased perished. On some of these occasions sermons have been delivered, breathing little of the spirit of the Prince of Peace. Men who had lost their lives in the act of voluntarily carrying fire and sword into a foreign country, have been held forth to the admiration of their countrymen, as having fallen in the *discharge of duty.* But these reverend patriots omitted to instruct their audience, that the Mexicans who fell in the act of defending their wives and children, were no less obedient to the commands of duty, than the American volunteer; nor did they avail themselves of the opportunity to draw the obvious inference that, as both Americans and Mexicans were but discharging their duty in killing each other; mutual slaughter is an acceptable sacrifice to the common Father of all, and in accordance with the precepts of the Divine Redeemer. Some of the clergy very consistently reduced to practice the doctrines they taught. Thus we had the announcement in a St. Louis paper, of "A BAPTIST PREACHER KILLED IN BATTLE," with an eulogy on his patriotism. The *New Orleans Picayune* thus noticed another officer of the Church militant:—"A company of about ninety men arrived here yesterday from the parishes, under the command of the Rev. Richard A. Stewart, as captain. Captain Stewart is a worthy clergyman, of the Methodist persuasion, who allows nothing to prevent his discharge of that duty every citizen owes his country in the hour of peril!" The Reverend Captain, it seems, so exerted himself in the hour of his country's peril, as to acquire at least that honor which cometh from man; for on his return from the wars, we again find him noticed in the *Picayune* of February, 1848. In an account of a Taylor meeting in New Orleans, it is said, "Mr. Stewart, of Iberville submitted a resolution, nominating General Zachary Taylor as a candidate for the Presidency of the United States. A member of the Convention rose to second the resolution, and said, 'that as the mover might not be known to all the Convention, he would announce him to them as the *Reverend Colonel* Stewart, of Iberville, the *fighting clergyman!*' (immense applause.)"

It is however due to justice to acknowledge, and to acknowledge with gratitude, that the sacred office has rarely been desecrated by a vindication of the Mexican war; and that in numerous instances ecclesiastical bodies and individual pastors have, with Christian boldness and fidelity, exposed and denounced its wickedness. Nor was opposition to the war confined to the clerical profession. The whole *religious* community, especially at the North, were, with few exceptions, unanimous in reprobating it; and indeed, had it not been for the acts and efforts of politicians, of men striving to keep the offices they had, and others striving to gain the offices they wanted, the great mass of the people would have regarded the war with abhorrence.

The moral sense of the nation was, moreover, impaired by the sentiment industriously cultivated by the politicians of both parties—"Our country, right or wrong." This sentiment was of course intended to vindicate each party, for the support it gave to the war, by insinuating that devotion to country is more imperative than moral obligation.

The war has also had a most unhappy influence in familiarizing the public ear to *falsehood*, and under circumstances tending to divest the sin of much of its vileness. Falsehood was dignified, both by the magnitude and importance of the objects it was intended to promote, and by the elevated position of those who condescended to use it as an instrument.

It was one of the lamentations of the Prophet, that "truth has fallen in the streets;" and in our days, the Mexican war has caused her to be trampled in the dust, not only in the streets of Washington, but in every highway throughout the republic. The Message of Mr. Polk (Dec. 1846), in vindication of the war, has been termed "a pyramid of mendacity". It would occupy too much space to examine in detail the various materials of this vast structure, we will merely give a few specimens which the attentive reader of the preceding pages will be qualified to analyze for himself.

"The existing war with Mexico was neither *desired* nor *provoked* by the United States; on the contrary, *all honorable means were resorted to to avert it.* After years of endurance of aggravated wrongs on our part, Mexico, in violation of solemn treaty stipulations *commenced* hostilities, and thus by her own act *forced* the war upon us. Long before the advance of our army to the left bank of the Rio Grande, we had ample cause of war against Mexico; and, had the United States resorted to this extremity, we might have appealed to the whole civilized world for the justice of our cause." "The *wrongs* which we have suffered from Mexico almost ever since she became an independent power, and the *patient endurance* with which we have borne them, are *without a parallel in the history* of modern civilized nations." "The annexation of Texas to the United States constituted no just cause of offence to Mexico." "Whilst occupying his (General Taylor's) position on the east bank of the Rio Grande *within the limits of Texas,* then recently admitted as one of the States of our Union, the Commanding-General of the Mexican forces, who, in pursuance of the orders of his Government, had collected a large army on the opposite shore of the Rio Grande, crossed the river, invaded *our territory,* and commenced hostilities by *attacking our forces.*" "Every honorable effort has been used by me to *avoid* the war that followed; but all have proved vain. All our attempts to preserve peace have been met by insult and resistance on the part of Mexico." "This war has not been waged with a view to conquest," &c., &c.

With a reckless consistency rarely paralleled, he announced to Congress on the 6th of July, 1848, that "the war in which our country was RELUCTANTLY involved in the NECESSARY vindication of the national rights and honor, has been terminated."

The fictions of Mr. Polk were reiterated by his party with all the gravity of sincere belief. The Whigs in Congress, with a few honorable exceptions, pursued a different policy. They fearlessly confessed that the war for which they voted was unnecessary and unjust, a war of aggression and not of defence; and that the assertion in behalf of which they enrolled their names in an enduring record, that the war existed "by the act of Mexico" was FALSE. To excuse their conduct, they also had *their* fiction. They voted to raise fifty thousand men, for the purpose of rescuing General Taylor and his little army from capture by the Mexicans!

The falsehoods respecting the Mexican war, coined in Washington, became a circulating medium throughout the country. They were found in almost every official despatch; they were uttered through the press; they were passed as genuine by Governors in their messages, and by Legislatures in their resolves. Who shall estimate the injury done to the morality of the nation by this wide-spread contempt for truth? The example of men conspicuous for talents, influence, and station, must be operative for good or for evil. "When the righteous are in authority the people rejoice; but when the wicked bear rule, the people mourn." It has been well said that truth and the confidence it inspires, is the basis of human society, and that error is the source of every iniquity. How deplorable, then, that the love of truth and abhorrence of falsehood should be weakened by the authority and example of those in high places! But with this subject are connected considerations more momentous than any that belong to this transitory scene;—we are all soon to enter upon an endless existence in a world in which sorrow and falsehood are alike unknown, or in a place from which joy and truth are for ever banished.

Surely, among the awful responsibilities resting upon the authors and supporters of the Mexican war, will be included the corruption of public opinion and the depravation of public morals to which it has given birth.

CHAPTER XXXIII.

ACQUISITION OF TERRITORY.

HAVING taken a retrospect of the pecuniary, political, and moral sacrifices made by the American people, in the war they have waged against Mexico, let us next inquire what equivalents they have received. It is difficult to imagine any which are not included in the TERRITORY and the GLORY they have acquired. The value of these acquisitions, we proceed to examine.

It appears from a document laid before Congress from the War Department and Land Office, that the alleged limits of Texas embrace 325,520 square miles; and those of New Mexico and California, as ceded by treaty, 526,078 more, making a grand total of 851,590 square miles. It is only by comparison that we can form an adequate idea of the extent of this prodigious area. The state of New York contains less than 50,000 square miles; of course the addition made to our possessions is equal to seventeen times the extent of the *Empire State.* It is four times the size of France, and five times that of Spain.*

Texas, it is true, was acquired by other means than open war. But no less than 125,520 square miles, included within her assumed boundaries, rightfully belonged to Mexico, and our title to them is founded, not on her claim, but on conquest, confirmed by the treaty of peace. Adding this territory to that of New Mexico and California, we have

* See American Almanac for 1842, p. 270

651,591 square miles, about one half of all that was left to Mexico, after the revolt of Texas, as the spoils of war. Such was "the magnanimous forbearance exhibited towards Mexico," of which Mr. Polk thought proper to boast in his Message to the Senate communicating the treaty which ceded to us this vast plunder.

How far this forbearance was magnanimous depends, of course, on the motives which prompted it. We have already seen that the insurgents of Texas, after some hesitation, *forbore* to include California within its boundaries. The reason assigned for this forbearance had no reference to right and justice; it was simply, that they had already taken as much as they wanted, and that more at present would be inconvenient. It is difficult to see wherein our forbearance was more magnanimous than that of our Texan brethren. We have taken precisely what we went to war to acquire; and a territory from which thirteen large slave States could be carved, was sufficient to give the slave power an entire control of the Federal Government. Mexico, moreover, is so enfeebled and despoiled, that all that is left may be absorbed by the mighty Republic, at any moment it may be deemed expedient to take possession.

But as Mexico was prostrated, and we might have annexed the whole Republic to our territory, was it not magnanimous to *pay her* for what we did take? It is true Mexico was prostrate, but she was not submissive. She could not resist our arms, but she could not be occupied and governed as American territory except by military force. The war was becoming unpopular, and the Administration was tottering, the popular branch of the National Legislature having declared against it. It was doubtful whether Congress would furnish supplies for new conquests. But, in any event, nothing more could be hoped from the farther prosecution of the war than what had been already effected—the military occupation of Mexico. Such an occupation for a single year would cost double or treble the sum we paid the Mexicans. It was obviously wiser and cheaper to pay a moderate sum for a quit-claim to the land we wanted, than to continue an expensive and dangerous litigation. In the prosecution of this litigation, we had already expended 20,000 lives, and more than a hundred millions of dollars. Hence, the means of acquiring *peaceable* possession of the land we had taken was a matter of political and pecuniary calculation, and the result affords but little proof of magnanimity.

The question, whether this territory is not worth all it has cost us, will be variously answered. By those who regard slavery as the corner-stone of our political liberties, who behold in it a divine institution illustrative of the wisdom and benevolence of the Deity, and an instrument by which those who possess it will be enabled to govern the whole Republic, and mould its policy for their own interest, the acquisition of territory which it was expected would give to slavery an indefinite extension, an assured perpetuity, and an overwhelming political preponderance, would of course be regarded as of priceless value. On the other hand, the addition of this territory, should it be used for the purpose for which it was acquired, cannot but be regarded as a direful curse by all who believe slavery to be hostile alike to the will of God and the happiness of man. We have had, in the preceding pages, most abundant proof that this territory would not have been acquired except with a view to the extension of slavery; and it is therefore just and fair, in estimating its value compared with its cost, to keep in mind for what object that cost was incurred.

The future is hidden from our view, but there is little reason for doubting, that not only Texas, but all New Mexico, will for a long period be doomed to the ignorance, degradation, and misery, which are inseparable from human bondage. Events unexpected and utterly unforeseen, even at the conclusion of the war, have since occurred, which will probably exempt at least a portion of California from the curse of slavery. That portion, however, it is to be feared, will find another and a sore curse in its recently-discovered gold. The mineral wealth in which it is said to abound will be shared by a promiscuous crowd from foreign lands as well as our own citizens. The eager search for gold in the mines in which it is buried has ever been found hostile to regular industry, and to habits of virtue and frugality. We have cause to apprehend that the population which will be attracted to this region will not be of a character to strengthen our republican institutions, or in any respect to elevate our national character.

But whatever may be the riches of these mines, and whatever may be the consequences resulting from them, it should be remembered that they formed no part of the motives which prompted the war—no part of the estimated value of the territories we have seized. The true question to be solved in this discussion is, did we pay, in blood, and treasure, and in the moral and political evils resulting from the war, a higher price than the territories were at the time supposed to be worth to us?

We had territory enough, as has already been shown, for unborn generations; and, with the exception of the extension of slavery, no plausible motive could be urged for the acquisition. No president would have dared to negotiate a treaty of cession at the price of one hundred millions, nor would any Senate have had the hardihood to ratify so preposterous a treaty, had it been made. Nor is it conceivable that Mexico would have refused so magnificent and prodigal an offer, had it been made. We have seen that Mr. Polk offered through Slidell $25,000,000 for the very territory for which the country has paid at least five times that amount in money, in addition to blood, misery, and crime.

The Port of Saint Francisco was the only portion of the acquired territory which we needed, as being convenient to our commerce in the Pacific; and that might doubtless have been acquired by friendly negotiation at a moderate price; or a right of deposit secured by treaty, without cost.

CHAPTER XXXIV.

GLORY.

He whose wisdom and benevolence are alike infinite, has taught us not to seek that glory which cometh from man, and has assured us, that "that which is highly esteemed among men, is an abomination in the sight of God." If we believe the record which God has given of himself, we must be constrained to admit that, of all the objects of human ambition and of human admiration, none can be more abominable in his sight than MILITARY GLORY. Such glory is founded on bravery, skill, and success, in causing the misery and death of our fellow-men. It is wholly independent of the moral character of the cause in which it is acquired. The soldier is by general consent absolved from all responsibility for the cruelty, injustice, and wickedness of his employers. Whether he fights for liberty or slavery—to defend his own country or to plunder another—his glory rests upon his bravery, skill, and success, in subduing and slaughtering his enemies.

Bravery is an animal quality, very common among all nations, and its possession has never been confined to the wise and good. Were honor to be awarded to the bravest, the most atrocious villains would not unfrequently bear the palm. Indeed, few military exploits can, in a scornful recklessness of life, compare with the assassination of Henry the Fourth. What General has, like Ravilliac, coolly and dispassionately welcomed an inevitable, horrible and shameful death. Mere bravery is no more entitled to praise than any other animal quality, and its exercise is often indicative of the vilest passions, and a sottish indifference to a future state. The bravery of the soldier amid the excitement of the battle field, stimulated by fear of shame, and the hope of reward, is pale and lustreless compared with that devotion to duty which triumphs over pain, and danger, and life itself. "I go bound in the spirit unto Jerusalem," said the Apostle, "not knowing the things that shall befall me there, save that the Holy Ghost witnesseth in every city, saying that bonds and afflictions abide me. But none of these things move me, neither count I my life dear to myself."

Military skill, of course, arises from experience and instruction combined with natural talent, and, even when carried to the highest possible perfection, affords no guarantee for the presence of a single virtue. Bravery and military skill, as well as infamy, are associated with the memory of Benedict Arnold. But success is essential to military glory. The warrior is crowned only by the hand of victory. Yet her gifts are often dispensed without regard to the bravery and skill of the recipient, and we have seen her permitting one of the most distinguished of her favorites, after leading half a million of veterans to Russia, secure his personal safety by a sudden flight in the night season, and under cover of a borrowed name; and we have seen this same favorite, after wielding the most potent sceptre ever grasped by man, wearing out his days in an Island-prison.

The American army, furnished with all the appliances of war which science, and art, and wealth could supply, gained a series of uninterrupted victories over a nation with a small, feeble, and sparse population, but little removed from semi-barbarism, without commerce, without arts, without money, and without credit. Now, the historical fact, that these victories have been achieved by the bravery and skill of the American forces, constitutes the GLORY which is regarded by some, as an ample compensation for all the misery and wickedness resulting from the war! This glory gives no food to the hungry, no raiment to the naked, and adds nothing to the wisdom, virtue and comfort of the American people. We are assured, however, that it will give us peace and security by deterring aggression. All history bears testimony to the utter futility of such an expectation. Military glory ever renders its possessor arrogant and intolerant, and others jealous and vindictive. Powerful martial nations are those which enjoy the least peace; assailing others, if not assailed themselves.

Let us listen to the peans of triumph as chanted on the floor of the United States Senate by General Cass: "Our flag has become a victorious standard, borne by marching columns over the hills and valleys, and through the cities and towns and fields of a *powerful* (!) nation, in a career of success of which few *examples can be found in ancient or modern warfare.*" After giving the dates of twenty-eight victories, he exclaims, "If we recorded our history upon stone, as was done in the primitive ages of the world, we should engrave this series of glorious deeds upon tables of marble. But we shall do better; we shall engrave it upon our *hearts,* and we shall commit it to the custody of the press, whose monuments, frail and feeble as they appear, are more enduring than brass or marble, than statues or pyramids, or the proudest monuments erected by human hands. Let modern *philanthropists* talk as they please, the instincts of nature are truer than the doctrines they preach. Military renown is one of the great elements of national strength, as it is one of the proudest sources of gratification to every man who loves his country, and desires to see her occupy a distinguished position among the nations of the earth."*

It seems unfortunate for the honor and glory of our country that our military operations are conducted on a Lilliputian scale, and our military renown is so very cheaply acquired. The trophies gained in our Mexican war, even if engraven on marble, would look exceedingly diminutive compared to some, which, however the General may suppose to the contrary, are really recorded in the history of modern warfare. Had it been the General's good fortune to belong to "the Grand Army," his patriotic heart would have swelled with still prouder gratification, while listening at Austerlitz, to the glowing applause of his Emperor: "Soldiers! I am content with you; you have covered your eagles with immortal glory. An army of one hundred thousand men, commanded by the Emperors of Russia and Austria, have been, in less than four hours, cut to pieces and dispersed—forty stand of colors—the standards of the imperial guard of Russia—one hundred and twenty pieces of cannon, twenty Generals, and more than thirty thousand prisoners, are the results of this day, for ever celebrated. Henceforth you have no longer any rivals to fear." With what delight would he have drank in the glorious story, related to the army on entering Berlin: "Soldiers—the forests, the defiles of Franconia, the Saale and the Elbe, which your fathers had not traversed in seven years, you have traversed in seven days, and in this interval you have fought four fights, and one pitched battle. You have sent the renown of your victories before you to Potsdam and to Berlin. You have made sixty thousand prisoners, taken sixty-five standards, six hundred pieces of cannon, three fortresses, and more than twenty Generals. And yet nearly one half of you regret

* Cong. Globe, January 5th, 1848.

not having fired a shot. All the provinces of the Prussian monarchy, as far as the banks of the Oder, will be in your power." At Friedland, his soul would have been "satisfied as with fat things," as the address of the hero fell upon his ears. "Soldiers—in ten days you have taken one hundred and twenty pieces of cannon, seven standards, killed, wounded, or captured, sixty thousand Russian prisoners; taken from the enemy all its hospitals, all its magazines, all its ambulances, the fortress of Konigsburg, the three hundred vessels that were in the port laden with every species of munitions, and one hundred and sixty thousand muskets that England had sent to arm our enemies."

The vast amount of glory and misery detailed in these addresses, affords a significant comment on "the instincts of nature," and the pacific doctrines of "modern philanthropists."

Military renown, the Senator tells us, is one of the greatest elements of national strength, and the proudest source of gratification to every man who loves his country, and desires to see her occupy a distinguished position among the nations of the earth. The first assertion is contradicted by history, and the latter by the declarations of thousands and tens of thousands of men, whose virtue and benevolence are unquestioned. If military renown ever belonged to any people, the precious boon was enjoyed by the French under Buonaparte. Yet France was, at that very time, bleeding and agonizing at every pore,—her commerce destroyed,—her manufactures languishing, her liberties crushed, her young men dragged by the conscription from the paternal hearth, and offered a bloody sacrifice on the altar of personal ambition; and finally this same great element of national strength consigned the nation to *the custody* of a foreign army, and its mighty emperor, to a lonely rock. It was on that rock, and while brooding over his fallen greatness, that this scourge of Europe uttered the memorable words, "*The love of glory is like the bridge which Satan threw over chaos, to pass from Hell to Paradise.*" Like that fabled structure, it has indeed furnished to "woes unnumbered," a ready entrance into our unhappy world. In losing her hero, and her glory, France parted with her sorest plagues; and humbled in her pride, and despoiled of her conquests, she enjoyed for a series of years, a degree of peace, comfort, and prosperity to which she had been a stranger from the foundation of her monarchy.

CHAPTER XXXV.

PATRIOTISM.

IMMEDIATELY after the expulsion of the Persians from Greece, the fleets of the States in alliance with Athens, were collected in a neighboring port. Themistocles appeared in the Athenian Assembly, and announced that he had a plan for securing the power and glory of Athens; but, that secrecy being essential to its success, he could not make it public, and asked for instructions. He was authorized to communicate it to Aristides, and, with his approbation, to put it in execution. The latter, on learning the plan, reported, that nothing could possibly conduce more to the grandeur and prosperity of Athens, but nothing could possibly be more unjust. The Assembly, without inquiring into particulars, ordered that the plan, whatever it was, should be abandoned. Which party displayed the purest patriotism—the Assembly, which refused to augment the power of the Republic by an act of injustice, or the illustrious scoundrel who proposed rendering his country the mistress of Greece by firing the assembled fleets of her allies? Should the question be decided by the sentiment so generally adopted by a christian people, "our country right or wrong," the decision would be adverse to the pagan Athenians. But perhaps it will be said, that the sentiment is intended to apply only in a state of war, and that it is only after a declaration of hostilities that we are bound to support and vindicate the acts and pretensions of the Government, however, villainous. It is not easy to understand, how the act of a King or a Congress can dissolve those obligations of truth, justice, and mercy which the Creator has imposed upon all his creatures. Yet the violation and contempt of those obligations, for the supposed interests of the public, seem by many to be regarded as the test of patriotism.

Few virtues are more universally professed, few are more imperfectly apprehended, and few are more rarely practised, than PATRIOTISM. From the time of Absalom to the last electioneering meeting, patriotic professions have been the cheap materials from which demagogues have attempted to construct their fortunes.

Counterfeits imply an original. There *is* such a virtue as patriotism, acknowledged and inculcated by both natural and revealed religion; and it is but a development of that benevolence which springs from moral goodness. To do good unto all men as we have opportunity, is an injunction invested with divine authority. Generally our ability to do good is confined to our families, neighbors, and countrymen; and the natural promptings of our hearts lead us to select these in preference to more distant objects, for the subjects of our kind offices. Our benevolence, when directed to our countrymen at large, constitutes PATRIOTISM; and its exercise is as much controlled by the laws of morality, as when confined to our neighbors or our families. A voice from Heaven has forbidden us, "to do evil that good may come." The sentiment, "our country right or wrong," is as profligate and impious as would be the sentiment, "our church, or our party, right or wrong." If it be rebellion against God to violate his laws for the benefit of one individual, however dear to us, not less sinful must it be to commit a similar act for the benefit of any number of individuals. If we may not, in kindness to the highwayman, assist him in robbing and murdering the traveller, what divine law permits us to aid any number of our own countrymen in robbing and murdering other people? He who engages in a defensive war, with a full conviction of its necessity and justice, may be impelled by patriotism, by a benevolent desire to save the lives, and property, and rights of his countrymen. But, if he believes the war to be one of invasion and conquest, and utterly unjust, by taking part in it, he assumes its guilt, and becomes responsible for its crimes.

But soldiers, it is said, are bound to obey orders, without inquiring into their morality. Where enlistments are voluntary, this obligation is assumed, not imposed, and it may well be questioned, whether any man is at liberty to promise unqualified obedience to others. But the obligation of the soldier, does not affect the duties of the citizen. The latter is free from the promises of the former. The Government has declared a war of invasion and conquest, one which the citizen believes to be most iniquitous—is he required by duty, that is, by the commands of God, voluntarily to aid the Government in prosecuting such a war, by the offer of his money and services? If he is, then all people are under a divine obligation to aid their respective Governments in all their wars, however piratical, and waged for any purpose, however detestable. Such indeed, is the sentiment advanced in the following lines.

"Stand thou by thy country's quarrel,
Be that quarrel what it may;
He shall wear the greenest laurel,
Who shall *greatest zeal* display"

Here we have an American poet, who would exult in the massacre of Glencoe, sing peans to the Duke of Alva, and crown with the greenest laurels the butchers of the Albigenses.

"Our country right or wrong," is rebellion against the moral Government of Jehovah, and treason to the cause of civil and religious liberty, of justice and humanity.

Actions springing from mere selfishness, rarely command the respect of mankind, and the patriotism that is self-denying and costly, is more likely to be genuine than that which is lucrative. Tried by this test, there is comparatively but little patriotism in the world. The demagogue, who echoes the clamor of the mob, and thus opens to himself an avenue to wealth and power, gives a very inconclusive proof of his patriotism; while he who, in promoting what he believes to be the public weal, exposes himself to obloquy and loss, may reasonably be regarded as governed by disinterested motives.

One of the most universal of popular delusions, is that which awards patriotism to the soldier. But soldiers frequently engage in wars in which their country has no interest whatever; and, although military skill, and valor of a high order, have often been displayed by mercenary troops, they are surely not entitled to the meed of patriotism.

It is well-known, that multitudes adopt the military profession as a livelihood, with the expectation of pay, promotion, and distinction. It is not obvious that in selecting this profession, they are more influenced by a desire to do good to their country, than the lawyer, physician, divine, or mechanic. No class of men have in the history of the world, been more ready instruments of oppression, cruelty, and tyrany, than soldiers; and scarcely ever have the liberties of a people been destroyed, but through their agency. Rarely, indeed, have the representatives of a people convened in Senates or Parliaments, surrendered their rights to an usurper, except when overawed and compelled by military force. That soldiers have been governed by a high sense of patriotism it would be folly to deny, but still greater folly to affirm that such is generally the case.

We are fond of dwelling on the patriotism of the soldiers of the Revolution; and yet we have high authority to prove that, in many instances, their claim to this virtue was exceedingly equivocal. Washington, in a long letter to Congress, 24th September, 1776, gives a melancholy picture of the demoralization of the army: "Thirty or forty soldiers will desert at a time, and of late a practice prevails of a most alarming nature, and which will, if it cannot be checked, prove fatal both to the country and the army. I mean the infamous practice of plundering; for under the idea of Tory property, or property that may fall into the hands of the enemy, no man is secure in his effects, and scarcely in his person. In order to get at them, we have several instances of people being frightened out of their houses, under pretence of their houses being ordered to be burned, and this is done with a view of seizing the goods; nay, in order that the villainy may be more effectually concealed, some houses have already been burned to cover the theft. I have used my utmost endeavors to stop this horrid practice; but under the present lust after plunder, and want of laws to punish offenders, I might almost as well attempt to move Mount Atlas." He then goes on to detail the difficulty he had, in getting a court-martial to convict an *officer* for stealing. Again, on the 3d May, 1777, he writes to Congress: "The desertions from our army of late have been *very considerable.*"

The same year, Adjutant-General Reed, writes to Congress: "When the hurry of retreat or action made it difficult to go through the forms of trial, all restraints seemed to be broken through. A spirit of desertion, cowardice, plunder, and shrinking from duty, when attended with fatigue or danger, prevailed but too generally through the whole army."*

It is true, a soldier perils his life; but other men do the same for money, without any reference to the good of their country. Says Washington, writing to Congress, February 9th, 1776: "Three things prompt men to a regular discharge of their duty in time of action—natural bravery, hope of reward, and fear of punishment. The two first are common to the uninstructed and the disciplined soldier; but the latter most obviously distinguishes the one from the other. A coward, when taught to believe that, if he breaks his ranks and abandons his colors, he will be punished with death by his own party, will take his chance against the enemy." Washington was too well acquainted with human nature, and too much devoted to truth, to attribute martial valor to patriotism. The patriotism of our soldiers in Mexico, is a never-failing topic of eulogy with our political aspirants; but from a report of the Secretary of War, made 8th April, 1848, it appears that the desertions in Mexico, up to the 31st December, 1847, so far as they could be ascertained from confessedly very imperfect returns, amounted very nearly to five thousand, about one-sixteenth of the whole number of troops employed. The newspapers represent the desertions, in the early part of 1848, as very numerous.

The records of history, as well as daily observation, teach us, that patriotism is as rarely the virtue of politicians as it is of soldiers. "To the victors belong the spoils," now the avowed maxim of American parties, reveals the true object of multitudes who are vociferous in their professions of devotion to the public interest. An active politician, who is not the possessor or the

* Life of Reed, I. 240

expectant of office, is a personage rarely to be found in our Republic. To pursue measures supposed to be popular, affords a very uncertain indication of virtuous motives.

It seems impossible that any candid person acquainted with the origin and causes of the Mexican war, should insist that its necessity and justice were so palpable as to exclude all doubt: or that the assertion that the Mexicans commenced the war by invading the United States, and shedding American blood upon American soil, is supported by such irrefragable testimony, that no well-informed man can honestly deny its truth. Many of the democratic members of Congress, in their reproaches of the Whigs for voting for a war which they denounced as *unjust*, declared *such a war* to be the greatest of crimes, and those who prosecuted it, guilty of murder. Even Mr. Polk's organ thus abused the Whigs for voting thanks to victorious Generals:—"None but the Whigs would think of rewarding men volunteering to fight in a war unconstitutionally commenced by one man, and prosecuted in contempt of national honor." Yet this same ready tool had been lavish of his charges of treason against *all* who opposed the war, whatever might be their conscientious opinion of its character. But if an unjust war be indeed a crime, involving its authors and abettors in the guilt of murder, it is most remarkable that not one Democrat in two successive Congresses, found his conscience burthened with the momentous question, whether the Mexican war was or was not unjust! Probably not two of these gentlemen entertained precisely the same opinion on the great truths of scripture, yet not a solitary individual of the party saw aught but verities in Mr. Polk's messages! When we remember the diversities of the human mind, and the complicated and contradictory testimony in relation to the origin of the war, and the wide difference of opinion respecting it, throughout the nation, the unanimous, unfaltering faith of these gentlemen is a moral phenomenon. Their faith, however, was counted to them, if not for righteousness, at least for obedience, and opened to many of them a vista to future office and power. Under such circumstances, their support of the war cannot be taken as irresistible proof of their patriotism. Nor is the evidence of the patriotism of their opponents afforded by their vote for an acknowledged falsehood, and their grant of men and money to wage a war admitted to be iniquitous, of a more conclusive character. The Democrats, according to the orthodox rule, showed their faith by their works, while the unbelieving Whigs rested their justification on their works alone. Denying the necessity, expediency, and justice of the war, as well as the wisdom and integrity of Mr. Polk, they surrendered to him the army and navy, with an additional force of 50,000 men, and all the money he desired, to carry fire and sword into Mexico, and to dismember that Republic. To have done all this with a single desire to benefit their own country, would have been at least a very questionable benevolence, and a very ambiguous patriotism.

Mr. Clay, the distinguished and beloved leader of the Whig party, in a public speech delivered in Kentucky, declared that the preamble to the war bill, "falsely attributed the commencement of the war to the act of Mexico." He then added—"*I have no doubt of the patriotic motives* of those who, after struggling to divest the bill of that flagrant error, found themselves constrained to vote for it; but I must say, that no earthly consideration would have ever tempted *me* to vote for a bill with a PALPABLE FALSEHOOD stamped on its face. Almost idolizing truth, as I do, I never, never could have voted for the bill." Of course, Mr. Clay's patriotism so far differs from that of the gentlemen alluded to, that it cannot lead *him* to sacrifice TRUTH for the cause of his country. He then goes on to remark, that the war of 1812, against Great Britain, was of a widely different character from the present, being a *just* war, and so admitted by its opponents, who, from motives of *policy*, refused to support it, and that in consequence, "they lost, and justly lost the public confidence," that is, they lost their political ascendency. He then asks the following very significant question: "Has not the apprehension of a *similar fate*, in a case widely different, repressed a fearless expression of their real sentiments *in some of our public men?*" This interrogatory has all the force of an assertion. To what public men does he refer? Surely not to Mr. Polk and his party. His remarks irresistibly confine his question to the "some" Whigs in Congress, who, from fear of losing their popularity, as the Federalists had before done, voted for the "palpable falsehood," the war and the supplies. If he intended to intimate, and on no other supposition is his language intelligible, that these Whigs voted as they did from *selfish* considerations, it is deeply to be lamented that a man almost idolizing truth, should have hazarded the declaration, that he had no doubt of their *patriotic motives*. We have already noticed the frank admission of the *American Review*, a Whig organ, that on this occasion the Whig members seemed more solicitous about "*personal popularity*" than for the cause of "TRUTH AND RIGHT."

Subsequent developments have abundantly confirmed the intimations of Mr. Clay and of the *Review*. It has been shown by the declarations of certain Whig members of Congress, published in the newspapers, that on the day war was declared, they were urged to vote for the bill, on the ground that "it would be *bad policy* to oppose the bill," and that this opinion was supported by a reference to the political fate of those who had opposed the war of 1812 against Great Britain. In a deliberate consent to sacrifice the peace of the country, to squander its treasures and its blood, and to trample under foot both truth and justice, from considerations of party policy, and for the purpose of acquiring personal popularity, and with it, office and its emoluments, it is not easy to detect those "*patriotic motives*" which Mr. Clay very courteously and undoubtingly attributes to the Whig members who voted for the war.

On the 13th May, 1846, Congress voted that "*By the act of the Republic of Mexico,* war existed between that Republic and the United States." On the 31st January, 1848, a new House of Representatives voted, that this same war was "unconstitutionally and unnecessarily begun *by the President of the United States.*" In the affirmative of this latter vote, we find recorded the names of *fifteen* Whig Members who had belonged to the late house, and whose names are also recorded in the affirmative of the *former vote.* The last declaration, however truthful, was no doubt considered equally *good policy* with the first, inasmuch as a presidential election was approaching, and it was expedient to throw odium on the rival party, and on Mr. Polk its acknowledged head.

One of the gentlemen who voted for *both* declarations thus expressed his opinion of this self-same war: "Entertaining these views upon the origin and purposes of the war, I can consider it in no other light than as a NATIONAL CRIME; but, independent of this, it is an offence against the *moral* spirit of our time, a retrograde step in the movement of humanity, a violent wresting of our national energy and national resources, to unnatural and mischievous uses. I have no desire that a single Mexican wife should be made a widow, a single Mexican child an orphan; and I would rather that my country should sit down in honest shame, than purchase, at the price of rapine, and tears, and blood, the 'unjust glory' of waving her flag over all the wide continent that stretches between the stormy Atlantic and the shores of the tranquil sea:

'One murder makes a villain, thousands a hero.' "*

A little timely reflection might have warned this gentleman that the fifty thousand troops he voted to place under the orders of Mr. Polk to prosecute "a national crime," might peradventure cause many Mexican widows and orphans, acquire by conquest "unjust glory," and make more than one "hero."

He alone who governs himself by the laws of God will act consistently; while he who follows the ever-varying monitions of party policy will often be found wandering in tortuous paths.

History and daily observation compel the conviction, that patriotism is more frequently professed than practised, and that much which assumes the name, and passes current with the world, is utterly spurious. Yet it is also true, that the patriotism which seeks the public good, in obedience to the Divine will, and in accordance with the precepts of the Gospel, far from being an imaginary, is a real and active virtue. It is, indeed, to be found in camps and senates, but these are not its exclusive nor its favorite haunts. This patriotism inspires many a prayer for the peace, virtue, and happiness of the nation, and prompts innumerable efforts and costly sacrifices of time and money for the temporal and spiritual welfare of our fellow-coun-

* Speech of Mr. Marsh, Feb. 18, 1848.—Con. Globe.

trymen. Were we permitted to trace effects to their causes, in the moral government of the world, we should doubtless find that much of our prosperity as a people flows from the labors of faithful pastors, self-denying Sunday-school teachers, and sincere, zealous, but humble Christian men and women. It is chiefly by such patriotism, gentle and noiseless as the dew of Heaven, that our land is clothed with moral verdure and beauty, and that those who sit under their own vine, with none to make them afraid, are indebted for the peace and security they enjoy.

Patriotism springing from obedience to God, guided by His laws, and exercised in official station for the national welfare, at the certain and willing loss of popular favor and personal advantage, is perhaps the highest perfection to which this virtue can attain. Our own recent history affords an illustrious instance of such patriotism. We proceed to trace the course of John Quincy Adams, because we find in it a sanction for almost every moral and political sentiment maintained in these pages; and also because his example is well calculated to quicken and to purify the love of country, and to convey to all lessons of virtue and true wisdom.

CHAPTER XXXVI.

JOHN QUINCY ADAMS.

CUSTOM has sanctioned certain funeral honors on the decease of a man who has been President of the Republic, which, like the salute given to a military officer, affords no evidence of respect for his personal character. The honors paid to the memory of Adams were the outpourings of the heart of a great nation. The strife of faction was stilled, the voice of party was dumb, and the whole American people acknowledged and deplored the departure of a PATRIOT. It is interesting, and may be useful, to inquire into the cause of this wonderful and universal attestation, in the midst of high political excitement, to the merits of a public man.

Mr. Adams had long been in public life; but his career, for the most part, had not been calculated to win the affections of the people. It was commenced in the Federal party. He incurred the deep hostility of that party by abandoning it at a critical and important juncture, and exposed his motives to suspicion by accepting office from his late opponents. The democratic party, which had welcomed him into its bosom, and had abundantly rewarded what was deemed his apostacy, he abandoned in turn, and, as a Whig, became its active and zealous foe. Much of his life was passed at foreign courts; and, although always able, he gathered no unusual laurels in the field of diplomacy. Having never borne arms, no military halo encircled his brow. In 1824, at a period of singular party disorganization, he was one of *four* candidates for the Presidency. He received *fewer* votes than one of his competitors, but, as neither had a majority of the whole number, the election devolved on the House of Representatives. By that body he was chosen President by the smallest possible majority, and the vote of one of the largest States was decided in his favor by a single ballot. Instantly the whole country resounded with charges against him of base corruption. His administration, although pure, did not give general satisfaction. He was a candidate for the succeeding term, and was defeated by a large majority; and he retired to private life, one of the most unpopular of all the prominent politicians of the country.

In 1831, to the surprise of all, and to the mortification of many of his friends, he accepted a seat in the House of Representatives. He came there avowedly, to use his own words, "bound in allegiance to no party, whether sectional or political." He was thus deprived of that countenance and support which parties give both to their leaders and their tools. He was, it is true, confessedly a Whig; but so independent was his course, that he was continually ridiculed as "running off the track," and regarded as a man not to be depended on. He exerted but little influence in the House, and attracted but little attention till about the year 1836.

At this time the agitation of the anti-slavery question roused the holders of slaves to great exasperation, and alarmed the two political parties at the North, lest their supposed sympathy with the cause of human freedom might weaken the friendship of their southern allies, and deprive them of their coöperation in the pursuit of office. Hence Whigs and Democrats contended which should show the most devotion to slavery, the most zeal in suppressing the liberty of the press, and the freedom of discussion. Both whig and democratic Governors assailed the Abolitionists in their official Messages, threatening them with the penalties of the law. Mobs were raised in the large cities, by the efforts of rival newspapers and politicians. Printing presses were destroyed, individuals assaulted, churches sacked, and the freedom of the Post-Office shamefully invaded with the connivance of a democratic President and cabinet, postmasters being permitted to abstract from the mails whatever they deemed offensive to the slaveholders. But vain would it be to suppress anti-slavery tracts and newspapers, if a few independent members were permitted to make anti-slavery speeches on the floor of Congress, and which the press would spread on the wings of the wind as a portion of the ordinary debates. Such speeches had been made, and they were called forth by anti-slavery petitions. Hence, it was resolved to abolish the right of petition, and the freedom of discussion in Congress, on all subjects relating to slavery. It was on the 26th May, 1836, that the House of Representatives passed, without debate, the celebrated rule, known from the name of its author, as the Pinkney Gag. From this moment, utterly discarding all considerations of political influence, Mr. Adams devoted himself to the defence of constitutional liberty, assailed by the southern slaveholders, and their northern allies.* On the question of the gag-rule, prostrating alike the right of petition, and the freedom of discussion on the floor of the House, Mr. Adams, being precluded by the previous question from offering any remark, refused to vote, exclaiming, when his name was called, "I consider this resolution as a direct violation of the rules of this House, of the Con-

* Of seventy-nine northern Democrats, sixty-two voted with the slaveholders, and only one of forty-four northern Whigs.

stitution of the United States, and of the rights of my constituents." He then demanded that his refusal to vote, and the reason assigned, should be entered upon the minutes. The boldness and independence which he exhibited on this occasion, so novel and unexpected, so utterly at variance with the usual deferential submission of northern politicians to southern dictation, instantly riveted upon him the gaze of his countrymen, nor was that gaze intermitted, till twelve years afterwards, it beheld his honored and revered remains deposited in the tomb of his ancestors. He declared, in the presence of its authors and supporters, that the gag-rule was "an infamous resolution." He fearlessly imputed it to corrupt motives, and waged against it, a most vigorous and unceasing warfare, in speeches, in public addresses, in letters through the press to his own constituents, and to the people of the United States, till in December, 1845, he had the glory of carrying a resolution for its abolition.

Of all abominations in the sight of southern members of Congress, the alleged right of slaves to offer petitions to the national legislature, was the most atrocious, striking, in their opinion, a fatal blow at the authority of the masters. Mr. Adams, however, told the House, "If slaves were laboring under grievances and afflictions not incident to their condition as slaves, but to their natures as human beings, born to trouble as the sparks fly upward, and it were in the power and competency of the House to afford them relief, and if the House would permit me, I most assuredly would present their petition; and, if that avowal deserves the censure of the House, I am ready to receive it. I would not deny the right of petition to slaves. I would not deny it to a horse or a dog, if they could articulate their sufferings, and I could relieve them."

When threatened with an indictment for his anti-slavery

course by a southern Member, he replied, "Did the gentleman think to frighten me from my purpose by his threat of a grand jury? *He mistook his man.* I am not to be frightened from the discharge of a duty by the indignation of the gentleman, nor by all the grand juries in the Universe."

As slavery demanded for its protection, the suppression of the right of petition and the liberty of speech, he freely canvassed its claims to such sacrifices, on the part of the free states. He spoke of it as "The God-defying institution." Mr. Clay had contended that that was property which the *laws* made so. "The soul of man," said Mr. Adams, "cannot by human laws, be made the property of another. The owner of a slave is the owner of a living corpse; but he is not the owner of a man." He declared, "unyielding hostility against slavery is interwoven with every pulsation of my heart. Resistance against it, feeble and inefficient as the last accents of a failing voice may be, shall still be heard, while the power of utterance shall remain." In the presence of the slaveholding members he avowed, that in his prayers to Almighty God he daily invoked Him for the abolition of slavery. The internal traffic did not escape his anathema: "If," said he, "the African slave trade was piracy, the American slave trade could not be innocent, nor could its aggravated turpitude be denied." From the admitted wickedness of the African slave trade, he very logically deduced the wickedness of slavery itself. "If," said he, "the African slave trade be piracy, human reason cannot resist, nor can human sophistry refute, the conclusion, that the essence of the crime consists not in the *trade*, but in slavery. Trade has nothing in itself criminal by the law of nature."

At a time when politicians and pretended patriots were endeavoring to suppress the discussion of slavery, as fatal to the preservation of the Union, he delivered a Fourth of July address, in which he declared, that the "free and unrestrained discussion of the rights and wrongs of slavery, far from endangering the union of these States, is the *only condition* upon which the Union can be preserved and perpetuated. Are you to bless the earth beneath your feet because it spurns the footstep of a slave, and then to choke the utterance of your voice lest the sound of liberty should be re-echoed from the Palmetto groves, with the discordant notes of disunion? No! No!"

In a letter to his constituents, he thus described the state of the country: "What see we now? Communities of slaveholding braggarts of freedom, setting at defiance the laws of nature and of nature's God, restoring slavery where it had been extinguished (Texas), and vainly dreaming to make it eternal. Forming in the sacred name of liberty, constitutions of government, and interdicting to the legislative authority, the most blessed of all human powers, the power of giving liberty to the slave! Governors of States urging upon their legislatures, to make the exercise of the freedom of speech to propagate the rights of the slave to freedom, felony without benefit of clergy. Ministers of the Gospel, like the priest in the parable, coming and looking at the bleeding victim of the highway robber, and passing on the other side! or baser still, perverting the pages of the sacred volume, to turn into a code of slavery the very Word of God! Infuriated mobs murdering the peaceful minister of Christ, for the purpose of extinguishing the light of a printing press, and burning with unhallowed fire, the hall of freedom, the orphan school, and the Church devoted to the worship of God! and last of all, both Houses of Congress turning a deaf ear to hundreds of thousands of petitioners, and quibbling away their duty to read and listen and consider in doubtful disputations whether they shall receive, or, receiving, refuse to read or hear the complaints of their fellow-citizens and fellow-men!" In a letter to the people of the United States, he avowed his humiliation in beholding "the ignominious transformation of the people who had commenced their career by the Declaration of Independence, into a nation of slaveholders, and slave-breeders."

Addressing the slaveholders on the floor of Congress, he said, "I know well that the doctrine of the Declaration of Independence, that 'all men are born free and equal,' is held at the South as incendiary doctrine, and deserves lynching—that the Declaration itself is a farago of abstractions. I know all this perfectly, and that is the very reason I want to put my foot upon such doctrine, that I want to drive it back to its fountain—its corrupt fountain—and pursue it, until it is made to disappear from this land, and from the world. Sir, this philosophy of the South, has done more to blacken the character of this country in Europe, than all other causes put together. They point to us as a nation of liars and hypocrites, who publish to the world that all men are born free and equal, and then hold a large portion of our own population in bondage." Again, "As its (slavery) basis rests exclusively upon physical force, to physical force will it resort, not only to sustain its own institutions, but to encroach upon the institutions of freedom elsewhere. This disposition is already manifested in many ways, in the brutal treatment experienced by citizens of the free States, if but suspected of favoring abolition in the slaveholding jurisdictions, in the insolent demands upon the free States to deliver up their citizens for alleged offences against the slave laws—in the conspiring of American slaveholders in a foreign land against the life of one of the great champions of human liberty*—in the ruffian threats of assassination addressed to members of Congress for daring to present your petitions—in the surrender of the post-office to lynching law—in the murder of Lovejoy —in the burning of Pennsylvania Hall—in Southern commercial conventions to force the National channels of trade from North to South—in Southern railways and banking companies combined to link the mammon of the West to to the Moloch of the South—and in the strains of commendation upon all land-robbing practices of the Anglo-Saxons, and their virtuous abhorrence of Custom-Houses, embellished by their blackleg revenue and punctuality for *their debts of honor.*"

Utterly discarding the base sentiment, "Our country, right or wrong," he denounced the foreign policy of the administration, in resisting the claim made by Great Britain to visit vessels bearing the national flag, and suspected of being engaged in the African slave trade, to ascertain whether the flag was not fraudulently assumed. He asserted that measures were systematically pursued or projected to force the country into a war with England, for the protection of the slave trade. "Under the pretext of resisting the right of search, the most false principles have been advanced as the law of nations. Great Britain has never claimed the right to search American vessels. No such thing—on the contrary, she has explicitly disclaimed any such pretension, and that to the whole extent we can possibly demand. We deny to her the right to board pirates who hoist the American flag—yes, to search British vessels, too, that have been declared pirates by the law of nations—pirates by the law of Great Britain—pirates by the laws of the United States—that is the de-

* In reference of the attempt of Mr. Stevenson, from Virginia, and Hamilton, of South Carolina, made in London to force Daniel O'Connell into a duel.

mand of our late Minister to London. Now, behind all this exceeding zeal against the right of search is the question not brought to view, and that is, the support and perpetuation of the African slave trade. That is the real question between the ministers of America and Great Britain—whether slave-trading pirates, by merely hoisting the American flag, shall be saved from capture. I must say, that if it be true that the interference of our Minister in France (General Cass) was the occasion of the refusal by France to ratify the Quintuple treaty (for the suppression of the African slave trade), I do not hold that procedure in much admiration; it comes too near success in doing wrong."

Now it should be recollected, that this denial of the right of visitation, and the interference of General Cass, were both sustained by the Whig party, through Mr. WEBSTER then Secretary of State.

Mr. Adams astounded the southern members, by insisting, in a formal argument, that in case of war, or insurrection, the General Government had a discretionary power to manumit the slaves, and also by his audacity in asking leave to propose the following amendment to the Constitution, to be submitted by Congress to the several States, viz.: "From and after the 4th day of July, 1842, there shall be, throughout the United States, no hereditary slavery, but on and after that day every child born in the United States shall be *free.*"

A bill having been brought in, giving the right of suffrage "to all free white males," of the age of twenty-one years, and who had resided a certain time within the limits of Alexandria, he moved to strike out the word *white,* and supported his motion in an able and sarcastic speech. He asked "If this principle of universal suffrage was to be adopted, admitting paupers, idiots, lunatics, and the refuse of the prisons, why a man whose skin is not white, but who performs all the duties of a good citizen, a good husband, a good father, and a kind neighbor, should not be entitled to vote as well as a white man? I ask what is a *white* man? Is it the color of the skin that constitutes a white man? Then there are twenty members of this House who are not white men by that criterion. I pledge myself to bring forward a hundred respectable colored men of this city with complexions whiter than those of twenty members of this House. Would you then say, would the courts say, that this should be settled by going into the genealogy of the person? In this country it is a strange idea to look into a man's genealogy to ascertain whether he has a right to vote. Tell me why you insist on giving this privilege to the worst of your own color, while you refuse it to the best of those who have a portion of the blood of another race?"

The southern members rejected with scorn all recognition of the Republic of Hayti, on account of the complexion of its citizens; and Mr. Adams incurred their indignation by zealously maintaining the duty and policy of forming diplomatic relations with it.

In 1839, between thirty and forty Africans, recently imported into Havana, on their way from that port to the plantations of their two purchasers, took possession of the vessel, and arrived with their captive masters in our waters. The whole sympathy of the Government and of the slaveholders was immediately enlisted in behalf of the two men, who, in defiance of law and treaties, had obtained possession of these Africans, as legally entitled to freedom as themselves, and who had attempted to avoid capture by British cruizers by means of false and fraudulent Custom House passports. The case was brought into the Supreme Court of the United States, and Mr. Adams volunteered his services as their counsel. He embraced the opportunity of exposing the inhuman subserviency of the Government to the slaveholding interest, and obtained a judgment in behalf of the freedom of the unfortunate Africans.

The reader need not be reminded of the scorn and detestation in which abolitionists at this time were held at the North as well as at the South, nor how *patriotic* were all attempts then deemed to silence them by insult and violence. One of the most despised portions of these despised people, the Massachusetts Anti-Slavery Society, at a season of high public excitement, invited Mr. Adams to attend one of their celebrations. He replied, "It would give me great pleasure to comply with the invitation," and after excusing himself on account of want of health and leisure, added, "I rejoice that the defence of human freedom is falling into younger and more vigorous hands. The youthful champions of the rights of human nature have buckled, and are buckling on their armor, and the scourging overseer, and the lynching lawyer, and the servile sophist, and the faithless scribe, and the priestly parasite, will vanish before them like Satan touched with the spear of Ithuriel. You have a glorious and arduous career before you; and it is among the consolations of my last days, that I am able to cheer you in the pursuit, and exhort you to be stedfast and immoveable."

But the crowning crime of the abolitionists, was their union with English abolitionists in anti-slavery conventions held in London.

A northern member of Congress, sent under his frank to Mr. Polk, then Governor of Tennessee, certain proceedings of the "World's Convention." The Governor returned an insulting answer, concluding, "It is a matter of sincere regret that any American citizen should be guilty of such HIGH TREASON to the first principles upon which the States became united." Mr. Polk published his epistle, and it no doubt prepared the way for his elevation to the Presidency. In May, 1843, as a delegate to an Anti-Slavery Convention in LONDON, was leaving Boston, he received the following lines :

"My dear sir—I have only time to say God bless you and *your enterprize*, for which I have no other prayer to make, than that its success may herald my *nunc dimittis*.

"J. Q. ADAMS."

When Mr. Polk declared it to be high treason for any American to countenance these foreign Anti-Slavery Conventions, he little anticipated, that he should hereafter deem it expedient, officially to pronounce the writer of such a note, "a great and patriotic citizen."

We have already noticed Mr. Adams's strenuous opposition to the annexation of Texas, and his stern denunciation of the policy long pursued towards Mexico, and we have found his name associated with the little band who dared to vote against the Mexican war, and who, in derisive but prophetic language, were called "The immortal fourteen."

But if to question the justice of the war, was giving "aid and comfort" to the enemy, how deep the treason while the war was waging, to refuse in aiding its prosecution! Yet a few weeks before his death, Mr. Adams voted for a resolution withdrawing our troops from Mexico, relinquishing all claims for the expenses of the war, and establishing the desert between the Nueces and the Rio Grande the boundary between the two countries; and almost the last vote he ever gave, was for an amendment to the bill raising a loan of sixteen millions, viz. :

"Provided that no part of the money received under

the authority of this act shall be applied to any expenses that shall hereafter be incurred by the prosecution of the war with Mexico."

If Mr. Adams shocked the slaveholders by the freedom of his language, he was no less regardless of the sensibilities of their allies. Irritated by their subserviency, and their constant endeavors to thwart him, he exclaimed on the floor, "There is no end to the devices and ingenuity of *the servile part of this house,* for the purpose of suppressing the right of petition. I do not mean by the servile part of this house, the slaveholding part of it." He asserted "Northern subserviency to southern dictation is the price paid by a northern administration (Mr. Van Buren's) for southern support. The people of the north still support, by their suffrages, the men who have truckled to southern domination. I believe it impossible that this total subversion of every principle of liberty should be much longer submitted to by the people of the free States of this Union. If they choose to be represented by slaves, they will find servility enough to represent and betray them." On another occasion, he pronounced the northern Democrats "The consistent Swiss guards of southern slavery." Nor was his notice of the northern Whigs much more flattering. They were thus characterized by him: "The languid, compromising non-resistants of the north, afraid of answering a fool according to his folly, and flinching from the attitude of defiance flung in their faces by the bullying threat of readiness to meet them 'here or elsewhere.'"

He was as fearless in his assaults upon individuals, as upon classes. Congressional duelling excited his especial abhorrence, both for its wickedness, and because, as he contended, it was resorted to by southern members for the purpose of intimidating northern representatives. In a debate, referring to the subject, he spoke of the death of a northern man who had fallen in a duel, as "a deliberate murder committed on a member of this house," and alluded to a gentleman present who had acted as a second in this duel, and was supposed to have instigated it, as a man having come into that house "with his hands and face dripping with the blood of murder, the blotches of which were yet hanging upon him."

He as freely condemned what he thought wrong in the character and conduct of his country, as he did in parties and individuals. On the floor of Congress he declared, "You make and break treaties with the Indian tribes, whenever either to make or break treaties with them happens to suit the purposes of the President and a majority of both houses of Congress." Again—"In the treatment of the African and native American races, we have subverted the maxims and degenerated from the virtues of our fathers." In a published letter, respecting a celebration of West India emancipation, he avowed he had not taken part in it, "from shame for the honor and good name of my country, whose government has been now, for a series of years, pursuing and maturing a counteraction of the purpose of universal emancipation, and organizing an opposite system for the maintenance and perpetuation of slavery throughout the earth." After referring to various disgraceful features in the conduct of the Government and people, he added, "O my friends, I have no heart to join in the festivity on the 1st of August, the British anniversary of disenthralled humanity. While all this, and infinitely more than I could tell, but that I would spare the blushes of my country, weigh down my spirits with the uncertainty, sinking into my grave, as I am, whether she is doomed to be numbered with the first liberators or the last oppressors of the race of immortal man."

It would have been an anomaly in the history of human nature, if a public man, thus outraging almost every popular prejudice, pouring contempt upon political meanness and corruption, spurning the commonly received tests of patriotism, and hurling defiance at all the demagogues of the day, had not excited against himself deep and wide-spread hostility. Truth, justice, virtue, and patriotism all forbid, as base and criminal, the suppression of the historical fact that, for years, John Quincy Adams was the most hated man in the American Republic. To the Whig party he was an encumbrance, perpetually interrupting the desired harmony between its northern and southern sections, by introducing the topic of slavery, and raising questions on which "policy" required the party to vote against him. Scorning the control of party discipline and caucus dictation, he pursued his own course, without asking or receiving permission from the leaders. At the organization of the last house of Representatives he ever attended, he dared to vote *against* the Whig nominee for Clerk, and by so doing, nearly secured the re-election of the late faithful and efficient, but democratic incumbent. The Whig party of his own State did not deem it expedient to assume the responsibility of his "fanaticism," by returning him to the Senate of the United States, as they had the power to do; and the Whig presses throughout the Union, with few exceptions, were nearly as strenuous in condemning his congressional conduct, as were his political opponents.

It can readily be understood, that the slaveholders looked upon him as an incendiary of the most odious as well as dangerous description; while the demagogues of every name and party were zealous in manifesting *their* patriotism, by pouring obloquy upon a man at once so distinguished and so unpopular. The northern Democrats especially, were careful to improve the opportunity of testifying their devotion to the cause of human bondage, by the most unmeasured hostility to its mighty opponent. Said the Albany *Argus* (the recognized organ of the New York serviles), " How discreditable is it to the country, that the MASSACHUSETTS MADMAN is permitted not only to outrage all order and decorum in the House, but to scatter incendiary evil and excitement throughout the country."

The *Richmond Inquirer*, then edited by the same person whom Mr. Polk afterwards selected to take charge of the official journal of the administration, announced that Mr. Adams was considered " A GENERAL NUISANCE, whom the voice of the House, if not of the people, must hereafter *abate*." The abatement intended was expulsion from Congress. A New York paper, alluding with approbation to this hint of expulsion, extended it to the few members who acted with Mr. Adams, and remarked— " But we are apprehensive there is not enough firmness or *patriotism* in Congress to adopt so stern and decisive a mode of rebuking the audacity of the MISCREANT TRAITORS."

The *Charleston Mercury*, the leading Journal in South Carolina, in reference to Mr. Adam's course in Congress, declared (1837): " Public opinion in the South, would now we are sure justify an immediate resort to force by the southern delegation, and even on the floor of Congress, were they forthwith to SEIZE AND DRAG FROM THE HALL any man who dared to insult them as that eccentric *old showman*, John Quincy Adams, has dared to do."

The *Washington Globe*, the acknowledged organ of the Democratic party at the seat of Government, spoke of Mr. Adams, as " a vulgar old man, who has forfeited all claim, by his incorrigible malevolence, to the respect otherwise due to his age and station," and declared "all his zeal, all his sympathies are against his country."

At a public dinner in Virginia, the company drank as a toast: "John Quincy Adams—once a man, twice a child, and now a DEMON." At a fourth of July dinner in South Carolina, the following toast was given: "May we never want a hangman to prepare a halter for John Quincy Adams." The company not only drank the toast, but accompanied it with nine cheers. In 1842, the democracy of Ohio, having the control of the Legislature, availed itself of the opportunity of making an acceptable offering at the shrine of slavery, by declaring in the name and by the authority of the State in joint resolution, that, "John Quincy Adams had subjected himself to the merited censure and reprehension of his countrymen;" and "that the House of Representatives of the United States owed it to themselves, to stamp his course and conduct with the severest marks of its indignant disapprobation and censure."

But the hatred felt against Mr. Adams, was not manifested only in indecent toasts, newspaper scurrility, and democratic obsequiousness to the slaveholders. Mr. Adams in a speech in the House (January 21st, 1839), observed: "I have received letters from various quarters of the country, with post-marks showing that they have been mailed at places very distant from each other, containing many of them positive threats of assassination; others of them filled with friendly advice, assuring me, that if I continued to present petitions similar to those I have heretofore presented in this House, my days are numbered, and I never shall survive the present session."

It was, however, on the floor of Congress, that the malignity towards him was excited to its greatest intensity. In a speech to his constituents (1842), alluding to the charge against him of using harsh language, he remarked: "So far as any friend or impartial person may have thought me blameable in that respect, I would ask him to consider that the adversaries with whom I have had to contend face to face, have pursued me with a violence and rancor unparalleled in the history of this country. That twice in the space of five years, I have for the single offence of persisting to assert the right of the people to petition, and the freedom of speech and of the press, been dragged before the House in which I was your Representative, as a culprit to be censured or expelled; and when, after ten days of the most unrelenting persecution, I have been barely released from its fury, I have been still denounced as the cause of the waste of time consumed by my persecutors in their struggle to accomplish my ruin. On both occasions, the fury of the whole mass of Southern slavery was concentrated over my head, for the avowed purpose of breaking down whatever of good name I had to leave as an inheritance to my children; in order that my signal ruin might strike terror to the heart of your every other Representative, and leave slavery the lord of the ascendant for all future time throughout the North American Union."

For the purpose of insult, a petition professing to be from *slaves*, asking for his expulsion, was sent to him by mail for presentation. On the 6th February, 1837, he informed the Speaker, that he had in his possession a petition purporting to come from slaves, and inquired whether it came within the gag-rule, excluding Anti-slavery petitions? Immediately, cries of "expel him," "expel him," were heard throughout the hall, and Mr. Thompson from South Carolina, moved: "That the Hon. John Quincy Adams, by the attempt just made by him to introduce a petition purporting on its face to be from slaves, has been guilty of a gross disrespect to the House, and that he be *instantly* brought to the bar to receive the severest censure of the Speaker." In his speech on the occasion, he observed: "If the *juries* of this District have, as I doubt not they have, proper intelligence and spirit, he may yet be made amenable to *another tribunal*, and we may yet see *an incendiary brought to condign punishment*."

After three day's discussion, the attempt to degrade Mr. Adams for asking a question, being found impracticable, was abandoned.

In 1842, Mr. Adams was again insulted by a petition from Georgia, forwarded to him through the mail, asking for his removal as Chairman of the Committee of Foreign Relations, on account of his monomania. He presented it to the House, and Mr. Hopkins of Virginia, immediately moved its reference to the committee, *with instructions to choose another Chairman.* Mr. Adams claimed to be heard in his defence, declaring that the feeling against him was "a slave-holding, slave-trading, and slave-breeding feeling." He was not allowed to proceed in his defence, and the motion of Mr. Hopkins was dropped. The brief calm that ensued, was but the precursor of a tempest; for, three days after, Mr. Adams presented a petition, praying Congress to take measures for dissolving the Union; and moved its reference to a committee, with instructions to report reasons why the prayer of the petition should *not* be granted.

The petition itself was brief, containing no allusion to slavery, and was, in fact, *an exact copy* of one that had some years before, been got up by certain of the South Carolina nullifiers.* The true paternity of the petition

* The reasons assigned in the petition were: "First, because

was at the time unknown to the House, and the Southern members, regarding it only in the light of an abolition document, seized the occasion, to bring disgrace upon Mr. Adams, under the pretext of their own extreme devotion to the Union. Mr. Gilmer of Virginia, and lately Governor of the State, immediately offered a resolution declaring "that in presenting to the consideration of the House, a petition for the dissolution of the Union, the member from Massachusetts, has justly incurred the censure of this House." In his speech he avowed he was endeavoring to stop the music of him, who,

> "In the space of one revolving moon
> Was statesman, poet, fiddler, and buffoon."

That evening between forty and fifty of the slaveholding members met in council to consider how they should proceed. Mr. Marshall, of Kentucky, made the meeting acquainted with the course he proposed taking in the morning, a course more decided than Mr, Gilmer's resolution. Accordingly the next morning he introduced a substitute for the resolution before the House, consisting of a long preamble, setting forth the perjury and treason to which Congress was invited by the Petition; together with a series of resolutions, concluding with, "Resolved, That the aforesaid John Quincy Adams, for this insult, the first of the kind ever offered to the Government, and for the wound he has permitted to be aimed through his instrumentality at the Constitution and existence of his country, the peace, security and liberty of the people of these States, might well be held to merit expulsion

no union can be agreeable or permanent, which does not present prospects of reciprocal benefits. Second, because a vast proportion of the resources of one section of the Union, is annually drained to sustain the views and course of another section Third, because, judging from the history of past nations, that union, if persisted in, in the present course of things, will certainly overwhelm the whole nation in utter destruction."

from the National Councils, and the House deem it an act of grace and mercy when they only inflict upon him their severest censures for conduct so utterly unworthy of his own past relations to the State, and his present position: This they hereby do, for the maintenance of their own purity and dignity; for the rest, they turn him over to his own conscience, and *the indignation of all true American citizens.*" On the reading of the resolutions, there was a *burst of applause from the Galleries and the House*, so much so, that the Speaker interfered to repress it.

The malignity of this assault upon Mr. Adams was equalled only by its absurdity and its impudence. In presenting the petition he had expressly declared his disapprobation of its object. Congress being authorized by the Constitution to propose unlimited alterations in that instrument, every citizen has a constitutional right to ask them to propose any alteration he desires, although it may virtually dissolve the Confederacy; and it is, moreover, preposterous to maintain that a union formed by consent of the partners, cannot by the same consent be severed. It must also be recollected that the assault proceeded from a sectional party, that for a long series of years, has been threatening to dissolve the Union, if not permitted to govern it. Instead of instantly spurning this ridiculous and wicked persecution, the House, by a formal vote of 118 to 75,* resolved to consider the charges against Mr. Adams. He was thereupon put on trial, and Mr. Marshall and Mr. Wise of Virginia, acted as the leading Counsel of the prosecution. The latter acquitted the accused of insanity, and avowed his conviction that "he was more wicked than weak;" but at the same time pronounced him "politically dead—dead as Burr—dead as Arnold. The people would look upon him with wonder,

* Only two northern Democrats voted in the negative!

would shudder and retire." The dead culprit, however, evinced most astonishing vitality. The accused became the accuser; his very persecution was proof of a conspiracy against the liberties of the North; and, abandoning the defence of himself, he arraigned the slave-holders at the bar of the nation for endeavoring to destroy the right of Habeas Corpus, the right of trial by jury, the freedom of the Post Office, the liberty of speech, of the press, and of petition, and in short, to destroy all the constitutional rights of the North adverse to human bondage—and that for the purpose of effecting these outrages, they had formed a coalition with the northern Democrats—that if the rights of the North could not be otherwise protected, the petitioners had acted properly, in asking for a dissolution of the Union.

The public watched with intense interest the progress of this momentous trial, and it was quickly perceived on which side victory was inclining. Mr. Gilmer, anxious to arrest a process from which the slave interest was suffering so severely, proposed a compromise—a *nolle prosequi* should be entered, provided the defendant would withdraw the petition he had presented. The proposition met with a positive and indignant refusal. Mr. Adams declared he would not, by withdrawing the petition, sanction the suppression of the right of petition, which was the real object of the prosecution; he had done only his duty, he defied the House, and spurned its proffered mercy. The trial continued to the 7th day, when, on motion of a *southern* member, all proceedings were discontinued.*

* Twenty-five of the southern members, and *all* the northern Whigs united in this vote; but the whole delegation of the northern democracy, with the exception of *six*, refused to unbind the victim whom they were anxious to offer a sacrifice on the altar of slavery, as an earnest and proof of their own fealty. Messrs. Thompson, Wise, and Gilmer, who had distinguished themselves by heaping obloquy upon Mr. Adams, were honored

The next day a new insult was offered to Mr. Adams All the southern members of the Committee of Foreign Relations, four in number, including Messrs. Gilmer and Hunter, of Virginia, and one northern "servile," resigned their seats, avowing that they could not condescend any longer to be associated with their Chairman. The Speaker appointed five southern gentlemen to fill the vacancies, and, of these, three, including Mr. Holmes, of South Carolina, refused the appointment—Mr. Holmes expressly declaring, in a letter to the Speaker, his repugnance to serve with Mr. Adams. Thus no less than eight members of the House professed to think it derogatory to their dignity to sit in the same Committee with John Quincy Adams. The object was to compel him to resign, or the House to remove him.

But this was the last spasm of impotent malice. From the commencement of his trial his reputation rose in public estimation, and it continued to rise, till at the time of his death, it had reached an elevation never surpassed by that of any man on the American Continent, with the single exception of WASHINGTON. The astonishing popularity of this lately defamed and persecuted man, is evinced by the strange and extraordinary praises it extorted from politicians of every description. On the announcement of his death, prominent men on the floor of Congress seized the occasion to make speeches in his honor. Among the eulogists were numbered no less than *three* gentlemen from the *South*. The speeches were, by order of the House, published in a pamphlet, and of this 20,000 copies, adorned with a portrait of the deceased, and a copy of his autograph, were distributed at public expense.

A panegyric on Napoleon, from which all allusion to

with important appointments, by and with the advice and consent of a *Whig* Senate, the two former to foreign missions, and the latter to the post of Secretary of the Navy his military achievements should be excluded, would be regarded as a unique performance, yet it would find its counterpart in these Congressional *oraisons funèbres.* In these the reader is told, in general terms, of the talents, virtue, and patriotism of the deceased; but not a hint is given of that course of conduct which in fact secured for him these very eulogies. This Congressional monument raised to the honor of Adams, gives no intimation that he was the champion of constitutional liberty, the restorer of the right of petition, the indomitable foe of human bondage. No allusion is made to his terrible conflicts and his glorious triumphs. Not a word discloses, that a slave ever breathed on the soil of America; that a slaveholding Republic had been added to the "area of freedom," or that a war was then raging, which Adams had denounced as waged for the extension of slavery, and from which he had voted to withhold supplies. Some of the speakers were minutely accurate in specifying the dates of Mr. Adams's appointments in former times, but all were marvellously oblivious of his *recent* services. One gentleman, preferring fiction to truth, favored the House with a beautiful and touching romance. Said Mr. McDowell, of Virginia—"No human being *ever* entered this Hall, without turning habitually and with heartfelt deference first to *him,* and few ever left it, without pausing as they went, to pour out *blessings* upon that spirit of consecration to the country, which brought and kept him there." Had Messrs. Gilmer, Hopkins, Hunter, and Wise been in their seats, they might possibly have dissented from the accuracy of the picture drawn by their colleague, and disclaimed for themselves the feelings and the acts so eloquently ascribed to all. But judging from the Lethean spirit in which the faculties of the speakers were apparently drowned, it is more probable, that these gentlemen, far from contradicting Mr. McDowell, would have testified to the truth of his statement. Mr. Holmes, of South Carolina, was another of the eulogists. He lamented that death had taken from among them "the gravest, wisest, most revered head"—one "adorned with virtue, learning, and *truth*;" and he called him "the Patriot Father, and the Patriot Sage." It did not, perhaps, occur to this gentleman, that as a few years before he disdainfully refused to be associated with this "Patriot Father, and Patriot Sage," in the Committee of Foreign Relations, it might be interesting to the public to know, how recently, and by what means he had discovered, that his was "the gravest, wisest, and most revered head" in Congress. This same gentleman (Mr. Isaac E. Holmes), as representing the veneration felt by *South Carolina* for the great champion of human rights, and her grief for his death, followed his remains from the city of Washington to their final resting-place in Massachusetts! Having eulogized the great Abolitionist, and paid the last honor to his memory, Mr. Holmes returned to Congress where, while laboring to extend slavery to the Pacific, he pronounced the emphatic words, "I hold it (slavery) to be the greatest blessing that God ever conferred upon man."

To no member of Congress did the charge of giving "aid and comfort" to the enemy apply with more force than to Mr. Adams; yet Mr. Polk, in an official order, declared him to be "a great and patriotic citizen;" and the official journal, robed in mourning, eulogized, as the "illustrious and venerable patriot and statesman," the very man who the editor had formerly affirmed was considered "a general nuisance."

Of course the whole press, of all parties and shades of party, was vocal in praise of the departed patriot; and one of the most profligate of the fraternity, who had ever thrown contempt upon all the objects most dear to his heart, thought it expedient to hold the following language: "Mr. Adams on all occasions we believe, has been open, pure, and uncontaminated, as single-hearted as a child, or an angel."

American citizens in Great Britain, were publicly invited by the American Minister, lately engaged in conducting the Mexican war as one of Mr. Polk's cabinet, to pay honors to the memory of John Quincy Adams: "A patriot, always loving his country above all lands of the earth," and this notwithstanding he was "a Mexican Whig." Public honors were paid to him even by the army in Mexico, although, if the assertions of some of its officers were true, he was a "knave" and a "traitor at heart."

A committee from the House of Representatives, of one from each State, attended the corpse from the capitol in Washington to the tomb in Quincy. The funeral *cortege* in its progress, was everywhere met by large concourses of citizens, municipal officers, and detachments of militia. The whole American people, as with one voice, acknowledged and deplored the departure of a great and virtuous patriot.

When it is recollected that Mr. Adams had changed no one of the many opinions that had exposed him to odium, that in no degree had he departed from that straight-forward course, which had so frequently brought him into violent collision with the Democrats of the North and the slaveholders of the South—and that in his last days he had outraged popular patriotism by opposing an existing war, and attempting to cut off supplies from our victorious armies—surely the revulsion of public opinion in his favor is marvellous and unparalleled.

Whence came it that the same unchanged, inflexible, and

dauntless man, scorning and defying public opinion, and scorning and defying it to his last breath—and who but lately was the object of such general hatred, that the representatives of the people spent a week in laboring to consign him "to the indignation of all true American citizens"—acquired such wonderful popularity, that rival politicians hurried to strew flowers upon his grave, and to let all the world know how very much they loved and admired him. The cause is to be found, first, in the entire confidence of the PEOPLE in his integrity, and their admiration of his talents and moral courage; and secondly, in the deference paid by politicians to public opinion "right or wrong."

The magnificent spectacle he exhibited when alone, unaided, and with but little sympathy he received and gloriously repelled the combined assault of the Northern Democracy and the slave interest, won for him the hearts of the common people.* They looked upon him as a moral phenomenon—a public man who never flattered, but often censured them—a politician who consulted duty and not "policy"—who feared God and not man—who talked as he voted, and voted as he talked—who went with his country and party when right, and *against them* when wrong—who was bold enough to be honest, and honest enough to be bold. This feeling in the community soon displayed itself. The year after his trial, he travelled from Boston to Cincinnati, and his journey was a triumphal progress. Even in the slave states, the tide had turned, and being expected at Wheeling, a crowd assem-

* The following extract from a Pittsburgh paper of 1843, affords a striking illustration of this remark: "As a token of respect for Mr. Adams, all the works in the city were closed yesterday, that the working men might have a chance to bid him welcome. The silence of the engines, the machinery, and the workman's tools was a mightier tribute to Mr. Adams, than the roar of cannon, the strains of music, or the eloquent address."

bled, not to insult, but to do him honor. The brave, frank, honest opponent was regarded with a respect never felt by the slaveholder for the fawning mercenary of the North. Mr. Adams had become the man of the PEOPLE, and was revered and beloved by them as *their* champion, the advocate of *their* rights. His great and acknowledged popularity, at length secured for him respectful treatment on the floor of Congress; and when the whole nation deplored his death, politicians of every name, and from every section of the country, deemed it advisable to unite in building his tomb.

The *facts* which have now been stated respecting Mr. Adams, however interesting in themselves, would have found no place in these pages, did they not illustrate some great truths, having a direct and important bearing on many of the sentiments advanced in the present work. They reiterate the lesson long since taught, of the utter worthlessness of public opinion as a standard of right and wrong. The demoniac cries, "Crucify him, crucify him!" were preceded by "Hosannas to the Son of David;" and the revulsion of feeling we have been considering shows that human nature is the same now as in the first century. Multitudes who, in 1848, did reverence to the "Patriot Father and the Patriot Sage," would have rejoiced ten years before to have caught him in the slave region.

We are taught in a most impressive manner, how exceedingly destitute are many of our public men of independent feelings and opinions. Whether Adams was a "*miscreant traitor*," or "*a great and patriotic citizen*," was a question to be determined, not by bringing his conduct to the test of any moral standard, but by the present feelings of the multitude. When he was supposed to be unpopular, no vituperation was too coarse—when known to be very popular, no praise was too gross, although ridiculously false.

The American people have by acclamation adjudged John Quincy Adams a PATRIOT, a judgment from which not one politician of any name has dared to appeal. This judgment sets aside, condemns, and repudiates almost every test of patriotism prescribed by the demagogues of the day. It has now been decided by a tribunal which these men admit to be infallible, that a man may be a patriot, nay, an "illustrious patriot" according to the official gazette, who openly repudiates the sentiment, "our country, right or wrong"*—who on a question of international law, sides with a foreign government against his own—who gives "aid and comfort" to the enemy by denouncing as unjust the war waged against him, and by striving to withhold supplies from the army sent to fight him—who mourns over the degeneracy of his country and doubts whether she is to be numbered "among the first liberators, or the last oppressors of the race of immortal man"—who, notwithstanding all "the compromises of the Constitution," denounces human bondage as a crime against God, and proposes so to change the Constitution as to effect the immediate abolition of hereditary slavery throughout the American Confederacy, and pouring contempt upon the lying Democracy of the day, claims for the black man the same rights of suffrage that are accorded to his white fellow-citizen.

Such is the character of a PATRIOT, as established by the latest decision of the American public; a decision in which every member of the vast tribunal, from Mr. Polk

* In some verses written by Mr. Adams, shortly before his death, and entitled "Congress, slavery, and an unjust war," are these lines—

"And say not thou, 'My country, right or wrong,'
Nor shed thy blood for an unhallowed cause."

down to the humblest caterer for war and glory, has concurred. It is, indeed, a decision which in its application to others, will be over-ruled, whenever "policy" or passion may require its abrogation; but it is nevertheless of vast importance. It has reversed many corrupt judgments previously given; it will cheer and encourage many weak-hearted patriots, and it may hint to some politicians, that it is possible to acquire popularity by adhering to duty, as well as by listening to the suggestions of "policy."

We have seen Mr. Adams, although constantly occupied in public life, bursting at pleasure the bonds of party, outraging public opinion, and apparently courting defeat and odium—

"Among innumerable false, unmoved—
Unshaken, unseduced, unterrified,
His loyalty he kept, his love, his zeal—
Nor number, nor example with him wrought
To swerve from truth, or change his constant mind."

Surely there must have been some potent principle of action which impelled him to pursue a path so divergent from those usually selected by political aspirants, one to all appearance leading him far from popular applause, and yet in the end conducting him to the very pinnacle of fame. There was such a principle, and it is shadowed forth in the moral with which Mr. M'Dowell "adorned his tale." "His life," said the Virginia eulogist, "has been a continuous and beautiful illustration of the great truth, that while the fear of man is the consummation of all folly, the fear of God is the beginning of wisdom." Unhappy is it for our country, that the reverse of this truth forms the maxim, by which so many of our public men apparently govern their conduct. But what was the secret of the great strength of this moral

Sampson? Since his death, certain letters to his son have been given to the press, and in these we find an answer to the inquiry. It appears, that while at the court of St. Petersburg, in 1811, he commenced a series of letters to his absent child, on the study of the Bible—"the Divine revelation," as he called it. In these he remarks, "I have myself, for many years, made it a practice to read through the Bible once every year. I have always endeavored to read it with the same spirit and temper of mind which I now recommend to you; that is, with the intention and desire that it may contribute to my advancement in wisdom and virtue. My custom is, to read four or five chapters every morning, immediately after rising from my bed. It employs about half an hour of my time, and seems to me the most suitable manner of beginning the day." The following advice to his son seems both indicative of his own future course, and prophetic of its glorious termination:—"Never give way to the pushes of impudence, wrong-headiness, or intractability, which would lead or draw you aside from the dictates of your own conscience and your own sense of right. Till you die, let not your integrity depart from you. Build your house upon the rock, and then let the rains descend, and the flood come, and the winds blow, and beat upon that house, it shall not fall. So promises your blessed Lord and Master." In a most wonderful manner was this promise fulfilled in his own case, even in the present world. But there is a day approaching, when the secrets of all hearts shall be laid open, and when every man shall come to judgment. Then will those who have in this life pursued expediency in preference to duty, learn, when too late, that "the wisdom of this world is foolishness with God."

CHAPTER XXXVII.

WAR, AND THE MEANS OF PREVENTION.

We have endeavored to give the reader some idea of the vast amount of crime and misery resulting from our hostilities with Mexico; yet those hostilities present but a faint image of WAR. All the American troops sent into Mexico, will not number as many as have often been killed and wounded in a single engagement. Had all the battles of the late war occurred at the same time, and on the same field, they would scarcely have equalled a skirmish between the outposts of two European armies. The total number of our troops *officially* reported to have been killed in battle, is less than two thousand! If we would know the horrors of war, not as waged in ancient times, when whole nations contended in arms, with heathen barbarity, but as waged within our own recollection, and by enlightened, civilized, and christian people, let us contemplate the details of only three of a multitude of modern battles.*

JENA—engaged, 200,000 men; killed and wounded, 34,000
EYLAU " 160,000 " " 50,000
BORODINO " 265,000; 1,230 cannon in the field,
25,000 killed, 68,000 wounded—93,000

Napoleon invaded Russia with 450,000 troops, of which number about 400,000 are supposed to have perished, only about 50,000 having returned to their native land. We shudder to reflect on the awful accumulated misery and crime necessarily resulting from such vast slaughter.

* See Alison.

Let it be also recollected that the horrors of the battle field, form but one item, and that comparatively a small one, in the long catalogue of woes, inflicted by war upon the human race. The limits of the present chapter forbid us to dwell on the anguish experienced by the friends and relatives of the killed and wounded—on the vast amount extorted from the avails of labor to defray the expense of war—on the ruin and desolation which mark the track of hostile armies, and the depravation of morals engendered by the license and temptations connected with the military profession. Nor have we space to exhibit the inefficiency and uncertainty of war, as a means of defence against injury, or as an instrument for enforcing justice. But we ask the attention of the reader to a topic seldom investigated, and yet possessing momentous interest—*the folly and the cost of military preparation.*

Of all the false and hoary maxims by which mankind have been deluded, perhaps none has ever exerted such baneful influence on human happiness as that scrap of counterfeit wisdom, "In peace, prepare for war." The proposed object of the counsel, is to *preserve peace* by being prepared to repel, and thereby to prevent aggression. The reasoning is contradicted by the testimony of history and by the character of human nature. No nation was ever better prepared for war than France under Napoleon, and no nation was ever more fiercely and violently attacked; and seldom has any nation been more humbled, compelled not only to receive a sovereign from the hands of her enemies, but to pay the expenses of a foreign army to whose custody she was consigned. Great military strength has no tendency to foster pacific dispositions in its possessor. While the character of man remains unchanged, his cupidity, oppression, and injustice will ordinarily be proportioned to his means of indulging them. Hence, in all ages those nations which have been the best prepared for war, have drank most deeply of its bloody cup. If we examine the history of Europe from 1700, to the general peace in 1815, we shall find that during the 115 years,

Great Britain was engaged in war . .	69 years.
Russia, ...	68 "
France, ...	63 "
Holland, ...	43 "
Portugal, ...	40 "
Denmark, ...	28 "

Pride, arrogance, and the lust of conquest, are the natural and bitter fruits of military preparation—fruits fatal to national peace and happiness.

Strange as may seem the assertion, it is, we believe, nevertheless true, that both Europe and America have expended more money in preparing for war, than in actual hostilities.

In the old world, every important city was anciently walled and fortified, and even in our own days, we have seen the French people already burthened with debt, lavishing millions in erecting a wall thirty miles in circumference around their Capital.*

When we examine the expenditures made in time of peace for military preparation, we are astounded by the stupendous results, and can scarcely credit the testimony of official statements.

* This work of prodigal folly has been falsely ascribed to the late King; it was demanded by the liberal or popular party, under the leadership of Mr. Thiers. The *Republic*, instead of lessening the burdens of the people, have actually, although unmenaced by a single State in Europe, *increased* their military preparations. On the 1st December, 1848, the effective force of the French army amounted to 502,196 men, and 100,432 horses; and to this was added a large navy, with between twenty and thirty thousand seamen.

The following facts are gleaned from a late English statistical work: *

For the six years ending with 1836, the average expenditures of the British Government, exclusive of payments for interest on the national debt, was	£17,101,508
Of this sum, there was paid on an average, for the army, navy, and ordinance,†	12,714,289
Leaving an average annual amount expenditure for civil purposes, of only	4,387,219

It thus appears that the annual payments for military preparations during this period, were no less than *seventy-four* per cent. of the current expenses of the Government, exclusive of £28,574,829, the yearly interest on the war debt!!

The Budget, for 1848, contained the following estimates, viz:

Army, ...	£7,540,405
Navy, ...	8,018,873
Ordinance, ...	2,947,869
Total, ...	£18,507,147

One would have thought that this enormous sum was quite enough to extort from the people of England in a single year for preparation for future and unseen hostilities. But no. The Duke of Wellington, in his speculations on steam navigation, suddenly conceived the idea, that a French army might, in an unexpected moment, be landed upon the British shores from a fleet of steamboats. A panic seized the venerable chief, and he trembled for

* Porter's Progress of the Nation, Vol. ii.

† The average for these six years, from some cause, was unusually small. The total outlay on army, navy, and ordinance, since the peace of 1815, to the year ending 5th January, 1848, is £484,231,985, being an annual average of £15,444,749. The actual payments for military preparation, during the year 1847, amounted to £18,503,146! See tract published by the "Edinburg Financial Reform Association."

the permanency of the Empire. The coasts of England ought immediately to be fortified, and a large home army ought to be forthwith organized and maintained, to fight the French whenever and wherever they might land from their steamers. The construction of the forts would of course furnish fat jobs for innumerable contractors, and the home army would supply younger sons with commissions, rank, and emolument. No wonder that multitudes of patriotic Englishmen were found to favor the insane project. The ministers, it is believed, were deterred from recommending the Duke's plan to Parliament, only by the sturdy opposition of the friends of peace.

A few years since, it was computed that the cost of the military peace establishments of the following Powers, was in the ratio named to the whole expenditure of the several Governments, *exclusive* of payments on account of debt, viz.:

Austria,	as	33 per cent.
France,	,,	38 per cent.
Prussia,	,,	44 per cent.
Great Britain,	,,	74 per cent.

We are fond of comparing our own republican frugality with monarchical prodigality. National vanity, like charity, covers not only a multitude of sins, but also a multitude of follies. The average expenditure of the Federal Government, for the six years, ending with 1840, *exclusive of payments on account of debt*, was $26,474,892. During the same years, the average payments for military and naval purposes, were $21,328,903. Being EIGHTY PER CENT. of the whole amount! A greater ratio than is expended by any monarchy in Europe, in preparing for war.*

* It is true, that during a portion of these six years, we were fighting a few Seminole Indians in Florida. If, then, we take the six years, ending with 1836, a time of profound peace, the ratio

It is with difficulty we can give our assent to the accuracy of such amazing disclosures; and yet our scepticism will vanish when we consider that fortifications, barracks, store-houses, arms, ammunition, and ships of war are all mostly constructed in time of peace. But this is not all. Men are also to be trained and instructed in the art of human slaughter, and kept ready to put in practice at a moment's warning, the lessons they have received.

In 1828, a time of general peace, the standing armies of Europe were estimated at 2,265,500 men.* If to the pay of these men, we add the cost of their food, clothes, lodging, and of the arms, ammunition, barracks, &c., with which they were furnished, and the value of their labor which is lost to the community, we shall not exaggerate their expense to the State when we estimate it at $500 a man, making the sum total of $1,132,750,000, an amount the mind cannot realize. But before we give vent to our indignation against Kings and Emperors for thus squandering the earnings of their subjects, let us once more look at home. Our young Republic, from the moment of her birth, has scarcely had a hostile neighbor. For about two years, Canada on the north, and for the same time, Mexico on the south, have been in a belligerent position towards us. Bounded for the most part by the ocean, and by interminable forests, we have had little to fear from invasion; and never, except in the war of 1812, has a hostile foot, other than that of a savage, pressed our soil. Yet with all our professions of economy, we have pursued the system of military preparation, after a royal fashion. Since the commencement of the Federal Government to the beginning of 1848, independent of

is *seventy-seven per cent.*, still greater than that of Great Britain. *See American Almanac for* 1845, *page* 143.

* *Balance Politique du Globe*, by M. Adrien Balbi.

the prodigious cost of arming and training the militia, there have been paid from the national treasury—

For the Army and Fortifications, - -	$366,713,209
For the Navy, and its operations, - -	209,994,428
	$576,707,637

Here we have half a billion of dollars taken from the people, with their own consent, for the purpose of being ready for war! To this immense sum may be added $61,169,834, expended in military pensions.

Were the money lavished in military preparation annihilated, all the mines in the world could not supply the requisite treasure. It is not annihilated, but it is wasted—that is, it is given for what yields no return of comfort and happiness to the nation at large. Let us suppose that the two millions of soldiers maintained in Europe, in 1828, had been employed at ordinary wages in building pyramids. Surely, none would deny that the money expended in raising structures so utterly worthless, was profligately wasted; and none will question that the people would have had good cause to rise in rebellion against rulers who robbed them of the fruits of their labor, for purposes so vain and ridiculous. Yet the treasures lavished on such piles, would have been far less in amount, and expended in a manner far less injurious to the public morals and happiness, than the money squandered on the armies.

M. Bouvet, in a recent speech in the French Assembly, remarking on the appropriation of 583 millions for the army and navy, about one-third of the whole estimate, well observed: "I cannot convey to you my sense of the irrational distribution of our resources, when I observe how comparatively unimportant we deem the elements of intelligence and public prosperity which is indicated by our budgets of instruction, commerce, and agriculture, amounting altogether to hardly thirty-six millions! What should you think of the father of a family, who possessing an income of 15,000 francs, should expend 5,000 in arms and horses, while he only appropriated 360 francs to the instruction of his children and the improvement of his estate? War, founded on force and restraint, is contrary to *liberty*. War, enabling the strong to triumph over the weak, is contrary to *equality*. War, shattering the law of love, which unites individuals and communities, is contrary to *fraternity*. Thus the Republic, to be consistent with its own constitution, ought henceforth to endeavor to suppress the military system, and to substitute for it an *international jurisdiction*. Such an object is so honest, so generous, so important to the public welfare, that France need not blush to make it the principal aim of its political existence."

The desire expressed by M. Bouvet, that international jurisdiction may be substituted for the military system, will find a cordial response in the breast of every true patriot, of every faithful disciple of the PRINCE OF PEACE. But what would be a practicable and safe and proper international jurisdiction? A "congress of nations," consisting of deputies from various States, and forming a court for the settlement of controversies arising between their several governments, has been proposed. However excellent such a tribunal may be in theory, and however useful it may hereafter be in practice, it cannot be disguised, that formidable difficulties oppose its speedy organization. Pacific sentiments must extensively prevail, before governments will be disposed to enter into such an arrangement; and the erection of such a tribunal must necessarily be preceded by tedious negotiations respecting the relative representation in the Congress, and the powers with which it should be entrusted. In the mean time, the military system would be continued, and its very continuance would render more difficult and distant the establishment of the Congress.

Happily there is a mode of "international jurisdiction," more simple, speedy, and practicable, and of which any two nations may at any time avail themselves, without waiting for the co-operation of others. This mode is faintly shadowed forth in our late treaty with Mexico, but in terms,—

> "Which keep the word of promise to the ear,
> And break it to the hope."

The 21st Article is as follows: "If unhappily any disagreement should hereafter arise between the Governments of the two Republics, whether with respect to the interpretation of any stipulation in this treaty, or with respect to any other particular concerning the political or commercial relations of the two nations, the said Governments, in the name of those nations, *do promise* to each other, that they will *endeavor* in the most sincere and earnest manner, to settle the differences so arising, and to preserve the state of peace and friendship, in which the two countries are now placing themselves, using for this end mutual representations and pacific negotiations; and if by these means they should not be enabled to come to an agreement, a resort shall not on this account be had to reprisals, aggressions, or hostilities of any kind, by the one Republic against the other, until the Government of that which deems itself aggrieved, shall have *maturely considered*, in the spirit of peace and good neighborship, whether it would not be better that such difference should be settled by the arbitration of commissioners appointed on each side, or by that of a friendly nation; and should such course be proposed by either party, *it shall be acceded* to by the other, *unless* deemed by it altogether incompatible with the nature of the difference, or the circumstances of the case."

This stipulation, it is obvious, amounts to nothing more than an acknowledgment that there is an equitable mode of preventing future hostilities, and a promise to adopt it, unless either party shall think it more *advantageous* to trust to the arbitrament of the sword.

Had the reference to arbitration been made imperative instead of discretionary, the treaty of peace would have done much to atone for the iniquity of the war. It would have secured Mexico from future spoliation, and by guaranteeing our own rights, would have removed all pretext for military preparation on our Mexican frontier; and it would, moreover, have set a glorious example of a victorious people debarring themselves from future conquests, and have taught the world how its swords might be beaten into ploughshares, and its spears into pruning-hooks.

Let us suppose that instead of this quibbling, shuffling, non-committal Article, the following had been substituted for it.

"It is agreed between the contracting parties, that, if unhappily any controversy shall arise between them, in respect to the true intent of any stipulation in this treaty, or in respect to any other matter, which controversy cannot be satisfactorily adjusted by negotiation, neither party shall resort to hostilities against the other, but the matter in dispute shall, by a special convention, be submitted to the arbitrament of some friendly power; and the parties do hereby agree to abide by the award which may be given in pursuance of such submission."

To such an Article, what valid objection can be offered?

The reference would be made only after negotiation had failed, of course it would be the alternative of WAR. Now whatever might be the award, each party would be the gainer, for each would be saved the expenditure of blood and treasure. The successful party would establish his claims without cost; and to the losing party, the remark of Franklin would be strictly applicable: "Whatever advantage one nation would obtain of another, it would be cheaper to purchase such advantage with ready money, than to pay the expense of acquiring it by war."

But it may be doubted by some, whether the award would be in accordance with justice. Why such a doubt? Would an impartial disinterested umpire, selected or agreed to by ourselves, and with the gaze of the world fixed upon him, be less able, or less inclined, to understand and determine the merits of the question submitted to him, than the Government of Mexico, or of our own country smarting under the irritation of real or imaginary wrong, seeking popularity by a show of patriotism and sensibility to national honor, and goaded on by politicians seeking for office, and by needy adventurers eager for the commissions, contracts, and spoils of war? The people at large have no interest in war; on the contrary, it is upon them its burdens press and its calamities fall.

We have seen how crushing is the weight of war-taxes upon the multitude; and yet they seem, for the most part, utterly ignorant of the true cause of their poverty and wretchedness. Deluded by demagogues, they ascribe their sufferings to kings, and nobles, and priests, but render a willing homage to SOLDIERS, who are in fact their real oppressors. The French people restless under the burthen of taxation, drove their monarch into exile, and seizing in their own hands the reins of Government, immediately enlarged their army, and have thus swelled their taxes beyond what they were under the monarchy. The suffering masses of England cry aloud against the political institutions of their country, and seek relief in annual parliaments, vote by ballot, &c., apparently unconscious that they are pressed to the earth by *war and military preparation.* Let them rid themselves of these plagues, and their taxes for the support of the Government, including all the appropriations for the maintenance of royalty in all its splendor, would be so trivial as to be scarcely perceptible. Does this statement excite the smile of incredulity? We appeal to facts.

The average expenditure of the British Government for the six years ending with 1836, including interest on the National-Debt, was	£45,676,357
Now of this immense sum, there was paid for the *civil* expenses of the Government, only	4,387,214
Leaving, for military preparation and interest on the war-debt - - - - - -	£41,289,143

Here we have disclosed the secret agent of those mighty upheavings which are causing the political world to reel to and fro like a drunken man. Men are wasting their lives and energies in toil, yet eat not the fruit of their labor, for it is wrested from them and offered on the altar of Moloch. Yet they perceive not the hand that robs them; and vainly attribute their poverty to defective political institutions. Hence, revolution follows revolution in rapid succession, like the waves of a troubled sea, but no relief is found. Agriculture is interrupted, commerce droops, industry is paralyzed, and soldiers and taxes are multiplied. Mexico, our own country, and France, bear witness that monarchs and nobles are not the exclusive devotees of war. Under all forms of Government have the wealth, the morals and the happiness of the people been sacrificed with their own consent, to their own insane admiration of glory, and their own foolish idea of the necessity of military preparation.

Let, then, the friends of human progress and of public peace, of happiness, and virtue, the patriot and the Christian, all unite in one loud and unceasing demand for treaties of arbitration. In this blessed reform any nation may take the lead; would that our own had seized the opportunity offered by the recent negotiation! Let Congress by a joint resolution, express its desire that an arbitration clause shall be inserted in all our future treaties, and the great work will be commenced. Such a resolution would be like the first beams of light breaking upon the darkness of night, and shining more and more unto the perfect day, gradually dispelling the baneful mists of military glory and ambition, and diffusing life, and joy, and abundance, among the suffering millions of our distracted world.

www.ingramcontent.com/pod-product-compliance
Lightning Source LLC
LaVergne TN
LVHW020214110826
845151LV00003B/708

* 9 7 8 1 4 2 5 5 3 3 7 0 0 *